ASIA BOND MONITOR
NOVEMBER 2021

ADB

ASIAN DEVELOPMENT BANK

ISBN 978-92-9269-160-8 (print), 978-92-9269-161-5 (electronic), 978-92-9269-162-2 (ebook)
ISSN 2219-1518 (print), 2219-1526 (electronic)
Publication Stock No. SPR210452-2
DOI: http://dx.doi.org/10.22617/SPR210452-2

The views expressed in this publication are those of the authors and do not necessarily reflect the views and policies of the Asian Development Bank (ADB) or its Board of Governors or the governments they represent.

ADB does not guarantee the accuracy of the data included in this publication and accepts no responsibility for any consequence of their use. The mention of specific companies or products of manufacturers does not imply that they are endorsed or recommended by ADB in preference to others of a similar nature that are not mentioned.

By making any designation of or reference to a particular territory or geographic area, or by using the term "country" in this document, ADB does not intend to make any judgments as to the legal or other status of any territory or area.

Corrigenda to ADB publications may be found at http://www.adb.org/publications/corrigenda.

Note:
ADB recognizes "China" as the People's Republic of China; "Hong Kong" and "Hongkong" as Hong Kong, China; "Korea" as the Republic of Korea; "Siam" as Thailand; "Vietnam" as Viet Nam; "Hanoi" as Ha Noi; and "Saigon" as Ho Chi Minh City.

Cover design by Erickson Mercado.

Contents

Emerging East Asian Local Currency Bond Markets: A Regional Update

Executive Summary vi

Global and Regional Market Developments 1

Bond Market Developments in the Third Quarter of 2021 12

Recent Developments in ASEAN+3 Sustainable Bond Markets 36

Policy and Regulatory Developments 40

Price Differences Between Labeled and Unlabeled Green Bonds 43

Market Summaries

    China, People's Republic of 46

    Hong Kong, China 51

    Indonesia 55

    Korea, Republic of 61

    Malaysia 67

    Philippines 73

    Singapore 79

    Thailand 83

    Viet Nam 89

Emerging East Asian Local Currency Bond Markets: A Regional Update

Executive Summary

Recent Trends in Financial Conditions in Emerging East Asia

Financial conditions in emerging East Asia weakened between 31 August and 5 November on the back of global inflationary concerns and a shift in monetary stance by the United States (US) Federal Reserve.[1] The Federal Reserve announced that it would scale back its bond purchases beginning in November, while rising global inflation is also pressuring central banks in the region to consider tightening monetary policies. This has led to bond yields rising, currencies weakening, and risk premiums edging up in most emerging East Asian economies during the review period. Nevertheless, a positive economic outlook and still-accommodative policy stances have supported financial conditions in the region, as evidenced by positive foreign capital flows into regional bond and equity markets during the third quarter (Q3) of 2021.

Compared with the prior quarter, Q3 2021 witnessed a moderation of gross domestic product growth in most emerging East Asian economies, largely due to a resurgence of coronavirus disease (COVID-19) cases. To support economic recovery, most central banks in the region maintained accommodative monetary stances. A few regional central banks also continued to support local currency (LCY) bond markets through LCY bond purchases, facilitating bond market functioning and government financing.

Recent Developments in Local Currency Bond Markets in Emerging East Asia

Emerging East Asia's LCY bond markets expanded in Q3 2021 to an aggregate USD21.7 trillion at the end of September, posting growth of 3.4% quarter-on-quarter (q-o-q), up from 2.9% q-o-q in the previous quarter. LCY bond issuance rose 6.8% q-o-q to USD2.4 trillion in Q3 2021.

The government bond segment dominates the region's LCY bond markets, accounting for 62.4% of total LCY bonds outstanding. Emerging East Asia's government bond stock reached USD13.6 trillion at the end of September, posting growth of 3.9% q-o-q in Q3 2021. The LCY government bond markets of members of the Association of Southeast Asian Nations (ASEAN) collectively stood at USD1.9 trillion, expanding 3.6% q-o-q and 14.4% year-on-year in Q3 2021. More than 60.0% of the LCY government bonds in ASEAN markets carried maturities of 5 years or more at the end of September. The outstanding amount of LCY corporate bonds in emerging East Asia reached USD8.2 trillion at the end of September, posting growth of 2.8% q-o-q. Domestic investors remain important players in the LCY bond markets of emerging East Asia. Financial institutions—such as banks, insurance companies and pension funds, and mutual funds—held an aggregate 51.0% of the region's government bonds outstanding at the end of September.

Sustainable bond markets in ASEAN+3 continued to expand to reach a size of USD388.7 billion at the end of September.[2] The issuance of sustainable bonds in the first 3 quarters of the year totaled USD165.5 billion. ASEAN+3 is home to the second-largest regional sustainable bond market in the world after Europe, accounting for 19.2% of the global sustainable bond total at the end of September. Green bonds, social bonds, and sustainability bonds accounted for 71.6%, 13.0%, and 15.3% of ASEAN+3 sustainable bonds outstanding, respectively. While the financial sector continued to be a major player in the region's sustainable bond market, a more diversified issuer base is emerging as the market develops.

---

[1] Emerging East Asia comprises the People's Republic of China; Hong Kong, China; Indonesia; the Republic of Korea; Malaysia; the Philippines; Singapore; Thailand; and Viet Nam.
[2] For the discussion on sustainable bonds, ASEAN+3 includes ASEAN members Indonesia, Malaysia, the Philippines, Singapore, Thailand, and Viet Nam plus the People's Republic of China; Hong Kong, China; Japan; and the Republic of Korea.

Special Topics on Emerging East Asian Local Currency Bond Markets

The November issue of the *Asia Bond Monitor* presents three boxes discussing relevant topics affecting the region's LCY bond markets. A theme chapter on pricing differentials between labeled and unlabeled bonds is also featured in this issue.

Box 1: Economic Outlook—Slightly Slower and Divergent Recovery

While the regional economic outlook remains positive, uneven vaccination progress and the outbreak of the Delta variant slightly weighed on the economic recovery in Q3 2021. In its *World Economic Outlook* released in October, the International Monetary Fund revised its 2021 growth forecast for emerging markets and developing economies to 6.4%, up marginally from 6.3% in July. The *Asian Development Outlook Update*, released in September 2021, downgraded its 2021 growth forecast for ASEAN, many of whose members suffered a major Delta outbreak during Q3 2021, to 3.1% from a July forecast of 4.4%. However, the growth forecasts for the People's Republic of China; Hong Kong, China; and the Republic of Korea—in all of which the Delta variant was more contained—were either maintained or upgraded.

Box 2: How Big Is the Risk of Another Taper Tantrum?

The Federal Reserve's announcement that it will scale back its asset purchases starting in November raised concerns globally of another taper tantrum. However, several factors indicate that the risk is more limited this time around, particularly in emerging Asia. First, the Federal Reserve has been more transparent in signaling its monetary policy trajectory. In contrast, the taper tantrum of May 2013 came following a surprise announcement. The Federal Reserve also recently stressed that the tapering of asset purchases would not be accompanied by interest rate hikes in the near term. Second, emerging Asian markets have more robust economic fundamentals compared to 2013, as reflected by indicators such as the real effective exchange rate and current account balance. Nonetheless, the risk of a taper tantrum cannot be entirely ruled out. Thus, the region's regulatory authorities should closely monitor potential sources of financial instability.

Box 3: Risks to Outlook—Downside Risks Outweigh Upside Risks

Downside risks continue to outweigh upside risks to the region's economic outlook. Uncertainty related to the pandemic was evident among some ASEAN economies when the Delta variant outbreak triggered the reintroduction of mobility restrictions that dampened economic growth. Slow vaccination rollouts in developing markets could trigger renewed COVID-19 waves. Global supply chain disruptions due to the pandemic pose another major downside risk for economic prospects since such disruptions hamper manufacturing activities. The supply disruptions also give rise to inflationary pressures, which if persistent may spur central banks to tighten monetary policy. On a positive note, rapid vaccination can loosen the link between new outbreaks and economic growth.

Theme Chapter: Price Differences Between Labeled and Unlabeled Green Bonds

The theme chapter analyzes the yield and price differences between labeled and unlabeled green bonds. Recent research empirically investigated the hypothesis that investors would pay more for labeled green bonds than unlabeled green bonds because the former have better information disclosure and lower reputational risk; thus, they are widely viewed as more credible green assets. The results confirm that a green label has a statistically significant negative effect on the yield of green bonds: the yields of labeled green bonds are 24–36 basis points lower than the yields of unlabeled green bonds with similar characteristics. An important policy implication is that widely accepted green bond labels (or certifications) benefit investors with lower information costs and reputational risks, and they benefit issuers with lower financing costs. Moreover, a well-functioning green bond market ecosystem helps issuers better utilize green labels and certifications, enhancing supply and promoting market development.

Global and Regional Market Developments

Inflation concerns and shifts in monetary policy in advanced economies drove up bond yields.

Between 31 August and 5 November, 2-year and 10-year government bond yields rose in nearly all markets in advanced economies and emerging East Asia.[1] The rise in bond yields was largely driven by inflationary concerns and a shift in the monetary stance of the United States (US) Federal Reserve (**Table A**). Inflationary pressures and a potential change in global liquidity weighed against financial conditions in emerging East Asia, with most currencies weakening and risk premiums edging up during the review period.

Yields on 10-year government bonds have risen rapidly in major advanced economies since late August. Bond yields in the euro area, Japan, and the United Kingdom stood higher on 5 November than their respective pre-pandemic levels of January 2020. But bond yields

in these advanced markets remained relatively low compared to average levels during the past decade (**Figure A**). The yield increases since August have largely reflected a robust economic recovery and inflationary pressures, although the momentum of the global economic recovery has slowed somewhat (**Box 1**).

The 2-year and 10-year yields in the US rose 19 basis points (bps) and 14 bps, respectively, during the review period from 31 August to 5 November, echoing a strong economic recovery, inflationary conditions, and an expected adjustment in monetary stance by the Federal Reserve. The US economic recovery remains strong, although annualized gross domestic product (GDP) growth slowed in the third quarter (Q3) of 2021 to 2.0% from 6.7% in the second quarter (Q2) as a rise in coronavirus disease (COVID-19) cases led to additional movement controls and delayed business reopenings. The unemployment rate fell to 4.6% in

Table A: Changes in Global Financial Conditions

	2-Year Government Bond (bps)	10-Year Government Bond (bps)	5-Year Credit Default Swap Spread (bps)	Equity Index (%)	FX Rate (%)
Major Advanced Economies					
United States	19	14	–	3.9	–
United Kingdom	19	13	0.2	2.6	(1.9)
Japan	2	4	1	4.5	(3.0)
Germany	(2)	10	(0.5)	1.4	(2.0)
Emerging East Asia					
China, People's Rep. of	(2)	4	17	(1.5)	1.0
Hong Kong, China	13	39	–	(3.9)	(0.07)
Indonesia	4	(0.3)	13	7.0	(0.4)
Korea, Rep. of	52	44	1	(7.2)	(2.2)
Malaysia	33	37	12	(4.3)	(0.1)
Philippines	46	86	16	7.1	(1.2)
Singapore	46	36	–	6.1	(0.4)
Thailand	22	35	3	(0.8)	(3.1)
Viet Nam	1	4	8	9.4	0.4

( ) = negative, – = not available, bps = basis points, FX = foreign exchange.
Notes:
1. Data reflect changes between 31 August 2021 and 5 November 2021.
2. A positive (negative) value for the FX rate indicates the appreciation (depreciation) of the local currency against the United States dollar.
Source: Bloomberg LP and Institute of International Finance.

---

[1] Emerging East Asia comprises the People's Republic of China; Hong Kong, China; Indonesia; the Republic of Korea; Malaysia; the Philippines; Singapore; Thailand; and Viet Nam.

Figure A: 10-Year Government Bond Yields in Major Advanced Economies (% per annum)

UK = United Kingdom, US = United States.
Note: Data coverage is from 1 January 2010 to 5 November 2021.
Source: Bloomberg LP.

October from 4.8% in September and 5.2% in August. Inflation remained elevated, with September and October inflation at 5.4% year-on-year (y-o-y) and 6.2% y-o-y, respectively. The Federal Reserve upgraded its economic growth forecasts for 2022 and 2023 to 3.8% and 2.5%, respectively, from its June forecasts of 3.3% and 2.4%. While the Federal Reserve kept the federal funds rate and the current asset purchase program unchanged at its Federal Open Market Committee meeting in September, it implied that it might begin hiking rates in 2022, compared with a previously indicated start date in 2023. At its November meeting, while the Federal Reserve noted that the rise in COVID-19 cases earlier this year had delayed recovery, it said that the economy continues to progress. The widely expected tapering in the Federal Reserve's bond purchases formally starts in November. Concerns of another possible taper tantrum eased as the risk is much smaller this time than in 2013 (**Box 2**).

Box 1: Economic Outlook—Slightly Slower and Divergent Recovery

The global coronavirus disease (COVID-19) landscape has witnessed a major positive development as well as a major negative development.[a] On the positive side, vaccination campaigns are making steady headway across the world. As of 16 October, 2.8 billion people, or 36.2% of the global population, had been fully vaccinated. However, progress has been uneven, with developing markets generally lagging advanced economies (**Figure B1**). For instance, the full vaccination rate reached 78.2% in Spain, but it was only 1.1% in Nigeria. On the negative side, the spread of the Delta variant has laid to rest any hopes that the world will return to the pre-pandemic normal in the short term. The variant, which was first detected in December 2020, is less deadly than the original virus, but it is highly contagious and has spread across the world like a wildfire.

On balance, the negative economic impact of the Delta variant outbreak has outweighed the positive economic impact of the global progress on COVID-19 vaccination. In response to the outbreak, some economies reintroduced or strengthened community quarantines and social distancing restrictions, with adverse effects on domestic demand, especially private consumption. The spread of the Delta variant has also dampened business and consumer confidence, which had been surging on hopes of a return to the pre-pandemic normal. In addition, the emergence of the highly transmissible variant has created a lot of uncertainty about the timetable for such a return.

Figure B1: Fully Vaccinated Share of the Population in Select Economies (%)

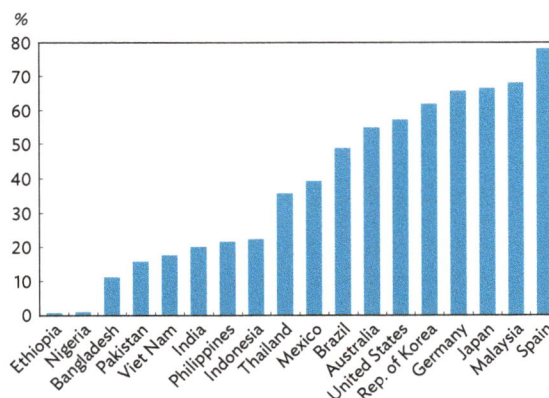

Note: Vaccination rates as of 16 October 2021.
Source: Our World in Data. COVID Vaccinations. https://ourworldindata.org/covid-vaccinations?country=OWID_WRL (accessed 17 October 2021).

On a positive note, thanks to vaccination progress, governments are responding in ways that are less detrimental to economic activity in response to new outbreaks. Vaccines do not fully protect individuals from infection, but they are highly effective against severe illness and death. Analysis in the *Asian Development Outlook 2021 Update*, released in September, reveals a strong negative cross-country correlation between vaccination rate and COVID-19

---

[a] This box was written by Donghyun Park (principal economist) in the Economic Research and Regional Cooperation Department of the Asian Development Bank.

continued on next page

Box 1: Economic Outlook—Slightly Slower and Divergent Recovery   *continued*

mortality rate. That is, markets that vaccinate more of their population suffer relative fewer deaths from the virus. In recognition of this reality, which implies a significantly lower humanitarian cost of new outbreaks, governments around the world are imposing less stringent restrictions when there is a new outbreak. This suggests that the impact of the pandemic on economic growth will decline over time.

According to the forecasts of the International Monetary Fund's *World Economic Outlook* (WEO), released in October, the world economy will grow 5.9% in 2021 and 4.9% in 2022, following a contraction of 3.1% in 2020 (**Table B1**). Relative to the WEO's July forecasts, the global growth forecast for 2021 was downgraded by 0.1 percentage points, while there was no change for the 2022 growth forecast. World trade volume shrank by 8.2% in 2020, but it is projected to bounce back strongly to expand 9.7% in 2021 before moderating to 6.7% growth in 2022. Relative to July, the WEO downgraded its growth forecast for advanced economies by 0.4 percentage points to 5.2% and upgraded its 2022 forecast marginally by 0.1 percentage points to 4.5%. The 2021 downgrade largely reflects a substantial downgrade for the United States, which experienced inventory reductions due to supply chain disruptions and weakening consumption. Emerging markets and developing economies are forecast to recover strongly and grow 6.4% in 2021 and 5.1% in 2022, after shrinking 2.1% in 2020. The October forecasts were almost the same as the July forecasts, with a marginal upgrade of 0.1 percentage points for 2021 and a marginal

downgrade of 0.1 percentage points for 2022. Inflation is projected to pick up in advanced economies from 0.7% in 2020 to 2.8% in 2021, before falling back to 2.3% in 2022. The corresponding figures for emerging markets and developing economies are 5.1%, 5.5%, and 4.9%.

The economic outlook for emerging East Asian economies is mixed and heavily dependent on pandemic containment. There is a dichotomy between East Asian economies such as the People's Republic of China (PRC) and Southeast Asian economies such as Indonesia, Malaysia, the Philippines, Thailand, and Viet Nam. While East Asian economies have effectively contained COVID-19, Southeast Asia was hit hard by the Delta variant in 2021. According to the *Asian Development Outlook 2021 Update*, the PRC is projected to grow 8.1% in 2021 and 5.5% in 2022, after growth had plummeted to 2.3% in 2020 due to the pandemic. The corresponding growth figures for the Republic of Korea and Hong Kong, China are 4.0% and 6.2% in 2021, 3.1% and 3.4% in 2022, and −0.9% and −6.1% in 2020. The 2021 growth forecast for the PRC released in September was unchanged from the April forecast, while the 2021 forecasts for the Republic of Korea and Hong Kong, China were upgraded by 0.5 and 1.6 percentage points, respectively. The *Asian Development Outlook 2021 Update* sharply downgraded its 2021 growth forecast for members of the Association of Southeast Asian Nations (ASEAN) from 4.4% to 3.1%, following a 4.0% contraction in growth in 2020. On the other hand, output in the ASEAN region is forecast to expand 5.0% in 2022.

Emerging East Asia's economic performance remains hostage to the trajectory of COVID-19 in the short term. This is evident in the downgrading of growth forecasts for ASEAN, which has suffered a tangible deceleration of growth momentum since April, when the Delta variant first emerged in the region. However, while there remains much pandemic-related economic uncertainty, progress in vaccination campaigns can significantly reduce the uncertainty. This is because vaccination reduces the need for draconian social distancing restrictions that crimp economic activity. Therefore, emerging East Asia's future economic performance will depend substantially on its progress in vaccination.

Table B1: Gross Domestic Product Growth Rate of World, Advanced Economies, and Emerging Markets and Developing Economies in 2020, 2021, and 2022 (%)

	2020	2021		2022	
	Actual	October Forecast	July Forecast	October Forecast	July Forecast
World	(3.1)	5.9	6.0	4.9	4.9
Advanced economies	(4.5)	5.2	5.6	4.5	4.4
Emerging markets and developing economies	(2.1)	6.4	6.3	5.1	5.2

( ) = negative.
Source: International Monetary Fund. 2021. *World Economic Outlook October 2021.* Washington, DC.

Box 2: How Big Is the Risk of Another Taper Tantrum?

On 22 October, United States (US) Federal Reserve Chair Jerome Powell said that the US central bank should start tapering its monthly USD120 billion purchases of Treasury bonds and mortgage-backed securities.[a] The Federal Reserve thus confirmed that it would begin to cut back on its asset purchases in November. An improving economic outlook and a worrisome rise in inflation is driving the shift in US monetary policy. The shift has triggered widespread concerns about a repeat of the taper tantrum episode of May 2013, when a similar announcement by the Federal Reserve that it would unwind its massive asset purchase program, known as quantitative easing, rocked the financial stability of several emerging markets with weaker fundamentals. In particular, emerging markets with large current account deficits—most notably Brazil, India, Indonesia, South Africa, and Turkey—suffered financial turbulence, sparking fears of a broader emerging market financial crisis. Given the similarity between the asset purchase tapering of 2013 and today, how big is the risk of another taper tantrum? Three factors suggest that the risk is more limited this time around.

First, the Federal Reserve has been much more transparent in signaling its expected monetary policy path. It has clearly communicated its intentions well in advance of major policy shifts, thus avoiding turbulence in financial markets. The Federal Reserve has emphasized that any scaling back of bond-buying this time would be carried out in a gradual and smooth manner. By contrast, the announcement in May 2013 came as a complete surprise to the market. In addition, the Federal Reserve has made it crystal clear that the tapering of asset purchases will not be accompanied by interest rate hikes, at least for the time being.

Second, emerging Asian markets have stronger economic fundamentals compared to 2013. One key fundamental is the real effective exchange rate (REER), which is an indicator of external competitiveness. An overvalued REER denotes weak external competitiveness, which increases the risk of capital outflows. The left-hand panel of **Figure B2**, which shows the REER prior to the 2013 taper tantrum and the current REER relative to historical averages, indicates that

Figure B2: Real Effective Exchange Rate Fundamentals and Current Account Balances in Selected Emerging Asian Markets

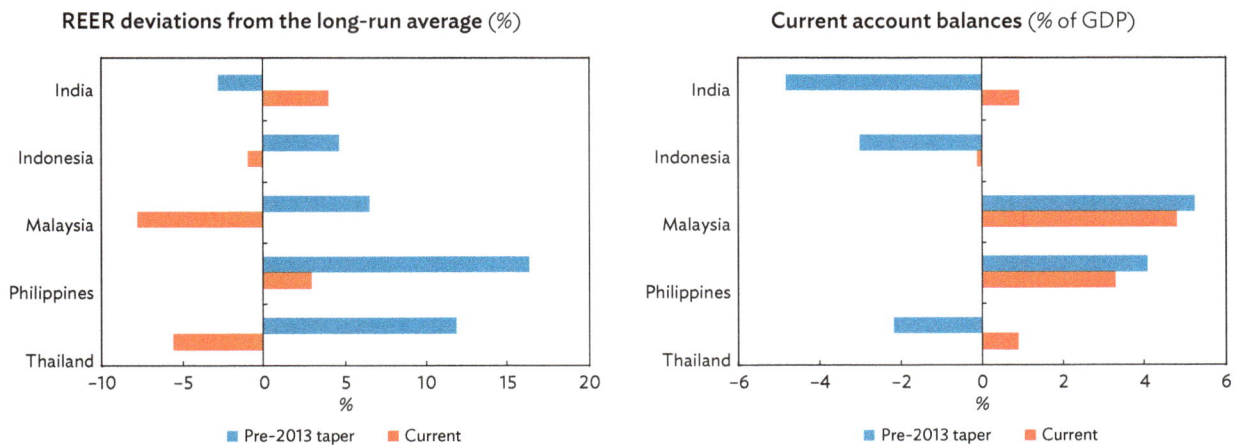

REER = real effective exchange rate.
Notes: Reported are the percentage deviations in the prevailing REER relative to an 8-year historical average using monthly data. Positive values denote an overvaluation; negative values denote an undervaluation. The pre-taper prevailing period is relative to April 2013, and the current prevailing period is relative to August 2021.
Source: Calculated using the Bank for International Settlements Statistics database.

GDP = gross domestic product.
Notes: "Pre-2013 taper" refers to the current account-to-GDP ratio in the first quarter of 2013. "Current" refers to the second quarter of 2021.
Source: Bloomberg, LP.

---

[a] This box is written by John Beirne. The content is based on Beirne, John. 2021. "Should Emerging Asia Worry about a "Taper Tantrum" Post-COVID-19?" *Asia Pathways Blog.* Asian Development Bank Institute. 20 September. https://www.asiapathways-adbi.org/2021/09/should-emerging-asia-worry-about-a-taper-tantrum-post-covid-19/.

continued on next page

Box 2: How Big Is the Risk of Another Taper Tantrum?   *continued*

the exchange rates of Indonesia, Malaysia, and Thailand are currently undervalued. The exchange rate remains overvalued in the Philippines but much less so than before the 2013 taper tantrum. India's currency has appreciated due to capital inflows, but the appreciation has been moderate. Overall, the region has not witnessed sharp currency appreciations this time around. This is significant because the emerging market currencies that appreciated sharply before the taper tantrum suffered the most in 2013.

Third, the right-hand panel in Figure B2 shows another key economic fundamental: the current account deficit. As noted earlier, countries with the largest current account deficits suffered the most financial instability during the taper tantrum. This explains why India and Indonesia were hit the hardest within emerging Asia. The chart shows that the current account balance of India is now positive while that of Indonesia is balanced. Malaysia, the Philippines, and

Thailand are all running surpluses of varying magnitudes. The absence of large deficits renders the region less vulnerable to external shocks such as the Federal Reserve's tapering of asset purchases.

To sum up, the risk of another taper tantrum is quite limited although we cannot rule it out altogether. At a broader level, there are two major reasons for such optimism. First, the Federal Reserve is expected to signal its intentions about tapering with much greater clarity and transparency than was the case in 2013, thus greatly reducing the risk of surprising financial markets. Second, emerging Asian economies currently have stronger economic fundamentals than they did during the taper tantrum, as evidenced by key indicators such as REER and the current account balance. Nevertheless, the region's regulatory authorities should closely monitor other potential sources of financial instability, such as high debt levels, to protect financial stability.

In the euro area, the economy continues to rebound. Quarter-on-quarter GDP growth accelerated to 2.2% in Q3 2021 from 2.1% in Q2 2021. On a y-o-y basis, GDP growth slowed to 3.7% in Q3 2021 from 14.2% in the previous quarter. The European Central Bank (ECB) upgraded its 2021 economic growth forecast to 5.0% in September from 4.6% in June, while adjusting the 2022 GDP growth forecast to 4.6% from 4.7%. The ECB also revised upward its respective inflation forecasts for 2021, 2022, and 2023 to 2.2%, 1.7%, and 1.5% in September from 1.9%, 1.5%, and 1.4% in June. Given the strengthening economic recovery and an uptick in inflation, the ECB is gradually turning hawkish. While the ECB has yet to adjust its policy rates, during its October meeting the ECB indicated a slower pace in its asset purchases under the pandemic response program in the fourth quarter of 2021 compared with prior quarters. The ECB also confirmed that the pandemic asset purchase program would end in March 2022. The ECB also offered some pushback, implying that a rate hike in 2022 was unlikely and, while the inflationary pressures are still transitory, inflation might persist longer than expected.

Japan's annualized Q3 2021 GDP contracted 3.0% after posting growth of 1.5% in Q2 2021. At its September and October meetings, the Bank of Japan left unchanged

its policy rate target and asset purchase program. The Bank of Japan also noted in its October meeting that in the near-term downward pressure remains. The 2021 GDP growth was revised to 3.4% from 3.8%, while the 2022 forecast was revised to 2.9% from 2.7%.

From 31 August to 5 November, 2-year and 10-year government bond yields rose in nearly all emerging East Asian economies, except for a marginal decline in the People's Republic of China's (PRC) 2-year yields and Indonesia's 10-year yields. This trend largely tracked rising bond yields in major advanced economies and inflationary concerns in many regional markets, as well as shifting monetary policy stances in advanced economies and in the region (**Table B**).

The region's largest increase in the 10-year yield was observed in the Philippines, with a gain of 86 bps. The rise was mainly driven by y-o-y inflation, which reached 4.9%, 4.8%, and 4.6% in August, September, and October, respectively, the highest monthly readings in the region. The Republic of Korea posted emerging East Asia's second-largest increase in the 10-year bond yield (44 bps) and the largest increase in the 2-year bond yield (52 bps). The Bank of Korea hiked the policy rate by 25 bps at its August meeting on the back of an improving economy and the need to prevent potential financial risks.

Table B: Inflation in Major Advanced Markets and Emerging East Asia

Economy	Inflation Rate (%)												
	Oct-2020	Nov-2020	Dec-2020	Jan-2021	Feb-2021	Mar-2021	Apr-2021	May-2021	Jun-2021	Jul-2021	Aug-2021	Sep-2021	Oct-2021
United States	1.20	1.20	1.40	1.40	1.70	2.60	4.20	5.00	5.40	5.40	5.30	5.40	6.20
Euro Area	(0.30)	(0.30)	(0.30)	0.90	0.90	1.30	1.60	2.00	1.90	2.20	3.00	3.40	4.10
Japan	(0.40)	(0.90)	(1.20)	(0.70)	(0.50)	(0.40)	(1.10)	(0.80)	(0.50)	(0.30)	(0.40)	0.20	0.10
China, People's Rep. of	0.50	(0.50)	0.20	(0.30)	(0.20)	0.40	0.90	1.30	1.10	1.00	0.80	0.70	1.50
Hong Kong, China	(0.40)	(0.30)	(1.00)	2.60	0.50	0.60	0.80	1.00	0.70	3.70	1.60	1.40	1.70
Indonesia	1.44	1.59	1.68	1.55	1.38	1.37	1.42	1.68	1.33	1.52	1.59	1.60	1.66
Korea, Rep. of	0.10	0.60	0.50	0.60	1.10	1.50	2.30	2.60	2.40	2.60	2.60	2.50	3.20
Malaysia	(1.50)	(1.70)	(1.40)	(0.20)	0.10	1.70	4.70	4.40	3.40	2.20	2.00	2.20	–
Philippines	2.50	3.30	3.50	4.20	4.70	4.50	4.50	4.50	4.10	4.00	4.90	4.80	4.60
Singapore	(0.20)	(0.10)	0.00	0.20	0.70	1.30	2.10	2.40	2.40	2.50	2.40	2.50	3.20
Thailand	(0.50)	(0.41)	(0.27)	(0.34)	(1.17)	(0.08)	3.41	2.44	1.25	0.45	(0.02)	1.68	2.38
Viet Nam	2.47	1.48	0.19	(0.97)	0.70	1.16	2.70	2.90	2.41	2.64	2.82	2.06	1.77

( ) = negative, – = not available.
Note: Data coverage is from October 2020 to October 2021 except for Malaysia.
Sources: Various local sources.

Subsequently, on 25 November, the Bank of Korea raised its policy rate again by 25 bps. Singapore also witnessed a relatively large increase in its 2-year and 10-year bond yields, which gained 46 bps and 36 bps, respectively. Monetary Authority of Singapore tightened monetary policy at its October meeting when it raised the slope of the exchange rate band.

Indonesia was the sole market in the region that saw a decline in its 10-year yield, albeit a marginal dip of 0.3 bps, while its 2-year yield gained 4 bps. Upward pressure on Indonesia's yields was curtailed by relatively low inflation. Investment sentiment also improved on a strengthened current account balance and revised tax regulations that are expected to generate more tax revenues and thus reduce the budget deficit.

Persistent inflation concerns and the tightening monetary stance of the Federal Reserve weighed down regional currencies and pushed up risk premiums. Most regional currencies depreciated in September following the Federal Reserve's discussion of unwinding its current asset purchase program as early as November. But sentiment gradually recovered in October and early November, supported by positive economic recovery prospects and accommodative policy stances (**Figure B.1**). The Thai baht posted the region's largest decline, falling 3.1% versus the US dollar from 31 August to 5 November due to a widening current account deficit. The Thai baht has also experienced the largest depreciation since January 2020

among all regional currencies (**Figure B.2**). The Korean won and the Philippine peso depreciated by 2.2% and 1.2%, respectively, during the review period. For the Republic of Korea, the weakening of the currency tracked concerns over a moderation in its export performance due to global supply chain disruptions. In the Philippines, inflationary concerns weighed down the currency.

Figure B.1: Changes in Spot Exchange Rates versus the United States Dollar

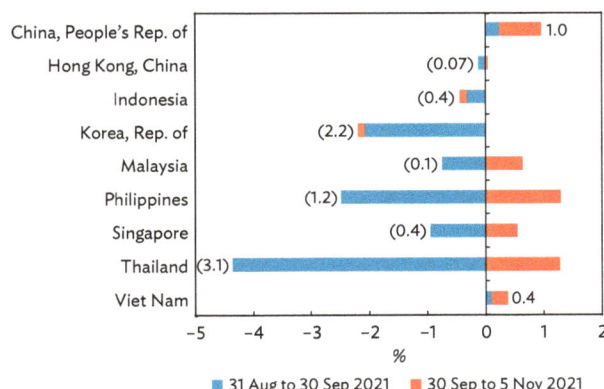

Notes:
1. Changes from 31 August 2021 to 30 September 2021, and from 30 September 2021 to 5 November 2021.
2. Numbers on the chart refer to the net change between the two periods.
3. A positive (negative) value for the foreign exchange rate indicates the appreciation (depreciation) of the local currency against the United States dollar.
Source: *AsianBondsOnline* computations based on Bloomberg LP data.

Figure B.2: Currency Indexes in Emerging East Asia and the United States

1 Jan 2020 = 100

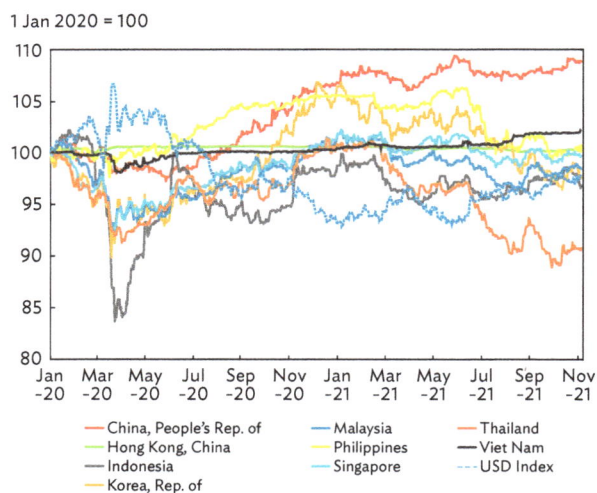

USD = United States dollar.
Note: Data coverage is from 1 January 2020 to 5 November 2021.
Source: *AsianBondsOnline* computations based on Bloomberg LP data.

Figure C.1: Credit Default Swap Spreads in Select Asian Markets (senior 5-year)

Midspread in basis points

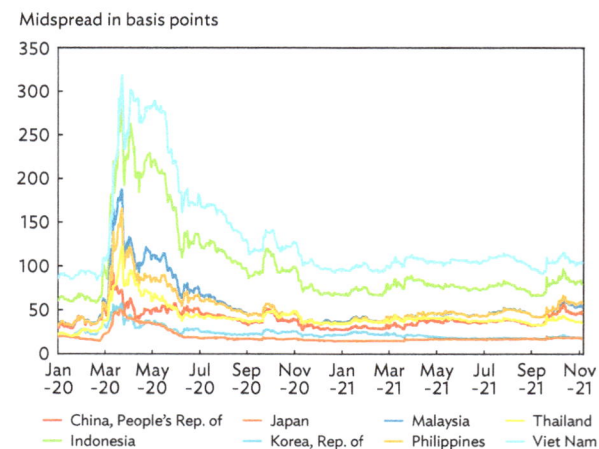

Notes:
1. Based on United States dollar-denominated sovereign bonds.
2. Data coverage is from 1 January 2020 to 5 November 2021.
Source: Bloomberg LP.

The Chinese yuan appreciated the most, gaining 1.0% during the review period. Next was the Vietnamese dong, which rose a marginal 0.4%.

Risk premiums, as proxied by credit default swap spreads and sovereign stripped spreads, steadily increased across the region's markets during the review period on heightened risk aversion largely due to global inflationary concerns (**Figures C.1** and **C.2**).

The region's equity markets witnessed net inflows of USD5.9 billion in September and USD3.1 billion in October (**Figure D.1**). However, equity markets in emerging East Asia posted mixed patterns between 31 August and 5 November (**Figure D.2**). Viet Nam reported the largest gain (9.4%), on reports that the Ministry of Planning and Investment intends to pass an economic recovery package worth VND800 trillion, while the Republic of Korea experienced the biggest decline (–7.2%), partly driven by investment outflows on the back of global supply chain disruptions.

Foreign capital flows into regional bond markets were negative in September in all Association of Southeast Asian Nations economies except Malaysia, amid rising bond yields and inflationary pressures (**Figures E.1**). As a result, the share of foreign holdings in most emerging East Asian markets declined in Q3 2021 (**Figure E.2**).

Figure C.2: JP Morgan Emerging Markets Bond Index Sovereign Stripped Spreads

Basis points

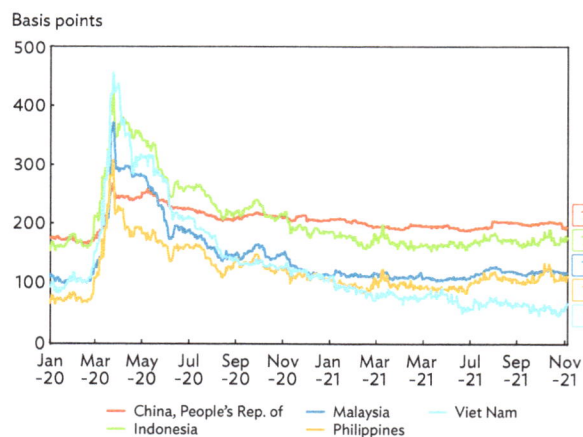

Notes:
1. Based on United States dollar-denominated sovereign bonds.
2. Data coverage is from 1 January 2020 to 5 November 2021.
Source: Bloomberg LP.

The PRC was the only market in the region that experienced an increase in its foreign holdings share, which rose slightly by 0.3 percentage points to reach 10.6% at the end of September. The PRC continued to open up its bond market and draw foreign investors with an attractive return profile, tax incentives, and the pending inclusion of its bond market in various global bond indices.

Figure D.1: Capital Flows into Equity Markets in Emerging East Asia

USD billion

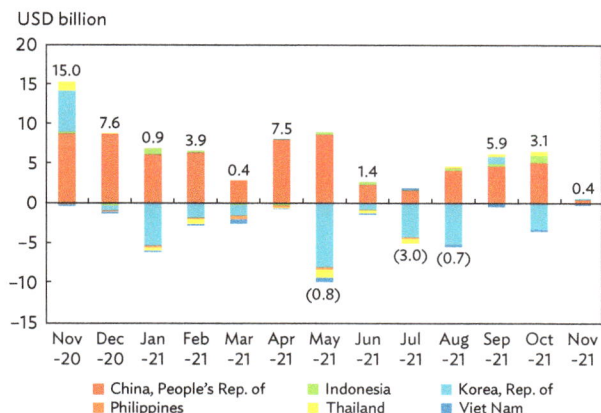

( ) = outflows, USD = United States dollar.
Notes:
1. Data coverage is from 2 November 2020 to 2 November 2021.
2. Numbers on the chart refer to net inflows (net outflows) for each month.
Source: Institute of International Finance.

Figure D.2: Changes in Equity Indexes in Emerging East Asia

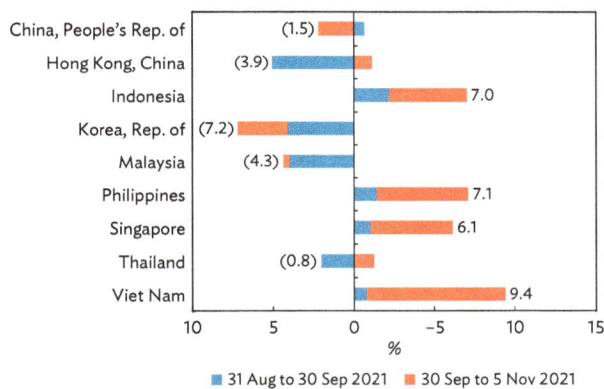

( ) = negative.
Notes:
1. Changes from 31 August to 30 September 2021 and from 30 September to 5 November 2021.
2. Numbers on the chart refer to the net change between the two periods.
Source: *AsianBondsOnline* computations based on Bloomberg LP data.

Figure E.1: Foreign Capital Flows in Local Currency Bond Markets in Emerging East Asia

USD billion

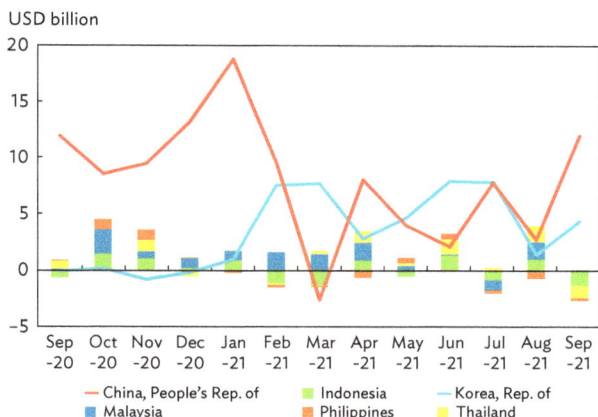

USD = United States dollar.
Notes:
1. The Republic of Korea and Thailand provided data on bond flows. For the People's Republic of China, Indonesia, Malaysia, and the Philippines, month-on-month changes in foreign holdings of local currency government bonds were used as a proxy for bond flows.
2. Data are as of 30 September 2021.
3. Figures were computed based on 30 September 2021 exchange rates to avoid currency effects.
Sources: People's Republic of China (*Wind Information*); Indonesia (Directorate General of Budget Financing and Risk Management, Ministry of Finance); Republic of Korea (Financial Supervisory Service); Malaysia (Bank Negara Malaysia); Philippines (Bureau of the Treasury); and Thailand (Thai Bond Market Association).

Figure E.2: Foreign Holdings Share in Local Currency Government Bond Markets in Select Emerging East Asian Economies

Change in share (%)

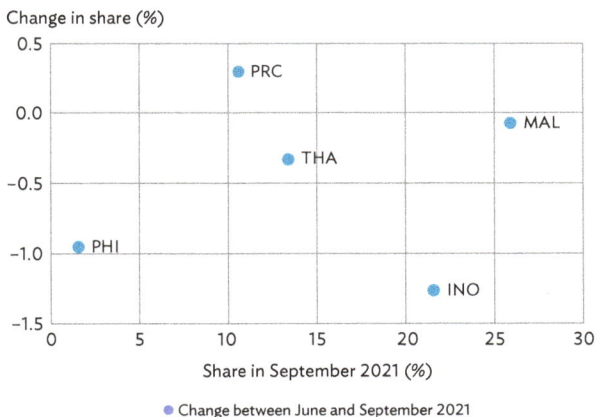

● Change between June and September 2021

INO = Indonesia, MAL = Malaysia, PHI = Philippines, PRC = People's Republic of China, THA = Thailand.
Note: Data reflect change in foreign holdings between the end of June 2021 and the end of September 2021.
Source: People's Republic of China (Bloomberg and CEIC Data Company); Indonesia (Directorate General of Budget Financing and Risk Management, Ministry of Finance); Malaysia (Bank Negara Malaysia); Philippines (Bureau of the Treasury); and Thailand (Bank of Thailand).

Domestic financial institutions—particularly banks, pension funds, and insurance companies—remain the cornerstone of regional local currency (LCY) government bonds markets, especially in Association of Southeast Asian Nations markets where foreign holdings are declining (**Figure F.1**). A few central banks also continue to support bond market liquidity and facilitate government financing via LCY asset purchase programs (**Figure F.2**). Although these programs have been effective in preserving market capacity while keeping bond yields low, they pose challenges in how to smoothly reverse these positions in the future. Regional central banks also face pressure to adjust their policies when their monetary stances diverge from that of the Federal Reserve. Inflationary pressures are an additional concern in a few regional markets. Since risks to the regional economic outlook and financial stability remain largely tilted to the downside, authorities need to closely monitor financial markets to avoid large swings in asset prices and to maintain financial stability (**Box 3**).

Figure F.2: Central Bank Purchases of Government Bonds

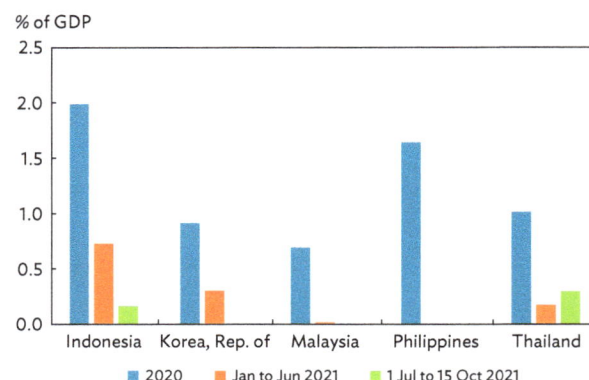

% of GDP

GDP = gross domestic product.
Notes:
1. Central bank purchases as a share of GDP for 2021 was computed based on June 2021 GDP.
2. For Indonesia, data cover the periods from 1 January 2021 to 15 June 2021, and from 16 June 2021 to 15 October 2021.
3. For the Republic of Korea, no additional purchases occurred from 1 July 2021 to 15 October 2021.
4. For the Philippines, data for 2021 are not available.
5. For Thailand, data cover the period from 1 January 2021 to 30 June 2021, and from 1 July 2021 to 18 October 2021.
Sources: CEIC Data Company, Haver Analytics, and various local sources.

Figure F.1: Investor Profiles of Local Currency Government Bonds in Select Emerging East Asian Markets

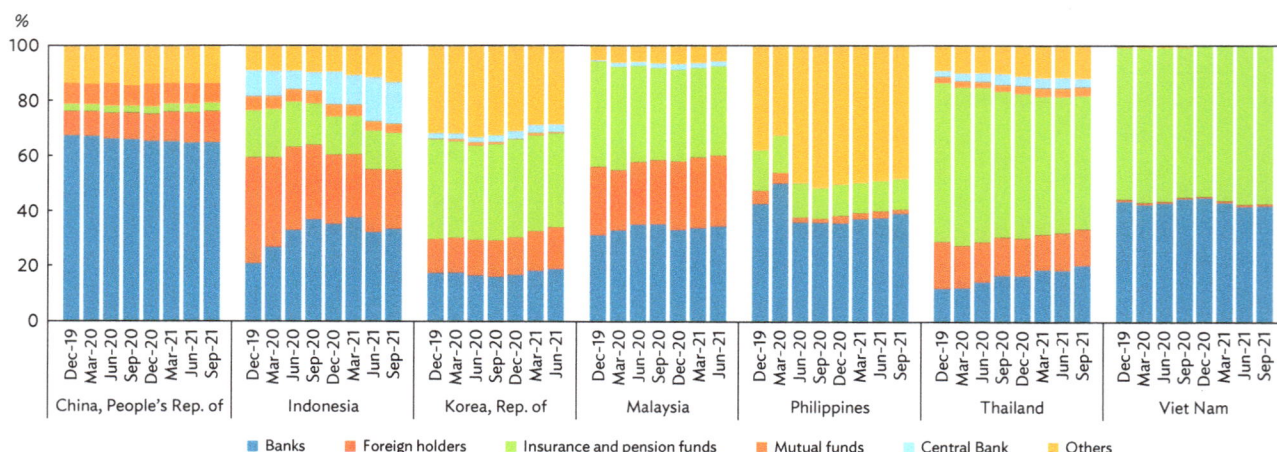

Notes:
1. Data coverage is from December 2019 to September 2021 except for the Republic of Korea and Malaysia (June 2021).
2. Data on central bank holdings are not available for the People's Republic of China, the Philippines, and Viet Nam.
3. Others include government institutions, individuals, securities companies, custodians, private corporations, and all other investors not elsewhere classified.
Source: *AsianBondsOnline* computations based on local market sources.

Box 3: Risks to Outlook—Downside Risks Outweigh Upside Risks

The short-term economic outlooks for the world and emerging East Asia remain positive, but downside risks continue to outweigh upside risks in the short term.[a] In particular, while vaccines offer the promise of an eventual return to something close to the pre-pandemic normal, the exact timetable for such a return remains highly uncertain. The global and regional economies are unsteadily but gradually regaining their footing after the unprecedented global health and economic shocks of the coronavirus disease (COVID-19) outbreak in early 2020. Nevertheless, a great deal of uncertainty remains about the trajectory of both the pandemic and its economic impact. Nowhere is this uncertainty more evident than among members of the Association of Southeast Asian Nations, which have been hit hard by a major Delta variant outbreak since April (**Figure B3**). Although the pandemic situation has improved in recent weeks, the unwelcome wave triggered new restrictions that dampened economic growth across the region.

The upshot is that notwithstanding the steady progress in vaccination, uncertainty surrounding COVID-19 is still the overarching risk to economic growth and financial stability in both emerging East Asia and the world. Just as the emergence of the Delta variant slowed the Association of Southeast Asian Nations' strong growth momentum, the future emergence of Lambda, Omega, and other variants with similarly significant

economic impacts cannot be ruled out. This lack of complete knowledge about COVID-19 and its containment suggests that the cycle of oscillation between hope and despair, between optimism and pessimism, will continue to beset the world economy and global financial markets.

Progress on vaccination is by far the single most important positive development in the world's fight against the pandemic. As noted earlier, vaccination reduces the humanitarian and economic costs of the disease. Vaccines weaken the link between COVID-19 outbreaks—be they Delta, Lambda, or Omega—on one hand, and social distancing restrictions and thus economic activity on the other. However, vaccines themselves are also a source of uncertainty. In particular, slower-than-expected rollouts of vaccines could trigger renewed COVID-19 waves and dampen the regional and global recovery. Vaccination progress has been noticeably slower in developing markets than in advanced economies. But given the contagious nature of the disease, which can easily spread across borders, all markets remain vulnerable unless all vaccinate their populations and bring the virus under control. Another major uncertainty related to vaccines is whether and for how long they are effective, especially against new variants.

A highly significant economic consequence of COVID-19, global supply chain disruptions, poses another major downside risk for global economic prospects. The International Monetary Fund's downgrading of its forecast for United States (US) gross domestic product growth in 2021 by a full percentage point—from 7.0% in July to 6.0% in October—was ultimately due to supply disruptions, which accelerated inventory drawdowns. The manufacturing sector of Germany, another large economy, has been affected by the lack of key inputs. These disruptions also contribute to softer consumption, for example, by limiting the availability of new cars amid the global semiconductor shortage.

A primary cause of the global supply disruptions, which have persisted longer than initially expected, are COVID-19 outbreaks in key links of global supply chains. These outbreaks have contributed to shortages of key parts and components such as semiconductors, which in turn have become a drag on manufacturing activity. Global supply chain disruptions have been exacerbated by global logistical challenges, as evidenced by congestion of epic proportions at US Pacific ports and skyrocketing trans-Pacific shipping freight rates.

Figure B3: April versus October Forecasts for 2021 GDP Growth in Select ASEAN Economies

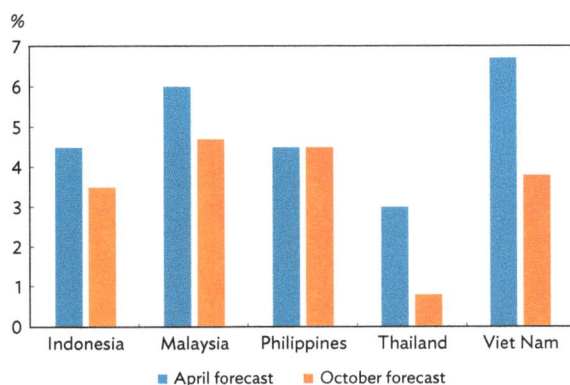

ASEAN = Association of Southeast Asian Nations, GDP = gross domestic product.
Source: Asian Development Bank. 2021. *Asian Development Outlook 2021 Update*. Manila.

---

[a] This box was written by Donghyun Park (principal economist) in the Economic Research and Regional Cooperation Department of the Asian Development Bank.

continued on next page

Box 3: Risks to Outlook—Downside Risks Outweigh Upside Risks   *continued*

Emerging East Asian economies, which are heavily dependent on trade and manufacturing, will be hit hard by the global supply disruptions.

Global supply chain disruptions are giving rise to another downside risk: increasing inflationary pressures. Negative supply shocks not only cause shortages but also higher prices. What is worse, under the current circumstances, is that the strengthening of demand will further exacerbate inflationary pressures. There are signs that the global demand that had been pent up due to social distancing restrictions needed to contain COVID-19 outbreaks is being unleashed as those restrictions are eased and economic activity recovers. The perfect storm of lower supply and higher demand is pushing up prices in both advanced economies and developing markets.

Growing inflationary pressures, in turn, are changing the calculus of global central banks regarding the trade-off between supporting economic growth versus containing inflation. In particular, global financial markets are closely monitoring whether the monetary policy actions of the US Federal Reserve signal a shift toward tightening. At

its 2-day meeting in September, the Federal Reserve indicated that it would soon begin to unwind its monthly USD120 billion purchases of US Treasuries and mortgage-backed securities. However, global and emerging East Asian financial markets have remained calm so far in response to the prospective tapering. Another potential shock to the region's financial stability is the ongoing liquidity crisis at Evergrande Group, one of the largest property developers in the People's Republic of China (PRC). Despite widespread concerns, Evergrande's financial problems have not yet affected the financial stability of the PRC or the region.

Overall, the balance of risks remains negative. The paramount risk to the world economy and global financial stability is the emergence of more intractable COVID-19 variants before the world achieves global herd immunity through vaccination. Yet, there are substantial upside risks too. Above all, rapid global vaccination can loosen the link between new outbreaks and economic growth sooner than expected. Another cause for optimism is the planned virtual meeting between the leaders of the PRC and the US, which may help to reduce the tension between the world's two giants. Any easing of the tension would significantly benefit the region and the world.

Bond Market Developments in the Third Quarter of 2021

Size and Composition

The outstanding amount of local currency bonds in emerging East Asia expanded to reach USD21.7 trillion at the end of September.

Emerging East Asia's local currency (LCY) bond market continued to grow in the third quarter (Q3) of 2021, reaching a size of USD21.7 trillion at the end of September.[2] Overall growth quickened to 3.4% quarter-on-quarter (q-o-q) in Q3 2021 from 2.9% q-o-q in the second quarter (Q2) (**Figure 1a**). The faster expansion stemmed from growth in both the government and corporate bond segments. Most of the region's governments continued to issue sovereign debt to finance economic relief measures amid the Delta variant-driven resurgence of coronavirus disease (COVID-19) cases. Growth in the region's corporate debt market was supported by robust issuance, as firms locked in low interest rates and most central banks in the region maintained accommodative monetary policies to support economic recovery.

All of the region's bond markets registered positive q-o-q gains in Q3 2021. Six out of nine markets showed faster q-o-q growth in Q3 2021 than in the previous quarter. The fastest-growing markets were those of Viet Nam and Singapore, while the markets of Malaysia and Hong Kong, China showed the weakest growth in Q3 2021.

On a year-on-year (y-o-y) basis, growth in emerging East Asia's bond market eased to 12.1% in Q3 2021 from 13.6% in Q2 2021 (**Figure 1b**). With the exception of Singapore, all of the region's bond markets experienced a slowdown in y-o-y growth in Q3 2021 compared with the previous quarter. Nevertheless, all nine markets posted positive y-o-y growth in Q3 2021. Indonesia and Viet Nam posted the fastest y-o-y expansions, while Hong Kong, China and Thailand had the slowest y-o-y growth.

The People's Republic of China (PRC) remained home to the region's largest LCY bond market with an outstanding

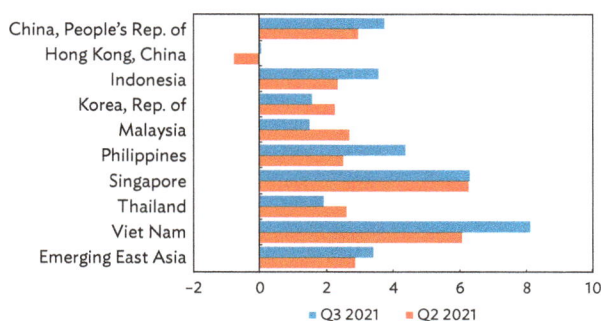

Figure 1a: Growth of Local Currency Bond Markets in the Second and Third Quarters of 2021 (q-o-q, %)

q-o-q = quarter-on-quarter, Q2 = second quarter, Q3 = third quarter.
Notes:
1. For Singapore, corporate bonds outstanding are based on *AsianBondsOnline* estimates.
2. Calculated using data from national sources.
3. Growth rates are calculated from local currency base and do not include currency effects.
4. Emerging East Asia growth figures are based on 30 September 2021 currency exchange rates and do not include currency effects.
Sources: People's Republic of China (CEIC Data Company); Hong Kong, China (Hong Kong Monetary Authority); Indonesia (Bank Indonesia; Directorate General of Budget Financing and Risk Management, Ministry of Finance; and Indonesia Stock Exchange); Republic of Korea (KG Zeroin Corporation and The Bank of Korea); Malaysia (Bank Negara Malaysia); Philippines (Bureau of the Treasury and Bloomberg LP); Singapore (Monetary Authority of Singapore, Singapore Government Securities, and Bloomberg LP); Thailand (Bank of Thailand); and Viet Nam (Bloomberg LP and Vietnam Bond Market Association).

bond stock of USD17.2 trillion at the end of September. The PRC's bond market accounted for a 78.9% share of the region's total bonds outstanding at the end of Q3 2021, up slightly from 78.7% at the end of Q2 2021. Growth in the PRC's LCY bond market picked up, rising to 3.8% q-o-q in Q3 2021 from 3.0% q-o-q in Q2 2021. The faster expansion in Q3 2021 stemmed from stronger growth in both the government and corporate bond segments. Growth in the government bond segment quickened to 4.0% q-o-q in Q3 2021 from 3.3% q-o-q in the previous quarter, driven by expansions in local government bonds, Treasury and other government bonds, and policy bank bonds. The expansion of the PRC's LCY government bond market was fueled by strong issuance of sovereign debt as the central and local governments continued to raise funds to support economic recovery and roll over maturing debt.

---

[2] Emerging East Asia comprises the People's Republic of China; Hong Kong, China; Indonesia; the Republic of Korea; Malaysia; the Philippines; Singapore; Thailand; and Viet Nam.

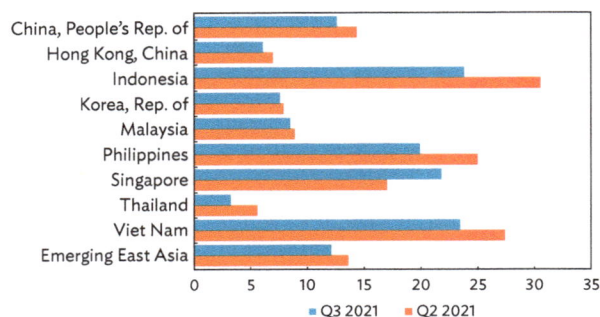

Figure 1b: Growth of Local Currency Bond Markets in the Second and Third Quarters of 2021 (y-o-y, %)

Q2 = second quarter, Q3 = third quarter, y-o-y = year-on-year.
Notes:
1. For Singapore, corporate bonds outstanding are based on *AsianBondsOnline* estimates.
2. Calculated using data from national sources.
3. Growth rates are calculated from local currency base and do not include currency effects.
4. Emerging East Asia growth figures are based on 30 September 2021 currency exchange rates and do not include currency effects.
Sources: People's Republic of China (CEIC Data Company); Hong Kong, China (Hong Kong Monetary Authority); Indonesia (Bank Indonesia; Directorate General of Budget Financing and Risk Management, Ministry of Finance; and Indonesia Stock Exchange); Republic of Korea (KG Zeroin Corporation and The Bank of Korea); Malaysia (Bank Negara Malaysia); Philippines (Bureau of the Treasury and Bloomberg LP); Singapore (Monetary Authority of Singapore, Singapore Government Securities, and Bloomberg LP); Thailand (Bank of Thailand); and Viet Nam (Bloomberg LP and Vietnam Bond Market Association).

Growth in the PRC's corporate bond stock also quickened, rising 3.3% q-o-q in Q3 2021 versus 2.3% q-o-q in the previous quarter. The growth in the corporate bond segment was underpinned by issuance of new corporate debt, which remained robust despite the risks brought about by the China Evergrande crisis that unfolded during the quarter. On a y-o-y basis, the PRC's LCY bond market's growth eased to 12.6% in Q3 2021 from 14.4% in Q2 2021.

The Republic of Korea's LCY bond market continued to be the second-largest in emerging East Asia, with an outstanding bond stock of USD2.4 trillion at the end of September. However, its share of the regional total dropped to 10.9% in Q3 2021 from 11.1% in the previous quarter. Growth in the Republic of Korea's total bond stock dropped to 1.6% q-o-q in Q3 2021 from 2.3% q-o-q in Q2 2021, driven by weaker growth in both the government and corporate bond segments. Government bonds outstanding rose 1.9% q-o-q in Q3 2021, down from 3.2% q-o-q in Q2 2021. Growth in central government bonds slowed to 3.0% q-o-q in Q3 2021

from 5.0% q-o-q in the prior quarter, as the government wound down debt issuance amid a strong economic recovery. Growth in the corporate bond stock also slipped to 1.4% q-o-q in Q3 2021 from 1.6% q-o-q in the previous quarter. In August, the Bank of Korea raised its policy rate from a record low of 0.50% to 0.75%, thus increasing borrowing costs. On a y-o-y basis, the Republic of Korea's LCY bond market growth inched down to 7.6% in Q3 2021 from 7.9% in Q2 2021.

Hong Kong, China's LCY bonds outstanding amounted to USD311.9 billion at the end of September. Total bonds outstanding posted 0.1% q-o-q growth in Q3 2021 after an 0.8% q-o-q drop in the previous quarter. The muted growth stemmed from a contraction in the corporate bond segment, which declined 2.9% q-o-q in Q3 2021 due to maturities and weak issuance. In contrast, growth in the government bond segment rose to 3.0% q-o-q in Q3 2021 from 2.4% q-o-q in the previous quarter. The growth was driven largely by a jump in the growth of outstanding Exchange Fund Bills (EFBs), which rose to 1.9% q-o-q in Q3 2021 from a marginal increase of 0.1% q-o-q in Q2 2021. In response to high demand due to ample liquidity in the financial system, the Hong Kong Monetary Authority (HKMA) increased its issuance of 91-day EFBs starting in September, fueling the rise in outstanding EFBs. On an annual basis, Hong Kong, China's LCY bond market rose 6.1% in Q3 2021, down from 7.0% in Q2 2021.

The total amount of LCY bonds outstanding of the member economies of the Association of Southeast Asian Nations (ASEAN) rose to USD1.9 trillion in Q3 2021 from USD1.8 trillion in Q2 2021.[3] Overall growth inched up to 3.6% q-o-q in Q3 2021 from 3.5% q-o-q in Q2 2021. The outstanding stock of government bonds totaled USD1.4 trillion, while the outstanding stock of corporate bonds amounted to USD0.5 trillion at the end of September. Singapore's bond market surpassed that of Thailand, becoming the largest among all ASEAN members. Thailand's bond market became the second largest, while Malaysia's bond market remained the third largest among all ASEAN members.

The outstanding amount of Singapore's LCY bonds climbed to USD434.6 billion at the end of September. Growth in total outstanding bonds was stable at 6.3% q-o-q in both Q2 2021 and Q3 2021. Growth

[3] LCY bond statistics for ASEAN include the markets of Indonesia, Malaysia, the Philippines, Singapore, Thailand, and Viet Nam.

in government bonds outstanding accelerated to 8.0% q-o-q in Q3 2021 from 4.8% q-o-q in the prior quarter. The expansion in government bonds stemmed from robust growth of outstanding Monetary Authority of Singapore (MAS) bills and Singapore Government Securities bills and bonds, which rose 12.9% q-o-q and 4.3% q-o-q, respectively. Meanwhile, growth in outstanding corporate bonds dropped to 3.0% q-o-q in Q3 2021 from 9.3% q-o-q in Q2 2021, driven in part by a contraction in issuance. On a y-o-y basis, Singapore's bond market growth rose to 21.9% in Q3 2021 from 17.1% in Q2 2021.

Thailand's LCY bond market reached a size of USD429.6 billion at the end of September. Overall growth eased to 1.9% q-o-q in Q3 2021 from 2.6% q-o-q in Q2 2021. The weaker expansion was driven primarily by slower growth in the corporate bond segment. Growth in outstanding government bonds rose to 2.2% q-o-q in Q3 2021 from 1.7% q-o-q in Q2 2021, as the government continued to issue sovereign debt to help fund its fiscal deficit and support stimulus measures to counter the prolonged impact of the pandemic on the tourism-reliant economy. In September, the Government of Thailand raised the ceiling of its public debt-to-gross domestic product (GDP) ratio to 70% from 60%, indicating that the government will continue to rely on borrowing to bolster economic recovery. Corporate bonds outstanding increased 1.2% q-o-q in Q3 2021, down from 5.1% q-o-q in the prior quarter, as the spread of the Delta variant heightened risks and dampened investor confidence. On a y-o-y basis, Thailand's LCY bond market growth eased to 3.3% in Q3 2021 from 5.6% in Q2 2021.

Malaysia's LCY bond market amounted to USD410.6 billion at the end of September. Overall growth weakened to 1.5% q-o-q in Q3 2021 from 2.7% q-o-q in Q2 2021. Growth in the government bond segment declined to 1.5% q-o-q in Q3 2021 from 3.9% q-o-q in the prior quarter. The expansion in the government bond segment was solely driven by growth in central government bonds, as there were no outstanding central bank bills at the end of September. Growth in the corporate bond segment was little changed, rising 1.4% q-o-q in Q3 2021 versus 1.3% q-o-q in Q2 2021. On an annual basis, Malaysia's LCY bond market expanded 8.5% y-o-y in Q3 2021, down from 8.9% y-o-y in the previous quarter.

Malaysia's *sukuk* (Islamic bond) market continued to dominate the *sukuk* market in emerging East Asia, with a total of USD262.0 billion of *sukuk* outstanding at the end of September. In Q3 2021, the stock of government *sukuk* reached USD109.6 billion on growth of 4.6% q-o-q. Meanwhile, outstanding corporate *sukuk* rose to USD152.4 billion on growth of 1.9% q-o-q.

Indonesia's LCY bond market reached a size of USD355.6 billion at the end of September, with growth rising to 3.6% q-o-q in Q3 2021 from 2.4% q-o-q in Q2 2021. The faster growth in Q3 2021 was supported by a stronger expansion in the government bond segment. Growth in the outstanding stock of LCY government bonds quickened to 4.0% q-o-q in Q3 2021 from 2.8% q-o-q in the previous quarter. Central government bonds drove much of the growth, rising 4.2% q-o-q in Q3 2021, while Bank Indonesia instruments posted a more modest 3.5% q-o-q growth. Corporate bonds outstanding continued to contract due to high maturities, dropping 0.2% q-o-q in Q3 2021 following a 2.4% q-o-q decline in the prior quarter. On a y-o-y basis, Indonesia's LCY bond market expanded 23.9% in Q3 2021, down from 30.6% in Q2 2021.

Outstanding Philippine LCY bonds totaled USD191.4 billion at the end of September. Overall growth increased to 4.4% q-o-q in Q3 2021 from 2.5% q-o-q in Q2 2021, supported by faster growth in the government bond segment. Outstanding government bonds rose 6.2% q-o-q in Q3 2021, up from 3.9% q-o-q in the prior quarter. Robust growth in outstanding Bangko Sentral ng Pilipinas securities (10.0% q-o-q) and Treasury bonds (8.3% q-o-q) drove the expansion in Q3 2021, while Treasury bills contracted 7.9% q-o-q. The contraction in the LCY corporate bond market steepened, declining 5.1% q-o-q in Q3 2021 after a 3.9% drop in the previous quarter, as movement restrictions intended to arrest the spread of the Delta variant continued to limit economic activities. On an annual basis, growth in the Philippine LCY bond market moderated to 20.0% y-o-y in Q3 2021 from 25.1% y-o-y in the previous quarter.

Viet Nam's LCY bond market remained the smallest in emerging East Asia with an outstanding bond stock of USD83.6 billion at the end of September. Overall growth rose to 8.1% q-o-q in Q3 2021 from 6.1% q-o-q in Q2 2021. The faster growth was driven by a rebound in the government bond segment, which expanded

4.2% q-o-q in Q3 2021 after a 0.5% q-o-q contraction in the previous quarter. Outstanding Treasury bonds rose 4.6% q-o-q in Q3 2021, driving much of the growth in the government bond segment. Government-guaranteed and municipal bonds posted a modest rise of 0.8% q-o-q, while there were no outstanding central bank bills at the end of September. Meanwhile, growth in outstanding corporate bonds moderated to 21.5% q-o-q in Q3 2021 from 36.6% q-o-q in Q2 2021. On a y-o-y basis, Viet Nam's LCY bond market growth eased to 23.5% in Q3 2021 from 27.5% in the prior quarter.

Government bonds continued to account for the majority of emerging East Asia's LCY bond stock, representing a 62.4% share of the total at the end of September. In nominal terms, the outstanding stock of government bonds in the region reached USD13.6 trillion at the end of Q3 2021 (**Table 1**). All nine government bond markets in the region posted positive q-o-q growth in Q3 2021. The q-o-q growth of the region's total government bond stock rose to 3.9% in Q3 2021 from 3.3% in Q2 2021, as most governments in the region continued to raise debt to support economic recovery amid the spread of the Delta variant. On a y-o-y basis, growth in the region's LCY government bond market slipped to 13.4% in Q3 2021 from 15.9% in Q2 2021.

The PRC and the Republic of Korea continued to be the two largest government bond markets in the region with a combined market share of 88.6% in Q3 2021. Meanwhile, the combined shares of ASEAN economies accounted for 10.2% of the region's government bonds stock. Among ASEAN economies, Indonesia had the largest stock of LCY government bonds at the end of September at USD326.1 billion. Thailand, Singapore, and Malaysia followed with outstanding LCY government bonds of USD313.1 billion, USD291.2 billion, and USD224.2 billion, respectively. The Philippines and Viet Nam had the region's two smallest government bond stocks at USD163.1 billion and USD62.1 billion, respectively.

The maturity structure of government bonds in emerging East Asia remained largely concentrated among medium- and long-dated tenors, except in the PRC and Hong Kong, China (**Figure 2**). In the PRC, the government issues bonds with tenors longer than 10 years less frequently due to a lack of liquidity. Investors in the PRC bond market are more inclined to trade shorter-dated bonds. This is also

true in Hong Kong, China, with the HKMA issuing Hong Kong Special Administrative Region bonds that carry 3-year tenors to meet strong demand from investors. Since 2020, the HKMA has increased its issuance of Silver bonds and iBonds, which carry 3-year maturities.

The outstanding stock of LCY corporate bonds in emerging East Asia totaled USD8.2 trillion at the end of September. Six of the region's nine corporate bond markets posted positive q-o-q growth in Q3 2021. The markets that posted q-o-q contractions during the quarter were those of Hong Kong, China; Indonesia; and the Philippines. Growth in the region's aggregate corporate bonds outstanding picked up, rising to 2.8% q-o-q in Q3 2021 from 2.2% q-o-q in Q2 2021. The faster growth stemmed primarily from an expansion in the PRC's corporate bond market, which is the region's largest market. Corporate bond market growth also marginally rose in Malaysia in Q3 2021 compared with Q2 2021. The rest of emerging East Asia's corporate bond markets posted weaker growth in Q3 2021 than in Q2 2021, but the faster growth in the PRC—and to a lesser extent, in Malaysia—propped up overall growth in the region's corporate bond market during the quarter.

ASEAN economies accounted for 6.4% of emerging East Asia's corporate bond market at the end of September. Within ASEAN, Malaysia, Singapore, and Thailand had the largest corporate bond markets with outstanding bond stocks of USD186.4 billion, USD143.4 billion, and USD116.5 billion, respectively. Indonesia and the Philippines followed, with outstanding bond stocks of USD29.5 billion and USD28.2 billion, respectively. Viet Nam's corporate bond market remained the region's smallest, with an outstanding stock of USD21.4 billion at the end of September.

The amount of LCY bonds outstanding in emerging East Asia was equivalent to 97.1% of the region's GDP at the end of September, up from 96.2% at the end of June and 95.9% in September 2020 (**Table 2**). The GDP equivalent of the government bond segment increased to 60.7% in Q3 2021 from 59.7% in Q2 2021, while corporate bonds remained unchanged at 36.5%. Most economies continued to raise debt from the bond market to support recovery, driving the overall increase in the debt stock.

Table 1: Size and Composition of Local Currency Bond Markets

	Q3 2020		Q2 2021		Q3 2021		Growth Rate (LCY-base %)				Growth Rate (USD-base %)			
							Q3 2020		Q3 2021		Q3 2020		Q3 2021	
	Amount (USD billion)	% share	Amount (USD billion)	% share	Amount (USD billion)	% share	q-o-q	y-o-y	q-o-q	y-o-y	q-o-q	y-o-y	q-o-q	y-o-y
China, People's Rep. of														
Total	14,457	100.0	16,507	100.0	17,159	100.0	5.4	19.9	3.8	12.6	9.6	26.2	3.9	18.7
Government	9,240	63.9	10,591	64.2	11,037	64.3	6.6	18.6	4.0	13.4	10.9	24.8	4.2	19.4
Corporate	5,217	36.1	5,917	35.8	6,123	35.7	3.2	22.2	3.3	11.4	7.4	28.6	3.5	17.4
Hong Kong, China														
Total	295	100.0	313	100.0	312	100.0	0.9	1.0	0.1	6.1	0.9	2.2	(0.2)	5.6
Government	149	50.6	157	50.1	161	51.6	0.1	(1.1)	3.0	8.2	0.1	0.04	2.7	7.7
Corporate	146	49.4	156	49.9	151	48.4	1.6	3.3	(2.9)	4.1	1.6	4.5	(3.1)	3.6
Indonesia														
Total	276	100.0	339	100.0	356	100.0	9.2	19.8	3.6	23.9	4.7	14.3	5.0	28.8
Government	246	89.3	310	91.4	326	91.7	10.1	22.6	4.0	27.3	5.5	17.0	5.3	32.3
Corporate	30	10.7	29	8.6	29	8.3	2.6	0.7	(0.2)	(4.2)	(1.7)	(3.9)	1.1	(0.5)
Korea, Rep. of														
Total	2,224	100.0	2,447	100.0	2,365	100.0	1.9	9.8	1.6	7.6	4.7	12.2	(3.4)	6.3
Government	914	41.1	1,028	42.0	996	42.1	3.0	12.1	1.9	10.4	5.8	14.6	(3.1)	9.1
Corporate	1,310	58.9	1,419	58.0	1,368	57.9	1.1	8.2	1.4	5.7	4.0	10.6	(3.6)	4.4
Malaysia														
Total	381	100.0	408	100.0	411	100.0	1.9	6.1	1.5	8.5	5.0	6.9	0.6	7.8
Government	204	53.6	223	54.6	224	54.6	2.3	8.0	1.5	10.6	5.5	8.8	0.6	9.8
Corporate	177	46.4	185	45.4	186	45.4	1.3	3.9	1.4	6.1	4.5	4.7	0.5	5.4
Philippines														
Total	168	100.0	192	100.0	191	100.0	8.8	21.5	4.4	20.0	11.8	29.9	(0.1)	14.0
Government	134	79.9	160	83.8	163	85.3	10.1	23.8	6.2	28.0	13.2	32.4	1.6	21.6
Corporate	34	20.1	31	16.2	28	14.7	3.8	12.9	(5.1)	(11.9)	6.7	20.7	(9.2)	(16.2)
Singapore														
Total	355	100.0	412	100.0	435	100.0	2.1	10.2	6.3	21.9	4.2	11.6	5.4	22.6
Government	229	64.7	272	65.9	291	67.0	2.4	13.0	8.0	26.3	4.5	14.4	7.1	27.0
Corporate	125	35.3	141	34.1	143	33.0	1.6	5.5	3.0	13.8	3.7	6.8	2.1	14.4
Thailand														
Total	444	100.0	443	100.0	430	100.0	4.2	8.3	1.9	3.3	44.9	59.7	(3.1)	(3.2)
Government	325	73.2	322	72.7	313	72.9	5.4	11.3	2.2	2.8	43.7	56.1	(2.9)	(3.6)
Corporate	119	26.8	121	27.3	117	27.1	1.1	0.9	1.2	4.5	48.3	70.2	(3.8)	(2.0)
Viet Nam														
Total	66	100.0	76	100.0	84	100.0	11.6	17.1	8.1	23.5	11.7	17.2	9.3	25.8
Government	56	83.7	59	77.2	62	74.4	8.9	6.8	4.2	9.7	9.0	6.9	5.3	11.7
Corporate	11	16.3	17	22.8	21	25.6	27.7	132.4	21.5	94.5	27.8	132.6	22.8	98.1
Emerging East Asia														
Total	18,666	100.0	21,138	100.0	21,741	100.0	4.8	17.5	3.4	12.1	9.2	23.5	2.9	16.5
Government	11,497	61.6	13,122	62.1	13,574	62.4	6.2	17.4	3.9	13.4	10.7	23.5	3.4	18.1
Corporate	7,169	38.4	8,017	37.9	8,168	37.6	2.8	17.9	2.8	10.0	7.0	23.6	1.9	13.9
Japan														
Total	11,492	100.0	11,520	100.0	11,428	100.0	1.3	2.3	(0.6)	4.9	3.7	4.8	(0.8)	(0.6)
Government	10,664	92.8	10,691	92.8	10,601	92.8	1.3	2.2	(0.7)	4.9	3.7	4.7	(0.8)	(0.6)
Corporate	828	7.2	829	7.2	828	7.2	1.9	4.1	(0.02)	5.5	4.3	6.6	(0.2)	(0.02)

( ) = negative, LCY = local currency, q-o-q = quarter-on-quarter, Q2 = second quarter, Q3 = third quarter, USD = United States dollar, y-o-y = year-on-year.
Notes:
1. For Singapore, corporate bonds outstanding are based on *AsianBondsOnline* estimates.
2. Corporate bonds include issues by financial institutions.
3. Bloomberg LP end-of-period LCY–USD rates are used.
4. For LCY base, emerging East Asia growth figures based on 30 September 2021 currency exchange rates and do not include currency effects.
5. Emerging East Asia comprises the People's Republic of China; Hong Kong, China; Indonesia; the Republic of Korea; Malaysia; the Philippines; Singapore; Thailand; and Viet Nam.
Sources: People's Republic of China (CEIC Data Company); Hong Kong, China (Hong Kong Monetary Authority); Indonesia (Bank Indonesia, Directorate General of Budget Financing and Risk Management, Ministry of Finance; and Indonesia Stock Exchange); Republic of Korea (KG Zeroin Corporation and The Bank of Korea); Malaysia (Bank Negara Malaysia); Philippines (Bureau of the Treasury and Bloomberg LP); Singapore (Monetary Authority of Singapore, Singapore Government Securities, and Bloomberg LP); Thailand (Bank of Thailand); Viet Nam (Bloomberg LP and Vietnam Bond Market Association); and Japan (Japan Securities Dealers Association).

Figure 2: Maturity Profiles of Local Currency Government Bonds in Emerging East Asia

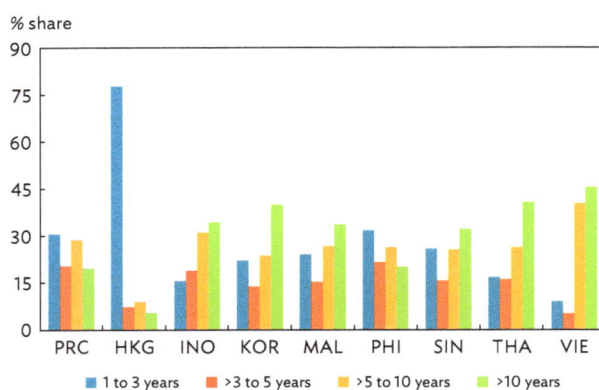

PRC = China, People's Rep. of; HKG = Hong Kong, China; INO = Indonesia; KOR = Korea, Rep. of; MAL = Malaysia; PHI = Philippines; SIN = Singapore; THA = Thailand; VIE = Viet Nam.
Notes:
1. Government bonds include Treasury bills and bonds.
2. Data as of 30 September 2021.
Source: AsianBondsOnline.

The PRC, Indonesia, the Republic of Korea, Malaysia, the Philippines, Singapore, Thailand, and Viet Nam saw increases in their bond market's share of GDP from Q2 2021 to Q3 2021. Hong Kong, China posted a decline.

In Q3 2021, three out of the nine markets in the region had their respective bond market's share of GDP exceed 100%, led by the Republic of Korea (148.1%). This was followed by Malaysia (125.2%) and Singapore (116.2%). Viet Nam's bond market, the smallest in the region, had a GDP share of 23.5%.

The government bond share of GDP in Singapore remained the largest in the region during the quarter at 77.8%, while that of Viet Nam was the smallest at 17.4%. The Republic of Korea had the largest corporate bond share of GDP at 85.7%, while Indonesia had the smallest at 2.6%.

Table 2: Size and Composition of Local Currency Bond Markets (% of GDP)

	Q3 2020	Q2 2021	Q3 2021
China, People's Rep. of			
Total	98.5	97.5	98.8
Government	63.0	62.5	63.5
Corporate	35.6	34.9	35.2
Hong Kong, China			
Total	84.2	87.2	85.9
Government	42.6	43.7	44.3
Corporate	41.6	43.5	41.6
Indonesia			
Total	26.5	30.8	31.0
Government	23.6	28.1	28.5
Corporate	2.8	2.6	2.6
Korea, Rep. of			
Total	141.2	147.2	148.1
Government	58.0	61.9	62.4
Corporate	83.2	85.4	85.7
Malaysia			
Total	116.7	121.9	125.2
Government	62.5	66.5	68.3
Corporate	54.2	55.4	56.8
Philippines			
Total	44.5	50.6	51.7
Government	35.6	42.4	44.1
Corporate	8.9	8.2	7.6
Singapore			
Total	101.5	112.4	116.2
Government	65.6	74.1	77.8
Corporate	35.9	38.3	38.3
Thailand			
Total	88.2	88.8	90.2
Government	64.5	64.6	65.7
Corporate	23.6	24.3	24.5
Viet Nam			
Total	24.9	22.8	23.5
Government	20.9	17.6	17.4
Corporate	4.1	5.2	6.0
Emerging East Asia			
Total	95.9	96.2	97.1
Government	59.1	59.7	60.7
Corporate	36.8	36.5	36.5
Japan			
Total	224.5	235.0	233.3
Government	208.4	218.1	216.4
Corporate	16.2	16.9	16.9

GDP = gross domestic product, Q2 = second quarter, Q3 = third quarter.
Notes:
1. Data for GDP is from CEIC Data Company.
2. For Singapore, corporate bonds outstanding are based on AsianBondsOnline estimates.
Sources: People's Republic of China (CEIC Data Company); Hong Kong, China (Hong Kong Monetary Authority); Indonesia (Bank Indonesia; Directorate General of Budget Financing and Risk Management, Ministry of Finance; and Indonesia Stock Exchange); Republic of Korea (KG Zeroin Corporation and The Bank of Korea); Malaysia (Bank Negara Malaysia); Philippines (Bureau of the Treasury and Bloomberg LP); Singapore (Monetary Authority of Singapore, Singapore Government Securities, and Bloomberg LP); Thailand (Bank of Thailand); Viet Nam (Bloomberg LP and Vietnam Bond Market Association); and Japan (Japan Securities Dealers Association).

Foreign Holdings

The foreign investor holdings share of LCY government bonds was down in all emerging East Asian markets except the PRC in Q3 2021.

The foreign holdings share decreased in the LCY government bonds markets of Indonesia, Malaysia, the Philippines, Thailand, and Viet Nam from Q2 2021 to Q3 2021, while it increased in the PRC (**Figure 3**). Although most markets in emerging East Asia experienced sustained net foreign fund flows into their government bond markets in Q3 2021, these were not substantial enough to raise the foreign holdings share. The anticipation of policy rate normalization in the United States (US) and other developed economies may have influenced the repositioning of offshore funds. The prospects of weaker regional currencies arising from an imminent tapering of monetary stimulus by the US Federal Reserve may also have affected foreign holdings. Moreover, the COVID-19 situation, while improving, continues to subject recovery prospects to uncertainty on risk of new waves of infection.

As mentioned, the PRC was the only market in emerging East Asia that had an increase in its foreign holdings share in Q3 2021. Foreign investors remained keen on PRC government bonds, lifting their holdings share to 10.6% from 10.3% at the end of June. The inclusion of PRC

government bonds in FTSE Russell's World Government Bond Index starting in October and foreign investment tax incentives may have attracted foreign investors to build their position in the market. Despite worries over China Evergrande's possible contagion effect, confidence in the PRC's overall LCY bond market seemed intact.

Indonesia and the Philippines had the largest decreases among the markets that experienced declines in their share of foreign investor holdings of government bonds. The downward movement was underpinned by foreign fund outflows from both markets in Q3 2021. The share in Indonesia fell by 1.3 percentage points to 21.6% at the end of September, the largest drop in the region. In the Philippines, foreign investors tapered their exposure to government bonds, with their holdings share decreasing by 0.9 percentage points to 1.6% at the end of September, reversing the gain in Q2 2021 when the share increased 0.2 percentage points to 2.5%. The Philippines has the second-smallest foreign holdings share in the region.

Relatively small declines in the foreign holdings share were seen in Malaysia, Viet Nam, and Thailand. The shares in Malaysia and Viet Nam fell by 0.1 percentage points each during Q3 2021. Malaysia's share was down to 25.9% at the end of September on the back of positive fund flows into the market, albeit of a lesser magnitude than in the previous quarter. Malaysia had the highest foreign holdings share in emerging East Asia at the end of September. However, political uncertainty may have caused foreign investors to slow their purchases of Malaysian government bonds. In Viet Nam, the foreign holdings share inched down to 0.7%, the smallest in the region, as opportunities for foreign investors are limited due to its small bond market. In Thailand, the foreign holdings share of government bonds slipped to 13.4% at the end of September after increasing to 13.7% at the end of June, ending the quarterly downward trend that had been in place since March 2019.

The Republic of Korea's foreign holdings share climbed to 15.4% at the end of June from 14.6% at the end of March (the latest quarter for which data are available for the Republic of Korea). The increase was underpinned by the largest inflows of foreign funds among emerging East Asian markets during Q2 2021. Amid cautiousness in most markets in the region and with Korean government bonds' attractiveness to foreign investors, they can be expected to continue increasing their exposure in the market.

Figure 3: Foreign Holdings of Local Currency Government Bonds in Select Asian Markets (% of total)

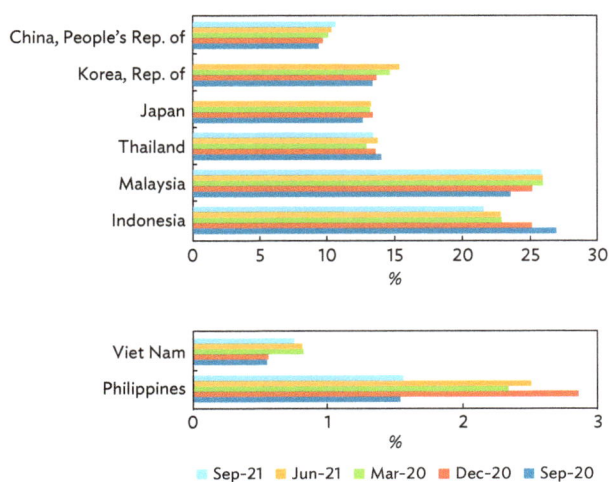

Note: Data for Japan and the Republic of Korea are as of 30 June 2021.
Source: *AsianBondsOnline*.

Foreign Fund Flows

Foreign buying of government bonds continued in most emerging East Asian markets in Q3 2021, albeit at a reduced pace compared with the previous quarter.

Emerging East Asia received total net inflows of USD35.0 billion in Q3 2021, down from USD36.3 billion in Q2 2021 and the lowest quarterly net inflows to date in 2021 (**Figure 4**). All markets in the region except for Indonesia and the Philippines recorded net foreign buying of government bonds during the quarter. In Q2 2021, on the other hand, all regional markets experienced net foreign buying. During Q3 2021, the largest inflows in the region were in July amounting to USD13.9 billion. Net inflows fell to their lowest level in August at USD7.4 billion before rebounding to USD13.8 billion in September.

Foreign fund flows into the region's bond market remained resilient despite the Federal Reserve's pronouncement that it would taper its monetary stimulus later this year, while also signaling that interest rate increases may follow more quickly than expected. The foreign fund inflows

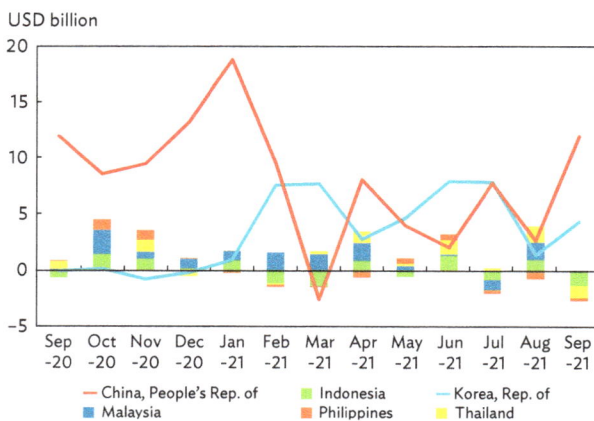

Figure 4: Foreign Capital Flows in Local Currency Bond Markets in Emerging East Asia

USD = United States dollar.
Notes:
1. The Republic of Korea and Thailand provided data on bond flows. For the People's Republic of China, Indonesia, Malaysia, and the Philippines, month-on-month changes in foreign holdings of local currency government bonds were used as a proxy for bond flows.
2. Data are as of 30 September 2021.
3. Figures were computed based on 30 September 2021 exchange rates to avoid currency effects.
Sources: People's Republic of China (*Wind Information*); Indonesia (Directorate General of Budget Financing and Risk Management, Ministry of Finance); Republic of Korea (Financial Supervisory Service); Malaysia (Bank Negara Malaysia); Philippines (Bureau of the Treasury); and Thailand (Thai Bond Market Association).

during Q3 2021 were likely supported by the improving COVID-19 situation in the region, as new cases declined and vaccination drives gained ground, which should translate to better recovery prospects absent new waves of infection. The relatively benign inflation environment and yield premiums in favor of emerging East Asian markets also buttressed the regional bond market's overall attractiveness to foreign investors.

The PRC's foreign fund inflows amounted to USD22.4 billion in Q3 2021, increasing from USD14.1 billion in the previous quarter. Foreign investors bought USD7.8 billion of government bonds in July and USD2.7 billion in August. In September, net inflows sharply increased to USD12.0 billion, the fastest pace of foreign buying since January (USD18.8 billion). Foreign funds entering the PRC's government bond market rose despite concerns over the fate of heavily indebted property developer China Evergrande. The upside, which is the inclusion of PRC government bonds in FTSE Russell's World Government Bond Index starting in October and tax incentives, likely outweighed default worries and resulted in foreign investors maintaining or building positions in the LCY bond market. The PRC had the largest net foreign fund inflows among emerging East Asian markets in Q3 2021 and was the major driver of the regional increase in foreign funds during the quarter.

The Republic of Korea had the second-largest net foreign fund inflows in emerging East Asia in Q3 2021, drawing in USD13.6 billion. This was, however, lower compared to USD15.4 billion in Q2 2021 when the Republic of Korea surpassed the PRC as the region's largest recipient of foreign funds. Foreign investors purchased USD7.8 billion of LCY bonds in July, USD1.4 billion in August, and USD4.4 billion in September. The attractive yield spread of Korean government bonds over rates in developed markets, amid expectations of tighter monetary policy following a policy rate hike in August, should continue to drive foreign interest in the market. Moreover, the Republic of Korea's sound external account position will make it less likely that foreign investments in the LCY bond market would abruptly lose value.

Malaysia and Thailand continued to register net inflows in Q3 2021, although both markets experienced significantly lower foreign buying compared to the previous quarter. In Malaysia, net inflows dropped to USD0.7 billion in Q3 2021 from USD2.2 billion in Q2 2021, posting the lowest quarterly net foreign buying since foreign funds returned to the Malaysian government bond market in Q2 2020. Political infighting and persistently high COVID-19 cases resulted in net foreign fund withdrawals of USD0.9 billion in July, which dragged down the quarterly inflows. Despite the downside risks, foreign buying resumed in August with USD1.5 billion of net inflows. However, this dwindled to USD0.1 billion in September. In Thailand, net inflows amounted to USD0.6 billion in Q3 2021, down from USD2.5 billion in Q2 2021. The Thai government bond market saw net foreign buying in July (USD0.3 billion) and August (USD1.4 billion), while it incurred net foreign selling of USD1.1 billion in September.

Indonesia and the Philippines were the two markets in emerging East Asia that experienced net foreign fund withdrawals in Q3 2021 after registering net inflows in the previous quarter. Indonesia's net outflows amounted to USD1.1 billion as a result of net foreign selling in July (USD0.8 billion) and September (USD1.3 billion), which offset net foreign buying in August (USD1.0 billion). While returns on Indonesian sovereign bonds are high relative to other markets in the region, this has not done much to lift foreign investor sentiment in the LCY bond market. Uncertainty over recovery prospects amid the COVID-19 situation continued to weigh down foreign investor appetite.

In the Philippines, foreign investors sold a net USD1.2 billion worth of government bonds in Q3 2021 after accumulating a net USD0.3 billion in Q2 2021. The Philippines is the only market in the region that incurred a net foreign sell-off in all 3 months of the quarter: July (USD0.3 billion), August (USD0.7 billion), and September (USD0.2 billion). Concerns over inflation, which registered a 32-month high of 4.9% y-o-y in August, may have discouraged fund inflows as inflation reduces returns. COVID-19 cases also peaked during the quarter, leading to the reimposition of the strictest quarantine measures and exacerbating uncertainty in the economy.

LCY Bond Issuance

Issuance of LCY bonds in emerging East Asia reached USD2.4 trillion in Q3 2021.

LCY bond issuance in emerging East Asia sustained its strong momentum in Q3 2021, with total issuance climbing to USD2.4 trillion from USD2.2 trillion in Q2 2021 (**Table 3**). Bond sales during the quarter were

buoyed by increased issuance from corporates and continued strong issuance from governments seeking to support relief and economic recovery measures amid new waves of COVID-19 cases in the region.

Since the start of the pandemic, issuance of LCY bonds has been robust, surpassing pre-pandemic levels and indicating the importance of LCY financing in sustaining economic resilience in the region. For the period from January to September, LCY bond issuance totaled USD6.6 trillion, equivalent to nearly 80% of the region's aggregate LCY bond issuance in 2020 (**Figure 5**).

During the quarter, five out of nine emerging East Asian markets recorded positive q-o-q issuance growth: the PRC, Indonesia, the Philippines, Singapore, and Thailand. While posting positive q-o-q growth in Q3 2021, issuance rates in the PRC, Singapore, and Thailand moderated from their respective q-o-q growth rates in Q2 2021. The four markets that recorded q-o-q contractions in issuance in Q3 2021 were Hong Kong, China; the Republic of Korea; Malaysia; and Viet Nam.

Both the corporate and government bond segments posted positive q-o-q hikes during the quarter, yet overall growth in LCY bond issuance moderated to 6.8% q-o-q from a 14.7% q-o-q hike in Q2 2021. This was largely due to a deceleration in issuance growth of Treasury and other government bonds, and central bank intruments during the quarter. In contrast, the issuance of corporate bonds surged in Q3 2021 compared with Q2 2021.

On a y-o-y basis, growth inched up to 2.5% in Q3 2021 from 2.2% in Q2 2021, buoyed by increased issuance in the PRC. Five markets, the PRC, Indonesia, the Philippines, Singapore, and Viet Nam, posted positive y-o-y growth. Contractions in y-o-y growth were noted in Hong Kong, China; the Republic of Korea; Malaysia; and Thailand.

In Q3 2021, total issuance in the region mostly comprised government bonds, which represented a 58.7% share of the total. This was down slightly from 59.7% logged in the prior quarter. Government bond issuance tallied USD1.4 trillion in Q3 2021, with growth easing to 5.0% q-o-q from 23.1% q-o-q as issuance growth of Treasuries and other government bonds decelerated from Q2 2021. Only the markets of Indonesia, the Philippines, and Thailand posted improved q-o-q growth in issuance of Treasury instruments and other government bonds in Q3 2021 compared with

Table 3: Local-Currency–Denominated Bond Issuance (gross)

	Q3 2020		Q2 2021		Q3 2021		Growth Rate (LCY-base %)		Growth Rate (USD-base %)	
	Amount (USD billion)	% share	Amount (USD billion)	% share	Amount (USD billion)	% share	Q3 2021		Q3 2021	
							q-o-q	y-o-y	q-o-q	y-o-y
China, People's Rep. of										
Total	1,574	100.0	1,492	100.0	1,668	100.0	11.6	0.6	11.8	6.0
Government	866	55.1	793	53.1	848	50.8	6.7	(7.1)	6.9	(2.1)
Central Bank	0	0.0	0	0.0	0	0.0	–	–	–	–
Treasury and Other Govt.	866	55.1	793	53.1	848	50.8	6.7	(7.1)	6.9	(2.1)
Corporate	707	44.9	699	46.9	820	49.2	17.1	10.1	17.4	16.0
Hong Kong, China										
Total	145	100.0	140	100.0	139	100.0	(0.8)	(3.7)	(1.1)	(4.2)
Government	117	80.8	110	78.5	113	81.8	3.2	(2.6)	3.0	(3.0)
Central Bank	117	80.7	106	75.9	109	78.9	3.0	(5.9)	2.7	(6.3)
Treasury and Other Govt.	0.1	0.1	4	2.6	4	2.9	9.9	3,000.0	9.6	2,985.5
Corporate	28	19.2	30	21.5	25	18.2	(15.8)	(8.6)	(16.0)	(9.0)
Indonesia										
Total	41	100.0	39	100.0	48	100.0	22.5	11.3	24.1	15.7
Government	39	93.9	37	96.6	46	95.2	20.7	12.8	22.3	17.3
Central Bank	9	21.6	21	55.3	27	57.0	26.2	193.4	27.9	205.0
Treasury and Other Govt.	30	72.3	16	41.3	18	38.2	13.3	(41.2)	14.8	(38.8)
Corporate	3	6.1	1	3.4	2	4.8	73.3	(12.7)	75.6	(9.3)
Korea, Rep. of										
Total	189	100.0	235	100.0	180	100.0	(19.5)	(3.7)	(23.4)	(4.8)
Government	85	44.8	101	43.2	78	43.4	(19.0)	(6.6)	(23.0)	(7.7)
Central Bank	31	16.2	31	13.3	27	15.0	(9.1)	(10.9)	(13.6)	(11.9)
Treasury and Other Govt.	54	28.6	70	29.9	51	28.4	(23.4)	(4.2)	(27.2)	(5.4)
Corporate	104	55.2	134	56.8	102	56.6	(19.9)	(1.3)	(23.8)	(2.5)
Malaysia										
Total	22	100.0	24	100.0	21	100.0	(14.2)	(3.5)	(15.0)	(4.2)
Government	12	57.4	13	55.3	12	55.9	(13.4)	(6.0)	(14.2)	(6.7)
Central Bank	0	0.0	0	0.0	0	0.0	–	–	–	–
Treasury and Other Govt.	12	57.4	13	55.3	12	55.9	(13.4)	(6.0)	(14.2)	(6.7)
Corporate	9	42.6	11	44.7	9	44.1	(15.3)	(0.2)	(16.1)	(0.9)
Philippines										
Total	25	100.0	42	100.0	42	100.0	4.5	74.4	0.002	65.8
Government	23	89.8	41	97.7	41	97.7	4.5	89.9	0.02	80.5
Central Bank	1	4.1	26	60.8	26	62.3	7.2	2,580.0	2.6	2,447.4
Treasury and Other Govt.	22	85.7	16	36.9	15	35.4	0.1	(28.0)	(4.3)	(31.6)
Corporate	3	10.2	1	2.3	1	2.3	5.1	(60.9)	0.6	(62.8)
Singapore										
Total	149	100.0	194	100.0	205	100.0	6.7	37.4	5.7	38.2
Government	145	97.5	185	95.4	200	97.4	8.9	37.3	8.0	38.1
Central Bank	119	80.2	155	80.0	174	84.8	13.2	45.4	12.1	46.2
Treasury and Other Govt.	26	17.3	30	15.4	26	12.6	(12.9)	(0.3)	(13.7)	0.3
Corporate	4	2.5	9	4.6	5	2.6	(39.8)	42.7	(40.3)	43.5
Thailand										
Total	93	100.0	69	100.0	69	100.0	5.8	(20.8)	0.6	(25.7)
Government	83	89.0	54	78.4	55	79.9	7.8	(28.9)	2.5	(33.4)
Central Bank	65	69.1	35	51.0	37	53.4	10.8	(38.9)	5.3	(42.7)
Treasury and Other Govt.	19	19.9	19	27.4	18	26.5	2.3	5.6	(2.8)	(1.0)
Corporate	10	11.0	15	21.6	14	20.1	(1.4)	45.0	(6.3)	36.0

continued on next page

Table 3 *continued*

	Q3 2020		Q2 2021		Q3 2021		Growth Rate (LCY-base %)		Growth Rate (USD-base %)	
							Q3 2021		Q3 2021	
	Amount (USD billion)	% share	Amount (USD billion)	% share	Amount (USD billion)	% share	q-o-q	y-o-y	q-o-q	y-o-y
Viet Nam										
Total	8	100.0	9	100.0	9	100.0	(6.0)	9.9	(5.0)	11.9
Government	5	63.7	4	47.7	5	53.2	4.8	(8.2)	6.0	(6.5)
Central Bank	0	0.0	0	0.0	0	0.0	–	–	–	–
Treasury and Other Govt.	5	63.7	4	47.7	5	53.2	4.8	(8.2)	6.0	(6.5)
Corporate	3	36.3	5	52.3	4	46.8	(15.9)	41.7	(15.0)	44.3
Emerging East Asia										
Total	2,246	100.0	2,245	100.0	2,381	100.0	6.8	2.5	6.1	6.0
Government	1,375	61.2	1,340	59.7	1,398	58.7	5.0	(1.3)	4.3	1.7
Central Bank	341	15.2	375	16.7	401	16.8	8.6	19.0	6.9	17.6
Treasury and Other Govt.	1,034	46.0	965	43.0	997	41.9	3.7	(7.6)	3.3	(3.6)
Corporate	871	38.8	905	40.3	983	41.3	9.4	8.5	8.7	12.9
Japan										
Total	533	100.0	505	100.0	502	100.0	(0.3)	(0.6)	(0.5)	(5.8)
Government	484	90.8	462	91.5	464	92.5	0.7	1.2	0.6	(4.1)
Central Bank	0	0.0	10	1.9	10	2.0	7.5	–	–	–
Treasury and Other Govt.	484	90.8	452	89.6	454	90.5	0.6	(1.0)	0.4	(6.2)
Corporate	49	9.2	43	8.5	38	7.5	(11.8)	(18.5)	(12.0)	(22.8)

( ) = negative, – = not applicable, LCY = local currency, q-o-q = quarter-on-quarter, Q2 = second quarter, Q3 = third quarter, USD = United States dollar, y-o-y = year-on-year.
Notes:
1. Corporate bonds include issues by financial institutions.
2. Bloomberg LP end-of-period LCY–USD rates are used.
3. For LCY base, emerging East Asia growth figures are based on 30 September 2021 currency exchange rates and do not include currency effects.
Sources: People's Republic of China (CEIC Data Company); Hong Kong, China (Hong Kong Monetary Authority); Indonesia (Bank Indonesia; Directorate General of Budget Financing and Risk Management, Ministry of Finance; and Indonesia Stock Exchange); Republic of Korea (KG Zeroin Corporation and and The Bank of Korea); Malaysia (Bank Negara Malaysia); Philippines (Bureau of the Treasury and Bloomberg LP); Singapore (Singapore Government Securities and Bloomberg LP); Thailand (Bank of Thailand and ThaiBMA); Viet Nam (Bloomberg LP, Hanoi Stock Exchange, and Vietnam Bond Market Association); and Japan (Japan Securities Dealers Association).

Figure 5: Local Currency Bond Issuance in Emerging East Asia

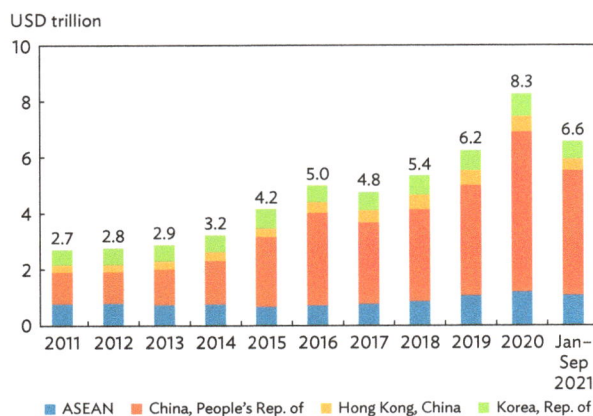

USD trillion

ASEAN = Association of Southeast Asian Nations, USD = United States dollar.
Source: *AsianBondsOnline*.

the previous quarter. Issuance growth of Treasuries and other government bonds moderated or contracted from the previous quarter in all other emerging East Asian economies in Q3 2021. Treasuries and other government bonds accounted for 71.3% of the regional government issuance total during the quarter. Compared with the same period a year ago, issuance of Treasuries and other government bonds contracted 7.6% y-o-y in Q3 2021 after rising a marginal 0.2% y-o-y in Q2 2021.

Central bank issuance also contributed to the region's government bond issuance growth, accounting for 28.7% of government bond issuance during Q3 2021. Issuance of central bank instruments in the region totaled USD401.2 billion, with growth moderating to 8.6% q-o-q in Q3 2021 from 9.3% q-o-q in Q2 2021. Fueling growth was increased issuance from the Hong Kong Monetary Authority, Bank Indonesia, the Bangko Sentral ng Pilipinas, MAS, and the Bank of Thailand. In contrast, the Bank of Korea reduced its issuance in Q3 2021, while there was an absence of issuance from the

People's Bank of China, Bank Negara Malaysia, and the State Bank of Vietnam. On a y-o-y basis, growth in central bank issuance inched up to 19.0% in Q3 2021 from 18.9% in Q2 2021.

Corporate bond sales in emerging East Asia were active in Q3 2021 as growth swelled to 9.4% q-o-q from 4.1% q-o-q in Q2 2021 to reach USD983.3 billion. Growth was buoyed by robust issuance of corporate bonds in the PRC. The only other markets that posted positive q-o-q growth rates in Q3 2021 were Indonesia and the Philippines, both of which recorded contractions in issuance in the preceding quarter. On an annual basis, corporate bond issuance in the region rebounded from a 1.5% y-o-y decline in Q2 2021 to a growth of 8.5% y-o-y in Q3 2021.

The PRC accounted for about 70% of the aggregate LCY bond issuance of emerging East Asian markets in Q3 2021. Total PRC bond sales summed to USD1,668.1 billion during the quarter, up 11.6% q-o-q. Growth, however, moderated from an expansion of 17.1% q-o-q recorded in Q2 2021. Much of the growth in issuance came from corporate bonds, with growth accelerating to 17.1% q-o-q in Q3 2021 from only 1.3% q-o-q in Q2 2021.

The lower growth rate for Q3 2021 was largely due to the upsurge in local government bond issuance that occurred in Q2 2021 as local governments sought to meet their quotas for bond issuance. Local government bond issuance remained strong but fell 7.0% q-o-q after a 173.5% q-o-q rise in Q2 2021. Policy bank bond issuance was also stable, with issuance in Q3 2021 roughly similar to that of Q2 2021. There was an uptick in the growth of Treasury bonds, with issuance rising 37.6% q-o-q. This was the main driver in the 6.7% q-o-q increase in total government bond issuance. Overall, issuance of Treasury bonds for the first 3 quarters in 2021 was about the same as last year.

Corporate bond issuance accelerated in Q3 2021 largely due to an increase in the issuance of commercial paper, which grew 17.1% q-o-q. Most of the corporate bond issuance for Q3 2021 was due to the refinancing of maturities, as corporate bonds outstanding only grew 3.3% q-o-q.

The Republic of Korea was one of the two markets in emerging East Asia that posted declines in issuance for all bond segments. Total bond sales reached USD180.0 billion in Q3 2021, reflecting a 19.5% q-o-q contraction after rising 14.2% q-o-q in Q2 2021. Corporate bond issuance during the quarter plunged 19.9% q-o-q from a 16.6% q-o-q hike in Q2 2021. Government bond issuance fell 19.0% q-o-q after 11.1% q-o-q growth in Q1 2021. The government eased its issuance of Treasury instruments during the quarter following large-volume issuance in the first half of the year to fund its annual budget, which included two supplemental budgets approved this year. Central bank issuance also declined 9.1% q-o-q in Q3 2021. On a y-o-y basis, bond issuance growth contracted 3.7% in Q3 2021 from a growth of 5.8% in Q2 2021.

In Hong Kong, China, LCY bond issuance continued to contract for the third straight quarter, falling 0.8% q-o-q in Q3 2021 after a 2.2% q-o-q decline in Q2 2021. Overall growth was dragged down by the decline in the issuance of corporate bonds, which slumped 15.8% q-o-q in Q3 2021. Growth in government bond issuance moderated to 3.2% q-o-q from a rise of 4.5% q-o-q in Q2 2021. Issuance growth of Treasury instruments sharply decelerated to 9.9% q-o-q from a 944.4% q-o-q hike in Q2 2021 due to a high base effect with the issuance of inflation-linked retail bonds, or iBonds in the previous quarter. On an annual basis, issuance in Hong Kong, China's LCY bonds declined 3.7% y-o-y in Q3 2021 following 2.1% y-o-y growth in Q2 2021.

Bond issuance among ASEAN member economies totaled USD394.4 billion, accounting for a 16.6% share of emerging East Asia's issuance in Q3 2021. LCY bond issuance growth in ASEAN markets decelerated to 6.3% q-o-q in Q3 2021 from 12.7% q-o-q in Q2 2021. During the same period, growth on a y-o-y basis eased to 18.2% from 30.9%. All ASEAN member economies increased their issuance volumes in Q3 2021 versus Q2 2021, except for Malaysia and Viet Nam. Singapore remained the largest source of new LCY bonds in Q3 2021, with its share of ASEAN total issuance at 52.1%. The next largest shares of ASEAN bond issuance were those of Thailand and Indonesia, with respective shares of 17.6% and 12.1%.

In Singapore, LCY bond sales climbed to USD205.4 billion in Q3 2021 on growth of 6.7% q-o-q, a moderation from the 15.3% q-o-q hike in the preceding quarter. Government bond issuance grew 8.9% q-o-q, driven solely by a faster increase in issuance of MAS bills. In contrast, issuance of Singapore Government Securities declined 12.9% q-o-q in Q3 2021 after rising 25.2% q-o-q in the prior quarter. Corporate bond issuance declined 39.8% q-o-q, dragged down by weak sentiment due to a delay in the reopening of Singapore's economy amid rising COVID-19 cases during the quarter. On an annual basis, growth in issuance of LCY bonds in Singapore slipped to 37.4% y-o-y in Q3 2021 from 38.4% y-o-y in Q2 2021.

Issuance in Thailand rose 5.8% q-o-q to USD69.3 billion in Q3 2021. Growth was driven solely by government bond issuance, which rose 7.8% q-o-q to USD55.4 billion. While Treasury and other government bond issuance rose 2.3% q-o-q, central bank bond issuance grew 10.8% q-o-q to USD37.0 billion. Growth in Thailand's bond issuance was dragged down by corporate bond issuance, which declined 1.4% q-o-q to USD14.0 billion. On a y-o-y basis, LCY bond issuance in Thailand continued to contract, declining 20.8% in Q3 2021 from 9.5% in Q2 2021.

LCY bond issuance in Indonesia totaled USD47.9 billion in Q3 2021, with growth accelerating to 22.5% q-o-q from 12.0% q-o-q in the prior quarter. Growth was largely driven by government bonds, which rose at a faster pace of 20.7% q-o-q in Q3 2021 versus 12.9% q-o-q in Q2 2021. The q-o-q expansion in government bond issuance was largely driven by increased issuance of Sukuk Bank Indonesia. The government also issued an increased volume of Treasury bills and bonds during the quarter to support a wider budget deficit brought about by pandemic-related stimulus. Corporate bonds surged 73.3% q-o-q in Q3 2021, a turnaround from an 8.5% q-o-q contraction in Q2 2021, as more corporates tapped the debt market to secure funding amid low borrowing costs and to refinance debt maturities. On a y-o-y basis, growth in issuance of LCY bonds moderated to 11.3% in Q3 2021 from 30.9% in Q2 2021.

LCY bond issuance in the Philippines rebounded in Q3 2021, posting growth of 4.5% q-o-q after contracting 4.0% q-o-q in Q2 2021. Total issuance tallied USD42.1 billion, with both government and corporate bonds recovering from contractions in Q2 2021. Government bond issuance rose 4.5% q-o-q, fueled by increased issuance of Bangko Sentral ng Pilipinas bills during the quarter, while issuance of Treasury bills and bonds were broadly unchanged from their levels in the previous quarter. Corporate bond issuance rose 5.1% q-o-q following a 20.2% q-o-q decline in Q2 2021.

On an annual basis, LCY bond issuance growth in the Philippines moderated to 74.4% y-o-y in Q3 2021 after rising 195.4% y-o-y in Q2 2021.

In Malaysia, LCY bond issuance totaled USD20.7 billion in Q3 2021, declining 14.2% q-o-q following a 1.0% q-o-q hike in Q2 2021. All bond segments posted q-o-q and y-o-y declines during the quarter. Government bond issuance fell 13.4% q-o-q in Q3 2021 after declining 1.8% q-o-q in the preceding quarter. Issuance solely comprised Malaysian Government Securities and Government Investment Issues, as Bank Negara Malaysia has yet to resume its issuance of central bank bills. Corporate bonds also fell 15.3% q-o-q after a 4.7% q-o-q gain in Q2 2021. On an annual basis, LCY bond issuance in Malaysia declined 3.5% y-o-y in Q3 2021, after rising 7.4% y-o-y in Q2 2021.

LCY bond issuance in Viet Nam fell to USD8.9 billion in Q3 2021 on a 6.0% q-o-q decline following a robust 271.1% q-o-q gain in Q2 2021. The contraction in issuance was due to the corporate bond segment, whose issuance fell 15.9% q-o-q. Growth in government bond issuance also moderated to 4.8% q-o-q in Q3 2021 from 160.9% q-o-q expansion in Q2 2021. The State Bank of Vietnam has yet to resume issuance of bills, which were last issued in the first quarter of 2020. On a y-o-y basis, LCY bond issuance in Viet Nam rose at a pace of 9.9% in Q3 2021, down from 57.1% in Q2 2021.

Cross-Border Bond Issuance

Cross-border bond issuance in emerging East Asia reached USD6.9 billion in Q3 2021.

Intraregional bond issuance in emerging East Asia reached USD6.9 billion in Q3 2021, an 8.6% q-o-q decline from the USD7.5 billion raised in the previous quarter, but a jump from the USD2.8 billion issuance volume registered in the same period in 2020. Institutions from Hong Kong, China continued to lead the issuance of cross-border bonds, with an aggregate share of 78.3% of the regional total in Q3 2021 (**Figure 6**). Other economies that registered cross-border bond issuances were the PRC, the Republic of Korea, the Lao People's Democratic Republic (Lao PDR), Malaysia, Singapore, and Thailand. Monthly issuance volume amounted to USD2.2 billion and USD2.9 billion in July and August, respectively. The month of September registered the lowest issuance volume for the quarter at USD1.8 billion, which can be

Figure 6: Origin Economies of Intra-Emerging East Asian Bond Issuance in the Third Quarter of 2021

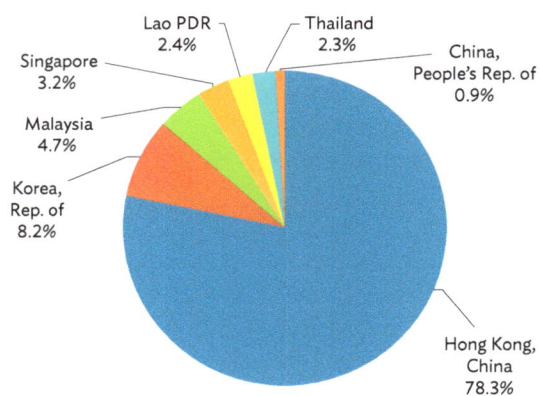

Lao PDR 2.4%
Thailand 2.3%
Singapore 3.2%
China, People's Rep. of 0.9%
Malaysia 4.7%
Korea, Rep. of 8.2%
Hong Kong, China 78.3%

Lao PDR = Lao People's Democratic Republic.
Source: *AsianBondsOnline* calculations based on Bloomberg LP data.

attributed to the rise in global yields making it more costly for institutions to issue bonds.

Hong Kong, China continued to dominate the region with an aggregate issuance of USD5.4 billion in Q3 2021, slightly lower than the USD5.6 billion raised in the previous quarter. Sixteen institutions from Hong Kong, China issued cross-border bonds, mostly denominated in Chinese yuan. Companies from the finance and consumer goods sectors led all others in cross-border issuance with shares of 38.0% and 35.4%, respectively. China Mengniu Dairy, a manufacturer and distributor of dairy products, was the single-largest issuer in both Hong Kong, China and the region with total cross-border bond issuance of USD1.4 billion, comprising CNY-denominated short-term bonds. The Hong Kong Mortgage Corporation followed with a total of USD1.2 billion with multiple issuances of CNY-denominated bonds. China National Travel Service (HK) Group was also one of the major issuers during the quarter with a total of USD465.5 million worth of 5-year CNY-denominated bonds. Another notable issuance was the USD368.3 million 5-year bond from Eastern Air Overseas (Hong Kong) Corporation Limited, which was denominated in Singapore dollars.

The Republic of Korea registered the second-largest issuance volume of cross-border bonds in Q3 2021, reaching USD560.4 million. However, this was a 30.9% q-o-q decline from USD811.5 million in the previous quarter. The Export–Import Bank of Korea was

the largest issuer in Q3 2021 with aggregate volume of USD324.6 million—of which USD206.1 million was denominated in Hong Kong dollars, USD79.3 million in Chinese yuan, and USD39.2 million in Philippine pesos. The bonds were issued in various tenors of between 1 year and 5 years. Another government-related institution that issued cross border bonds was the Korea Development Bank, raising USD25.7 million via 4-year HKD-denominated bonds. The remaining issuer of cross-border bonds in the Republic of Korea was Hyundai Capital Services with a total of USD210.1 million worth of 3-year bonds issued in both Chinese yuan and Hong Kong dollars.

In Malaysia, two banks issued cross-border bonds in Q3 2021 with a total volume of USD319 million. Malayan Banking raised USD220.3 million via issuance of 1-year and 3-year bonds, denominated in Hong Kong dollars and Chinese yuan, while CIMB Bank issued USD98.6 million worth of 5-year HKD-denominated bonds.

Only three institutions issued cross-border bonds in Singapore in Q3 2021 for a total of USD219.9 million. DBS Group raised USD179.8 million via issuance of a 5-year HKD-denominated bond, while DBS Bank issued USD1.3 million of HKD-denominated short-term bonds. Korea Development Bank Singapore issued a USD38.8 million 1-year CNY-denominated bond.

In the Lao PDR, state-owned EDL Generation Public Company, which owns and operates electric generation and transmission assets, issued USD167.0 million worth of 3-year and 4-year bonds denominated in Thai baht. In Thailand, CIMB Thai Bank was the sole issuer of cross-border bonds, raising USD157.7 million worth of 10-year bonds denominated in Malaysian ringgit. In the PRC, manufacturing company Xtep International Holdings issued USD64.2 million worth of 6-year HKD-denominated bonds.

The top 10 issuers of cross-border bonds in the region had an aggregate issuance volume of USD5.1 billion and accounted for 74.9% of the regional total. Nine firms on the list were from Hong Kong, China. They issued a total of USD4.8 billion, led by Mengniu Dairy, the Hong Kong Mortgage Corporation, and China Travel Service HK Group. The remaining firm on the list that was not from Hong Kong, China was the Export–Import Bank of Korea.

The Chinese yuan remained the predominant currency of cross-border bonds in emerging East Asia in Q3 2021, with an aggregate issuance volume of USD5.1 billion and a share of 74.6% of the regional total (**Figure 7**). Firms that issued in this currency were from Hong Kong, China; the Republic of Korea; Malaysia; and Singapore. The second most widely used currency during the quarter was the Hong Kong dollar with an aggregate issuance volume of USD788.9 billion and an 11.5% share of the regional total. Other currencies were the Singapore dollar (USD589.2 million, 8.6%); Thai baht (USD167 million, 2.4%); Malaysian ringgit (USD157.7 million, 2.3%); and the Philippine peso (USD39.2 million, 0.6%).

In Q3 2021, financial companies continued to dominate the intraregional bond market in emerging East Asia, reaching an aggregate volume of USD3.1 billion and comprising almost half of the regional total (**Figure 8**). The largest issuers from this category include the Hong Kong Mortgage Corporation and the Export–Import Bank of Korea. Companies involved in consumer products had the second-largest share at 28.6%, reaching a total volume of USD2.0 billion, and also registered the largest gain in sectoral share, driven by the increased issuance of cross-border bonds by China Mengniu Dairy. Utilities' share inched up to 11.5% on a total issuance volume of USD787.6 million, led by issuances from electric generation companies China Power International Development and the

Lao PDR's EDL Generation Public Company, and water company Beijing Enterprises Water Group. The issuance volume of real estate companies fell almost in half to USD654.5 million in Q3 2021, and its share fell to 9.6% from 16.9% in the previous quarter. In July, China Everbright Greentech, a PRC government-related institution based in Hong Kong, China, issued USD155.2 million worth of CNY-denominated 5-year green bonds referred to as "carbon neutrality and rural vitalization medium-term notes." China Everbright Greentech was also the sole issuer of cross-border bonds in Q3 2021 in the energy sector.

G3 Currency Issuance

G3 currency bonds issued in emerging East Asia during January–September amounted to USD302.5 billion.

G3 currency bonds issued in emerging East Asia amounted to USD302.5 billion during the January–September period, growing 4.7% y-o-y from the USD289.0 billion raised during the same period in 2020 (**Table 4**).[4] Higher volumes of G3 issuance in some of the region's economies compared to the previous year contributed to this expansion. This was in spite of the growing systemic risk stemming from the struggles of

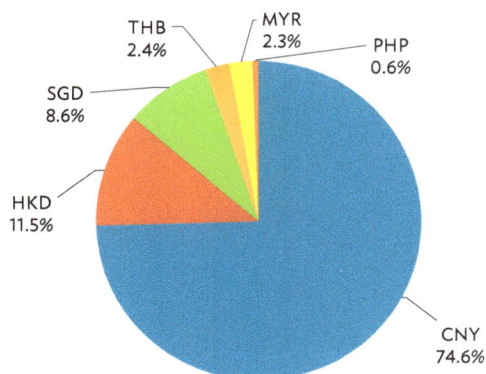

Figure 7: Currency Shares of Intra-Emerging East Asian Bond Issuance in the Third Quarter of 2021

CNY = Chinese renminbi, HKD = Hong Kong dollar, MYR = Malaysian ringgit, PHP = Philippine peso, SGD = Singapore dollar, THB = Thai baht.
Source: *AsianBondsOnline* calculations based on Bloomberg LP data.

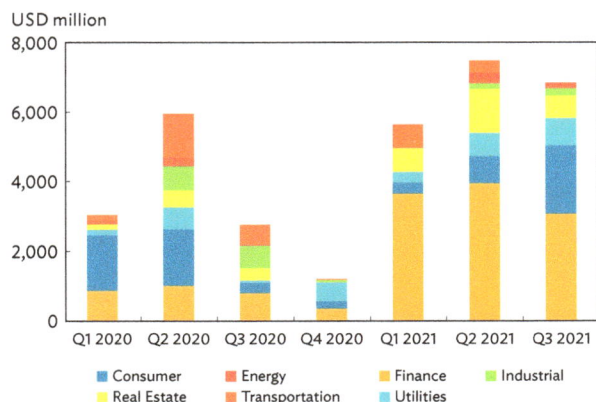

Figure 8: Intra-Emerging East Asian Bond Issuance in the Third Quarter of 2021, by Industry

Q1 = first quarter, Q2 = second quarter, Q3 = third quarter, Q4 = fourth quarter, USD = US dollar.
Note: Figures were computed based on 30 September 2021 exchange rates to avoid currency effects.
Source: *AsianBondsOnline* calculations based on Bloomberg LP data.

[4] G3 currency bonds are denominated in either euros, Japanese yen, or US dollars. For the discussion on G3 currency issuance, emerging East Asia comprises Cambodia; the People's Republic of China; Hong Kong, China; Indonesia; the Republic of Korea; Malaysia; the Philippines; Singapore; Thailand; and Viet Nam.

Table 4: G3 Currency Bond Issuance

2020			January–September 2021		
Issuer	**Amount (USD billion)**	**Issue Date**	**Issuer**	**Amount (USD billion)**	**Issue Date**
Cambodia	**0.4**		**Cambodia**	**0.0**	
China, People's Rep. of	**232.3**		**China, People's Rep. of**	**169.8**	
Industrial and Commercial Bank of China 3.58% Perpetual	2.9	23-Sep-20	Industrial and Commercial Bank of China 3.200% Perpetual	6.2	24-Sep-21
Bank of China 3.60% Perpetual	2.8	4-Mar-20	China Development Bank 0.380% 2022	2.0	10-Jun-21
Bank of Communications 3.80% Perpetual	2.8	18-Nov-20	Prosus 3.061% 2031	1.9	13-Jul-21
Others	223.8		Others	159.8	
Hong Kong, China	**34.8**		**Hong Kong, China**	**34.4**	
AIA Group 3.200% 2040	1.8	16-Sep-20	NWD Finance 4.125% Perpetual	1.2	10-Jun-21
MTR Corporation 1.625% 2030	1.2	19-Aug-20	Hong Kong, China (Sovereign) 1.375% 2031	1.0	2-Feb-21
AIA Group 3.375% 2030	1.0	7-Apr-20	Bank of Communications 2.304% 2031	1.0	8-Jul-21
Others	30.9		Others	31.2	
Indonesia	**27.9**		**Indonesia**	**23.3**	
Indonesia (Sovereign) 3.85% 2030	1.7	15-Apr-20	Indonesia (Sovereign) 3.05% 2051	2.0	12-Jan-21
Indonesia (Sovereign) 4.20% 2050	1.7	15-Apr-20	Perusahaan Penerbit SBSN Indonesia III 1.50% 2026	1.3	9-Jun-21
Indonesia (Sovereign) 0.90% 2027	1.2	14-Jan-20	Indonesia (Sovereign) 1.85% 2031	1.3	12-Jan-21
Others	23.4		Others	18.8	
Korea, Rep. of	**30.0**		**Korea, Rep. of**	**34.7**	
Korea Housing Finance Corporation 0.010% 2025	1.2	5-Feb-20	Posco 0.00% 2026	1.2	1-Sep-21
Korea Development Bank 1.250% 2025	1.0	3-Jun-20	Korea Housing Finance Corporation 0.01% 2026	1.2	29-Jun-21
Export–Import Bank of Korea 0.829% 2025	0.9	27-Apr-20	SK Hynix 1.50% 2026	1.0	19-Jan-21
Others	26.9		Others	31.3	
Malaysia	**17.2**		**Malaysia**	**12.9**	
Petronas Capital 4.55% 2050	2.8	21-Apr-20	Petronas Capital 3.404% 2061	1.8	28-Apr-21
Petronas Capital 3.50% 2030	2.3	21-Apr-20	Petronas Capital 2.480% 2032	1.3	28-Apr-21
Others	12.2		Others	9.9	
Philippines	**15.5**		**Philippines**	**8.3**	
Philippines (Sovereign) 2.65% 2045	1.5	10-Dec-20	Philippines (Sovereign) 3.20% 2046	2.3	6-Jul-21
Philippines (Sovereign) 2.95% 2045	1.4	5-May-20	Philippines (Sovereign) 1.75% 2041	0.9	28-Apr-21
Others	12.6		Others	5.1	
Singapore	**14.7**		**Singapore**	**14.0**	
United Overseas Bank 0.010% 2027	1.2	1-Dec-20	Temasek Financial I 2.75% 2061	1.0	2-Aug-21
Oversea-Chinese Banking Corporation 1.832% 2030	1.0	10-Sep-20	BOC Aviation 1.625% 2024	1.0	29-Apr-21
Others	12.5		Others	12.0	
Thailand	**5.3**		**Thailand**	**3.7**	
Bangkok Bank in Hong Kong, China 5.0% Perpetual	0.8	23-Sep-20	Bangkok Bank 3.466% 2036	1.0	23-Sep-21
PTT Treasury 3.7% 2070	0.7	16-Jul-20	GC Treasury Center 2.980% 2031	0.7	18-Mar-21
Others	3.8		Others	2.0	
Viet Nam	**0.1**		**Viet Nam**	**1.4**	
Emerging East Asia Total	**378.1**		**Emerging East Asia Total**	**302.5**	
Memo Items:			Memo Items:		
India	14.3		India	21.7	
Vedanta Holdings Mauritius II 13.00% 2023	1.4	21-Aug-20	Vedanta Resources 8.95% 2025	1.2	11-Mar-21
Others	12.9		Others	20.5	
Sri Lanka	0.4		Sri Lanka	0.8	
Sri Lanka (Sovereign) 6.57% 2021	0.1	30-Jul-20	Sri Lanka (Sovereign) 7.95% 2024	0.2	3-May-21
Others	0.3		Others	0.6	

USD = United States dollar.
Notes:
1. Data exclude certificates of deposit.
2. G3 currency bonds are bonds denominated in either euros, Japanese yen, or US dollars.
3. Bloomberg LP end-of-period rates are used.
4. Emerging East Asia comprises Cambodia; the People's Republic of China; Hong Kong, China; Indonesia; the Republic of Korea; Malaysia; the Philippines; Singapore; Thailand; and Viet Nam.
5. Figures after the issuer name reflect the coupon rate and year of maturity of the bond.
Source: *AsianBondsOnline* calculations based on Bloomberg LP data.

China Evergrande, the PRC's second-largest real estate company, to meet its debt obligations. Taking their cue from the US Federal Reserve's shifting stance, issuers took advantage of the low-interest-rate environment, wary that the Federal Reserve may ease its bond purchase program earlier than expected.

Of the total G3 currency bond issuance in the first 3 quarters of 2021, 93.5% was issued in US dollars, 5.9% in euros, and 0.6% in Japanese yen. During the review period, USD282.8 billion worth of USD-denominated bonds was raised in emerging East Asia, increasing 5.2% y-o-y, driven by issuance from Hong Kong, China; the Republic of Korea; and Singapore. Issuers also rushed their debt offerings to take advantage of low borrowing costs ahead of the US Federal Reserve shifting its monetary stance with the tapering of asset purchases to commence in November. Issuances in euros amounted to USD17.9 billion in January–September, declining 1.8% y-o-y as EUR-denominated fundraising efforts by the PRC and the Republic of Korea slowed. Bonds issued in Japanese yen totaled USD1.9 billion, a contraction of 9.1% y-o-y as Hong Kong, China's JPY-denominated issuance fell and Malaysia's stopped during the review period.

The PRC issued more than half of the region's G3 currency bonds during the review period, issuing USD169.8 billion worth in January–September. The Republic of Korea followed with USD34.7 billion, and then Hong Kong, China with USD34.4 billion. The US dollar was the G3 currency of choice for all economies in the region.

In the first 9 months of 2021, y-o-y growth in G3 currency bond issuance was posted in Singapore (46.9%); the Republic of Korea (43.2%); and Hong Kong, China (26.0%). A decline in the issuance of G3 currency bonds was recorded in the Philippines (−28.7%), Thailand (−16.8%), Malaysia (−14.8%), Indonesia (−4.1%), and the PRC (−1.3%). Cambodia did not issue any G3 currency bonds during the review period after issuing during the same period in 2020. Viet Nam, on the other hand, issued bonds denominated in G3 currencies after not issuing in January–September 2020.

Of the total issuance volume of G3 currency bonds in emerging East Asia during the review period, 56.1% came from the PRC. Furthermore, USD162.1 billion was issued

in US dollars and USD7.7 billion equivalent in euros. In September, the Industrial and Commercial Bank of China raised USD6.2 billion from its USD-denominated issuance of perpetual bonds. With an annual distribution rate of 3.2%, proceeds from the issuance will be regarded as additional tier 1 capital of the bank to meet regulatory requirements. In the same month, China Development Bank's branch in Hong Kong, China issued 3-year USD-denominated green bonds worth USD500.0 million and with a coupon rate of 0.625%. Funds raised from the issuance will be used to finance eligible green projects.

The Republic of Korea accounted for 11.5% of all issuances of G3 currency bonds during the review period. This was made up of USD31.6 billion in US dollars, the equivalent of USD3.1 billion in EUR-denominated bonds, and USD0.04 billion worth of bonds denominated in Japanese yen. Steelmaker Posco issued a 5-year EUR-denominated convertible zero-coupon bond worth USD1.2 billion in September. The issue was a green bond and funds raised from it will be used for green projects such as financing renewable energy and electric vehicle batteries. The issuance was also the largest equity-linked deal in the Republic of Korea. Commercial bank Kookmin Bank raised USD100.0 million in the same month from two 1-year USD-denominated bonds with coupon rates of 0.34% and 0.35%.

An 11.4% share of the region's G3-denominated bonds issued during the review period was from Hong Kong, China. In terms of currency, USD-denominated bonds amounted to USD33.3 billion, while EUR-denominated issuances totaled USD0.9 billion, and bonds denominated in Japanese yen reached USD0.2 billion. Financial company AIA Group sold about USD900.0 million worth of 12-year callable bonds denominated in euros. With a regular distribution rate of 0.88%, the amount raised from the issuance will be considered as tier 2 capital of the bank and will be used for general corporate purposes. In each of August and September, financial services company Guotai Junan International issued a 1-year USD-denominated bond worth USD100.0 million and with a coupon rate of 0.7%.

Issuance of G3 currency bonds by ASEAN member economies in January–September 2021 dropped 2.7% y-o-y.[5] The region's G3 currency bond issuance amounted to USD63.7 billion, down from the

---

[5] For the discussion on G3 currency issuance, data for ASEAN include Cambodia, Indonesia, Malaysia, the Philippines, Singapore, Thailand, and Viet Nam.

USD65.4 billion issued in January–September 2020, as most economies in the ASEAN region had a low level of fundraising activities. As a percentage of total G3 currency bond issuance in emerging East Asia in the first 3 quarters of 2021, ASEAN accounted for 21.0%, which was less than the 22.6% share posted in the previous year. Indonesia had the largest G3 currency bond issuance among all ASEAN members, despite the decline in its issuance during the review period, followed by Singapore, Malaysia, the Philippines, Thailand, and Viet Nam.

Issuances of G3 currency bonds in Indonesia in January–September 2021 accounted for 7.7% of emerging East Asia's total with USD20.1 billion in US dollars, the equivalent of USD2.3 billion in euros, and JPY-denominated bonds worth USD0.9 billion. The Government of Indonesia issued a dual-currency callable bond totaling USD1.2 billion in September. The issuance had a 13-year EUR-denominated and 40-year USD-denominated tranche with coupon rates of 1.3% and 3.2%, respectively. Proceeds from the issuance will be used for budgetary purposes, mainly to fund relief measures to fight the COVID-19 pandemic. Government-owned Bank Negara Indonesia sold USD600.0 million worth of USD-denominated perpetual bonds to top up its additional tier 1 capital and to manage the duration of its funding structure.

With a 4.6% share of total issuances of G3 currency bonds in emerging East Asia during the January–September period, entities in Singapore issued USD12.3 billion of bonds in US dollars, USD1.5 billion of bonds denominated in euros, and USD0.2 billion worth of JPY-denominated bonds. In August, Temasek Financial issued a triple-tranche callable bond denominated in US dollars amounting to USD2.5 billion. The issuance, which was drawn from the company's guaranteed global medium-term note program, had tenors of 10 years, 20 years, and 40 years. Proceeds from the issuance will be used in the ordinary course of business. In September, multinational banking and financial services company DBS Group Holdings raised USD800.0 million from its issuance of a 5.5-year USD-denominate bond. With a coupon rate of 1.194%, the issuance was drawn from the company's global medium-term note program.

Malaysia's issuance of G3 currency bonds was 4.3% of the total for emerging East Asia during the first 3 quarters of 2021, with issuance solely in US dollars amounting to USD12.9 billion. Financial institutions Malayan Banking and CIMB Bank added to Malaysia's

stock of USD-denominated bonds through their issuance of 5-year bonds. Malayan Banking's bond was worth USD35.0 million with a coupon rate of 1.27%, while CIMB Bank raised USD20.0 million from their bond with a 1.35% periodic distribution rate. Both banks issued their bonds from their respective medium-term note programs.

The Philippines had a 2.8% share of total G3 currency bond issuance in emerging East Asia in January–September 2021. Bonds issued denominated in US dollars totaled USD5.4 billion, bonds denominated in euros were worth USD2.4 billion, and JPY-denominated bonds amounted to USD0.5 billion. In September, AYC Finance and ACEN Finance each issued USD400.0 million worth of perpetual callable bonds denominated in US dollars. AYC Finance's bond had a coupon rate of 3.9% and the proceeds will refinance some of its USD-denominated commitments. ACEN Finance's issuance was a green bond with a coupon rate of 4.0%, the proceeds of which will be used to finance the company's green projects.

Thailand's share of all G3 currency bonds issued in the region was 1.2% during the review period, issuing solely in US dollars totaling USD3.7 billion. In September, Bangkok Bank raised USD1.0 billion from its 15-year USD-denominated callable bond with a coupon rate of 3.466%. Funds raised from the issuance will be considered as additional tier 2 capital of the bank. In August, Kasikornbank sold USD350.0 million of its callable perpetual bond with a periodic distribution rate of 4.0%. Proceeds from the issuance will be used for general corporate purposes.

In January–September 2021, 0.5% of all G3 currency issuance in emerging East Asia came from entities in Viet Nam issuing USD-denominated bonds worth USD1.4 billion. In September, hospitality company Vinpearl Joint Stock Company issued a USD425.0 million 5-year sustainable bond with a coupon rate of 3.25%. Funds raised from the issuance will be used by the company for various sustainable projects and for refinancing its parent company Vingroup's existing facilities.

Figure 9 presents the monthly issuance of G3 currency bonds in emerging East Asia from September 2020 to September 2021. After a high issuance volume in June and July 2021, offerings dipped temporarily in August as issuance activities fell across all economies in the region as the Delta variant spread around the world. The

Figure 9: G3 Currency Bond Issuance in Emerging East Asia

USD billion

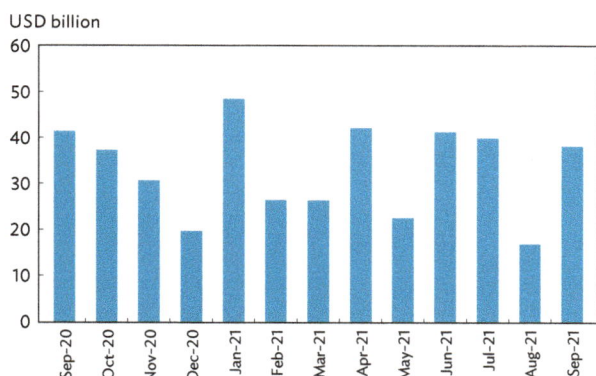

USD = United States dollar.
Notes:
1. Emerging East Asia comprises Cambodia; the People's Republic of China; Hong Kong, China; Indonesia; the Republic of Korea; the Lao People's Democratic Republic; Malaysia; the Philippines; Singapore; Thailand; and Viet Nam.
2. G3 currency bonds are bonds denominated in either euros, Japanese yen, or US dollars.
3. Figures were computed based on 30 September 2021 currency exchange rates and do not include currency effects.
Source: *AsianBondsOnline* calculations based on Bloomberg LP data.

threat of this deadlier COVID-19 variant forced many governments to reimpose mobility restrictions, slowing down already sluggish economic activities globally. G3 currency bond issuance recovered immediately in September, spurred by increased issuances from most economies in the region.

Bond Yield Movements

Local currency government bond yields in emerging East Asia mostly rose on global inflationary fears as well as the shifting monetary stances of advanced economy central banks.

Among advanced economies, the central bank whose monetary policies are shifting the most is currently the Federal Reserve. During its 21–22 September meeting, while its monetary policy rate was left unchanged, the Federal Reserve indicated that if the US economy continued to improve, a reduction in its asset purchases would be likely. In addition, updated economic forecasts for September from June showed that the Federal Reserve now expects a rate hike in 2022 at the earliest, instead of 2023 as forecast previously. During its 2–3 November meeting, the Federal Reserve said that it would begin tapering its asset purchases starting November.

The European Central Bank is also shifting its policy stance. While it left its monetary policy rate and asset purchase program unchanged during its 20 October monetary meeting, it said that it would slow the pace of purchases under the pandemic emergency purchase program in the fourth quarter of 2021 compared to prior quarters. The Bank of Japan's monetary stance has remained unchanged since its 21 September meeting, but the central bank noted that Japan's economy continued to progress.

In addition to tightening monetary stances in advanced economies, there has been a rise in global inflationary fears, exacerbated by a rise in energy prices. These factors have led yields in emerging East Asia to rise as well.

The 2-year bond yield trended upward in emerging East Asia between 31 August and 15 October. The steepest rise was in the Republic of Korea as the Bank of Korea raised policy rates in August (**Figure 10a**). Singapore also had a sharp rise in its 2-year yield, following monetary tightening by MAS. The rise in 2-year yields was not as noticeable in Indonesia, where yields had trended downward before showing a slight rise and then leveling toward the middle of October (**Figure 10b**). In Indonesia, investor sentiment was buoyed by stronger exports of palm oil, following rising energy prices. In addition, interest rates are higher in Indonesia compared to its peers and inflation remains below forecast, reducing pressure for Bank Indonesia to raise the policy rate.

For the 10-year yield, steep increases were noted in Hong Kong, China; the Republic of Korea; and Singapore (**Figure 11a**). Both the Republic of Korea and Singapore had tightening monetary stances while Hong Kong, China's yields strongly tracked US yield movements. The Philippines had the steepest rise in its 10-year yield, largely due to inflationary concerns as its inflation rate was the highest in the region during the review period (**Figure 11b**).

The yield curves of emerging East Asia shifted upward for all markets from 31 August to 15 October, tracking trends in the 2-year and 10-year yield movements (**Figure 12**). The steepest average yield increases were noted in Thailand and the Philippines, with their yield curves rising by an average of 34 basis points (bps) each, respectively. For the Philippines, the rise in its yield curve was tempered by yield movements for tenors of longer than 10 years. If these were not included then the overall

Figure 10a: 2-Year Local Currency Government Bond Yields

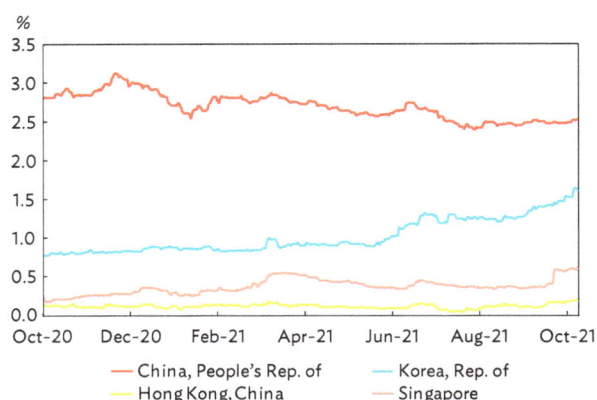

Note: Data coverage is from 1 October 2020 to 15 October 2021.
Source: Based on data from Bloomberg LP.

Figure 10b: 2-Year Local Currency Government Bond Yields

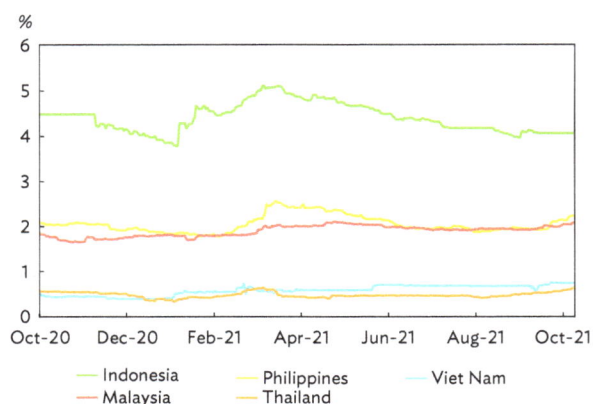

Note: Data coverage is from 1 October 2020 to 15 October 2021.
Source: Based on data from Bloomberg LP.

Figure 11a: 10-Year Local Currency Government Bond Yields

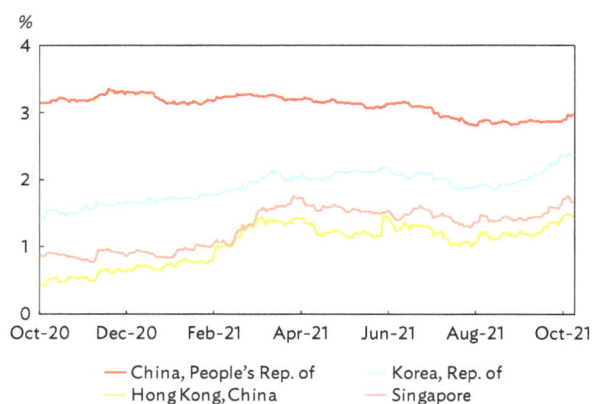

Note: Data coverage is from 1 October 2020 to 15 October 2021.
Source: Based on data from Bloomberg LP.

Figure 11b: 10-Year Local Currency Government Bond Yields

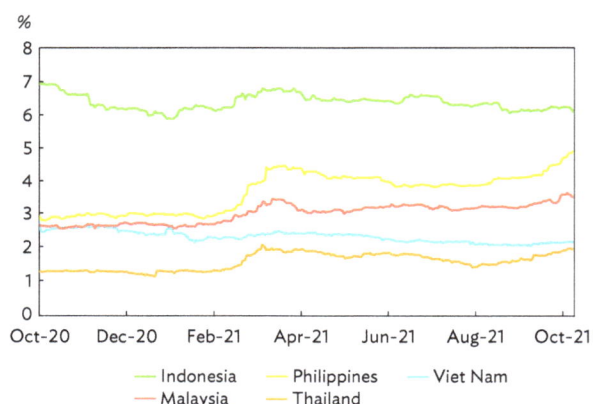

Note: Data coverage is from 1 October 2020 to 15 October 2021.
Source: Based on data from Bloomberg LP.

rise in the Philippine yield curve would have been more dramatic, with its 10-year yield rising 84 bps during the period. In addition to the shift in monetary stance in the US, yields in the Philippines were driven by persistently high inflation. In Thailand, yields were influenced by US monetary policy as well, but its economic performance has also led to market concerns that government debt supply would increase.

In the PRC, the upward shift in its yield curve was not as pronounced as in other markets, owing to concerns that the PRC's economy is showing signs of weakness. The Manufacturing Purchasing Managers Index fell to

49.2 in October from from 49.6 in September, both below the 50-point threshold demarcating expansion and contraction.

The yield curves of Indonesia and Viet Nam barely shifted during the review period. In Indonesia, investor sentiment has rebounded with an improving current account balance and inflation remaining at manageable levels.

The 2-year versus 10-year yield spread for emerging East Asia rose in all markets, except in Indonesia and Singapore, as the region's yield curves steepened on the back of changing US monetary policy (**Figure 13**).

Figure 12: Benchmark Yield Curves—Local Currency Government Bonds

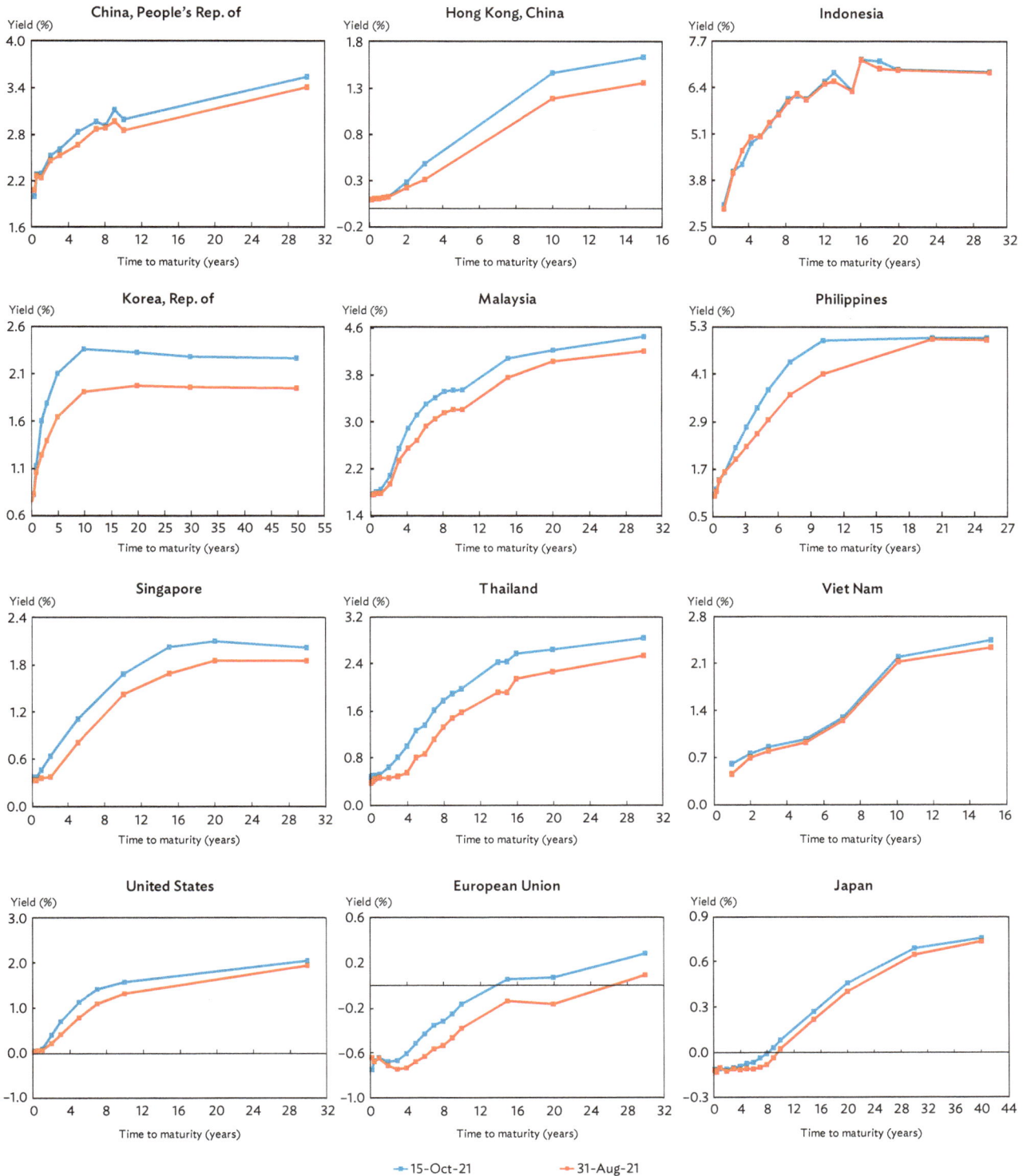

Sources: Based on data from Bloomberg LP and Thai Bond Market Association.

Recent GDP releases show a moderation in growth compared to the previously strong Q2 2021 performance with some markets posting contractions for Q3 2021. In the PRC, GDP growth slowed to 4.9% y-o-y in Q3 2021 from 7.9% y-o-y in the previous quarter, raising concerns that the PRC's economy is slowing. Hong Kong, China's

GDP growth slowed to 5.4% y-o-y in Q3 2021 from 7.6% y-o-y in the previous quarter due to base effects. The Republic of Korea's GDP growth fell to 4.0% y-o-y in Q3 2021 from 6.0% y-o-y in Q2 2021 amid a decline in consumption due to reimposed social distancing measures. In the Philippines, GDP growth declined to 7.1% y-o-y in Q3 2021 from 12.0% y-o-y in the previous quarter. In Singapore, GDP growth slowed to 7.1% y-o-y from 15.2% y-o-y during the same review period due to a low base effect. GDP contracted in Malaysia (−4.5% y-o-y), Thailand (−0.3% y-o-y), and Viet Nam (−6.2% y-o-y) in Q3 2021 due to mobility restrictions during the quarter that curtailed economic activities.

While inflation expectations are rising, inflation trends have been largely mixed, with inflation in some markets either leveling off or declining after previous months of increases. Indonesia's inflation has been stable and is below Bank Indonesia's forecast (**Figure 14a**). Other markets have stable inflation but at elevated levels. While Singapore's inflation has been fairly stable, inflation levels are high compared to the first quarter of 2021. The Philippines' inflation rate has been stable but is currently the highest in the region (**Figure 14b**). The Republic of Korea also experienced higher inflation during the review period than earlier in the year.

As a result, after a period of maintaining existing monetary policies, some emerging East Asian central banks are indicating a tightening shift. Other than inflation, the

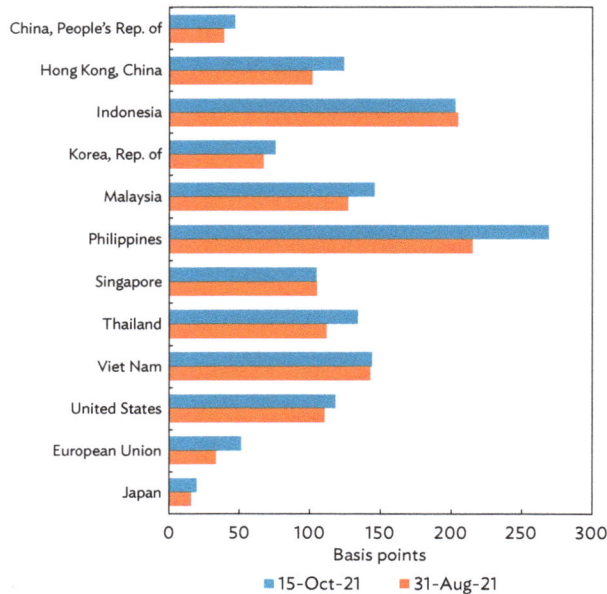

Figure 13: Yield Spreads between 2-Year and 10-Year Government Bonds

Source: *AsianBondsOnline* computations based on Bloomberg LP data.

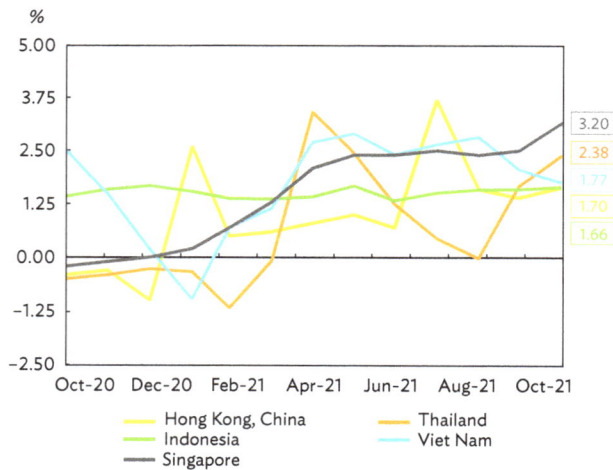

Figure 14a: Headline Inflation Rates

Note: Data coverage is from October 2020 to October 2021.
Source: Based on data from Bloomberg LP.

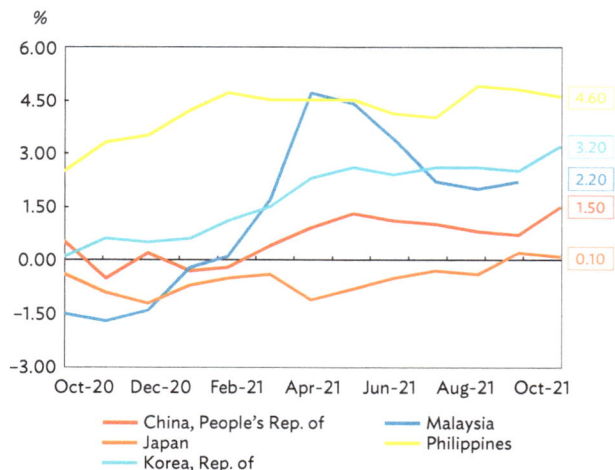

Figure 14b: Headline Inflation Rates

Note: Data coverage is from October 2020 to October 2021 except for Malaysia (September 2021).
Source: Based on data from Bloomberg LP.

Table 5: Policy Rate Changes

Economy	Policy Rate 30-Sep-2020 (%)	Rate Change (%)												Policy Rate 31-Oct-2021 (%)	Change in Policy Rates (basis points)
		Oct-2020	Nov-2020	Dec-2020	Jan-2021	Feb-2021	Mar-2021	Apr-2021	May-2021	Jun-2021	Jul-2021	Aug-2021	Sep-2021		
United States	0.25													0.25	0
Euro Area	(0.50)													(0.50)	0
Japan	(0.10)													(0.10)	0
China, People's Rep. of	2.95													2.95	0
Indonesia	4.00		↓0.25			↓0.25								3.50	↓ 50
Korea, Rep. of	0.50											↑0.25		0.75	↑ 25
Malaysia	1.75													1.75	0
Philippines	2.25		↓0.25											2.00	↓ 25
Thailand	0.50													0.50	0
Viet Nam	4.50	↓0.50												4.00	↓ 50

( ) = negative.
Notes:
1. Data coverage is from 30 September 2020 to 31 October 2021.
2. For the People's Republic of China, data used in the chart are for the 1-year medium-term lending facility rate. While the 1-year benchmark lending rate is the official policy rate of the People's Bank of China, market players use the 1-year medium-term lending facility rate as a guide for the monetary policy direction of the People's Bank of China.
Sources: Various central bank websites.

changing stance in advanced economies could pressure central banks in the region to raise policy rates to maintain parity on interest rates. The Republic of Korea was the first to do so, with the Bank of Korea raising its policy rate by 25 bps during its meeting on 26 August (**Table 5**). As widely expected, the Bank of Korea raised rates again in November. In addition, while Singapore has no interest rate policy, during its 14 October meeting it adjusted the slope of the Singapore dollar nominal effective exchange rate policy band to allow a slight appreciation.

Other markets that are showing economic weakness are being pressured to ease further. In the PRC, slowing growth and problems in the property market led to some market participants expecting the central bank to ease; however, the People's Bank of China has not yet done so. In Thailand, there were expectations in August of a possible rate cut, and while the Bank of Thailand left policy rates unchanged on on 4 August, 29 September, and 10 November, minutes of the 4 August meeting showed two policy members in favor of a rate reduction.

Corporate spreads rose in the PRC, were mixed in the Republic of Korea, and fell in Malaysia and Thailand.

The spread between AAA-rated yields and government yields rose in the PRC, following heightened credit concerns largely due to potential defaults in the property sector. The spread also rose in the Republic of Korea but fell in Malaysia and Thailand (**Figure 15a**).

For lower-rated bonds, the spread again rose in the PRC due to the abovementioned investor concerns. The spread was roughly unchanged in the Republic of Korea, while it fell in Malaysia and Thailand (**Figure 15b**).

Figure 15a: Credit Spreads—Local Currency Corporates Rated AAA versus Government Bonds

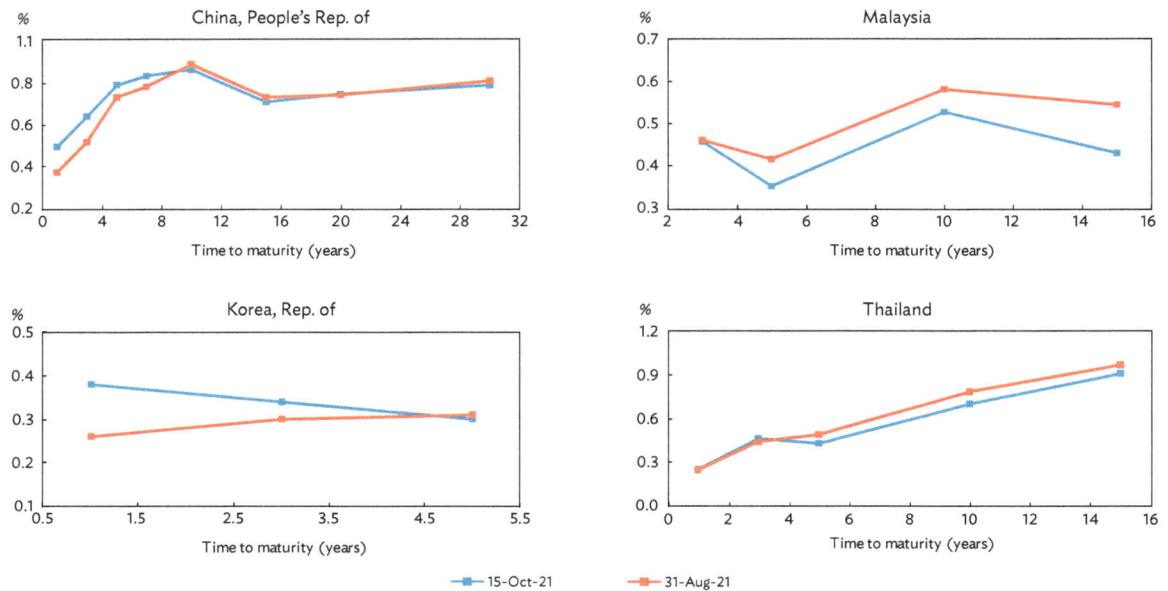

Notes:
1. Credit spreads are obtained by subtracting government yields from corporate indicative yields.
2. For Malaysia, data on corporate bonds yields are as of 30 August 2021 and 14 October 2021.
Sources: People's Republic of China (Bloomberg LP); Republic of Korea (KG Zeroin Corporation); Malaysia (Fully Automated System for Issuing/Tendering Bank Negara Malaysia); and Thailand (Bloomberg LP).

Figure 15b: Credit Spreads—Lower-Rated Local Currency Corporates versus AAA

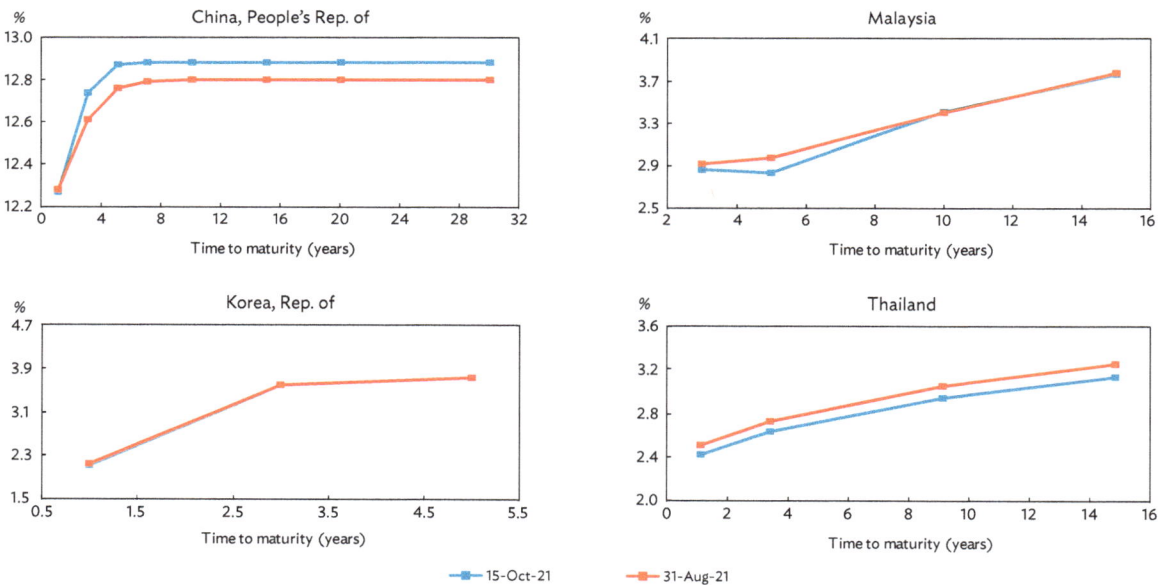

Notes:
1. Credit spreads are obtained by subtracting government yields from corporate indicative yields.
2. For Malaysia, data on corporate bonds yields are as of 30 August 2021 and 14 October 2021.
Sources: People's Republic of China (Bloomberg LP); Republic of Korea (KG Zeroin Corporation); Malaysia (Fully Automated System for Issuing/Tendering Bank Negara Malaysia); and Thailand (Bloomberg LP).

Recent Developments in ASEAN+3 Sustainable Bond Markets

ASEAN+3 sustainable bond markets—which comprise green bonds, social bonds, and sustainability bonds—continued to post robust growth in the third quarter (Q3) of 2021.[6] The outstanding amount of sustainable bonds in the region climbed to USD388.7 billion at the end of September, with growth moderating to 10.6% quarter-on-quarter (q-o-q) in Q3 2021 from 15.6% q-o-q in the second quarter (Q2) of 2021 (**Figure 16**). On a year-on-year (y-o-y) basis, sustainable bond market growth in the region remained strong at 54.2% while easing slightly from 57.2% in Q2 2021.

By region, ASEAN+3 continued to have the second-largest sustainable bond market in the world, accounting for 19.2% of the global total at the end of September (**Figure 17**). At the end of September, the global sustainable bond market reached a size of USD2.0 trillion. The largest sustainable bond market in the world by region, Europe, accounted for 49.3% of the global total.

Green bonds outstanding in ASEAN+3 markets reached USD278.5 billion at the end of September, accounting for a 71.6% share of the regional sustainable bond total. The region's green bond market posted growth of 9.9% q-o-q in Q3 2021, moderating from 11.6% q-o-q in Q2 2021, while the annual growth rate in Q3 2021 quickened to 39.0% y-o-y from 36.0% y-o-y in Q2 2021. The People's Republic of China accounted for 69.0% of the region's green bond total, while ASEAN markets collectively accounted for 5.9% (**Figure 18**).

Figure 16: Outstanding Amount of Green, Social, and Sustainability Bonds in ASEAN+3 Markets

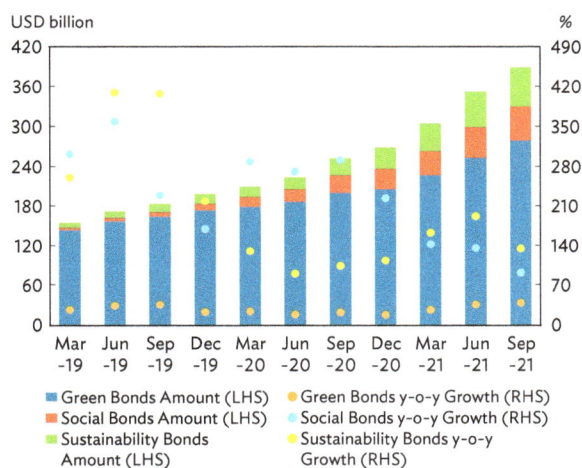

ASEAN = Association of Southeast Asian Nations, LHS = left-hand side, RHS = right-hand side, USD = United States dollar, y-o-y = year-on-year.
Notes:
1. ASEAN includes the markets of Indonesia, Malaysia, the Philippines, Singapore, Thailand, and Viet Nam.
2. ASEAN+3 includes ASEAN members plus the People's Republic of China; Hong Kong, China; Japan; and the Republic of Korea.
3. Data include both local currency and foreign currency issues.
Source: *AsianBondsOnline* computations based on Bloomberg LP data.

Figure 17: Outstanding Amount of Global Sustainable Bond Markets at the End of September 2021

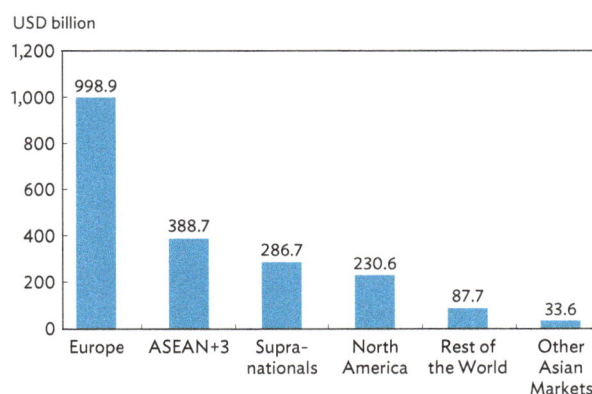

ASEAN = Association of Southeast Asian Nations, USD = United States dollar.
Notes:
1. ASEAN includes the markets of Indonesia, Malaysia, the Philippines, Singapore, Thailand, and Viet Nam.
2. ASEAN+3 includes ASEAN members plus the People's Republic of China; Hong Kong, China; Japan; and the Republic of Korea.
3. Data include both local currency and foreign currency issues.
Source: *AsianBondsOnline* computations based on Bloomberg LP data.

---

[6] For the discussion on sustainable bonds, ASEAN+3 includes Association of Southeast Asian Nations (ASEAN) members Indonesia, Malaysia, the Philippines, Singapore, Thailand, and Viet Nam plus the People's Republic of China; Hong Kong, China; Japan; and the Republic of Korea.

Figure 18: Outstanding Green, Social, and Sustainability Bonds in ASEAN+3 by Economy (share of total)

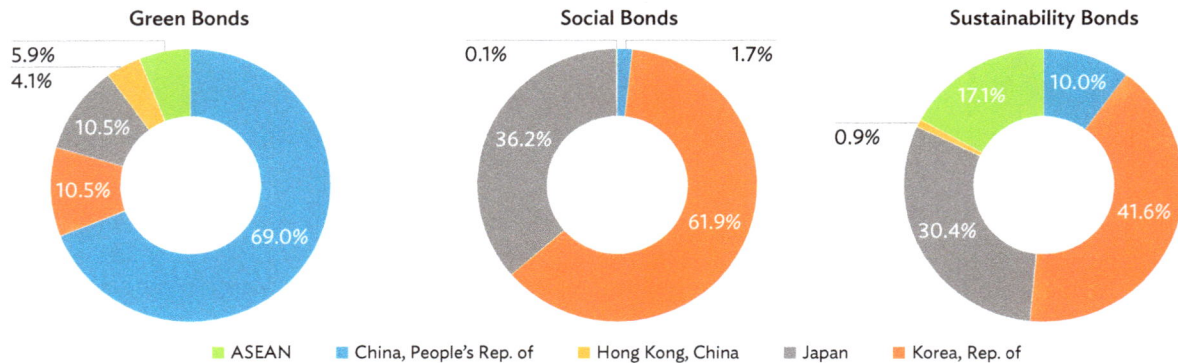

Green Bonds
- 5.9%
- 4.1%
- 10.5%
- 10.5%
- 69.0%

Social Bonds
- 0.1%
- 1.7%
- 36.2%
- 61.9%

Sustainability Bonds
- 17.1%
- 10.0%
- 0.9%
- 30.4%
- 41.6%

■ ASEAN ■ China, People's Rep. of ■ Hong Kong, China ■ Japan ■ Korea, Rep. of

ASEAN = Association of Southeast Asian Nations.
Notes:
1. ASEAN includes the markets of Indonesia, Malaysia, the Philippines, Singapore, Thailand, and Viet Nam.
2. ASEAN+3 includes ASEAN members plus the People's Republic of China; Hong Kong, China; Japan; and the Republic of Korea.
3. Data for green, social, and sustainability bonds as of the end of September 2021 and include both local currency and foreign currency issues.
Source: *AsianBondsOnline* computations based on Bloomberg LP data.

The share of social and sustainability bonds in the region's overall sustainable bond market continued to expand in Q3 2021. The collective share of social and sustainable bonds climbed to 28.4% at the end of September from 27.9% at the end of June, and 20.5% in September 2020, reflecting rising investor interest in such bonds. In nominal terms, the stocks of social and sustainability bonds in the region rose to USD50.6 billion and USD59.6 billion at the end of September, respectively, accounting for 13.0% and 15.3% of ASEAN+3's sustainable bond total. The social bond market grew by 10.9% q-o-q and 92.1% y-o-y in Q3 2021, while the sustainability bond market expanded 13.7% q-o-q and 135.0% y-o-y during the same period. The Republic of Korea and Japan led all social and sustainable bond markets in ASEAN+3 in terms of the size of their respective bond stocks, while ASEAN markets accounted for 0.1% and 17.1% of regional social and sustainability bonds outstanding at the end of September.

Sustainable bond issuance maintained its strong momentum in 2021, with issuance in the first 3 quarters of 2021 reaching USD165.5 billion, which was equivalent to around 180% of the 2020 full-year issuance volume (**Figure 19**). For all three sustainable bond categories, issuance in the first 9 months of the year already exceeded the total 2020 issuance volume.

Corporates remained the largest player in the ASEAN+3 sustainable bond market, accounting for 80.5% of the sustainable bond market at the end of September

Figure 19: Issuance Volume of Green, Social, and Sustainability Bonds in ASEAN+3

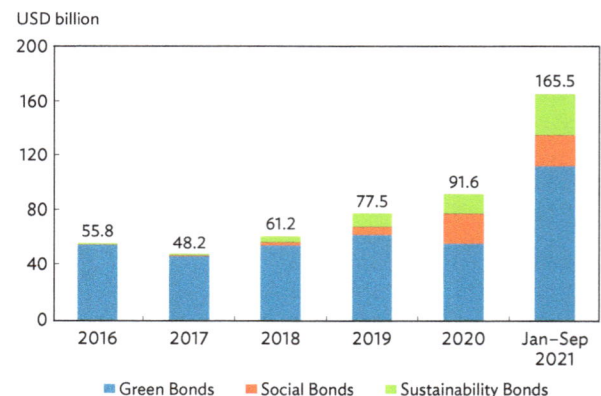

USD billion

- 2016: 55.8
- 2017: 48.2
- 2018: 61.2
- 2019: 77.5
- 2020: 91.6
- Jan–Sep 2021: 165.5

■ Green Bonds ■ Social Bonds ■ Sustainability Bonds

ASEAN = Association of Southeast Asian Nations, USD = United States dollar.
Notes:
1. ASEAN includes the markets of Indonesia, Malaysia, the Philippines, Singapore, Thailand, and Viet Nam.
2. ASEAN+3 includes ASEAN members plus the People's Republic of China; Hong Kong, China; Japan; and the Republic of Korea.
3. Data include both local currency and foreign currency issues.
Source: *AsianBondsOnline* computations based on Bloomberg LP data.

(**Figure 20**). By type of bond, corporates dominated, representing 88.1% of the green bond market and 76.2% of the sustainability bond market. However, corporate issuances are less dominant in the social bond market, as reflected in a share of 43.8% at the end of September, though this was a slight increase from 39.1% at the end of 2020.

Figure 20: Outstanding Green, Social, and Sustainability Bonds in ASEAN+3 by Type of Bond

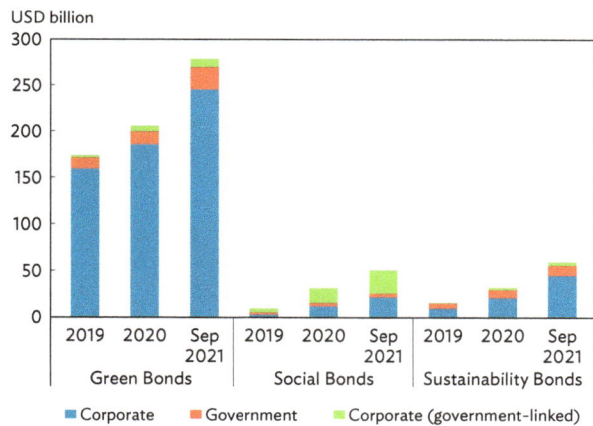

ASEAN = Association of Southeast Asian Nations, USD = United States dollar.
Notes:
1. Corporate denotes bonds issued by private sector corporations. Government bonds include bonds issued by sovereigns, regional governments, and local governments. Corporate (government-linked) denotes corporations with government affiliations.
2. ASEAN includes the markets of Indonesia, Malaysia, the Philippines, Singapore, Thailand, and Viet Nam.
3. ASEAN+3 includes ASEAN members plus the People's Republic of China; Hong Kong, China; Japan; and the Republic of Korea.
4. Data include both local currency and foreign currency issues.
Source: *AsianBondsOnline* computation based on Bloomberg LP data.

The financial sector continued to lead the region in terms of sustainable bonds outstanding in Q3 2021 (**Figure 21**). However, the sector's dominance in the green bond market slipped to a share of 41.5% at the end of September from 48.3% at the end of December 2020, as the green bond market matured with greater sector diversification. At the same time, the financial sector maintained its majority share of the social (63.7%) and the sustainability (53.4%) bond markets. In terms of currency denomination, a majority of green bonds and social bonds were denominated in local currency at the end of September, with domestic currencies accounting for shares of 65.5% and 79.5%, respectively (**Figure 22**). Regional sustainability bonds were denominated mostly in foreign currency (58.1%) at the end of September.

Most sustainable bonds in ASEAN+3 were not rated, as a majority of the issuances were denominated in local currency (**Figure 23**). Among those that were rated, most were investment grade.

Figure 21: Outstanding Green, Social, and Sustainability Bonds in ASEAN+3 by Sector of Issuer (share of total)

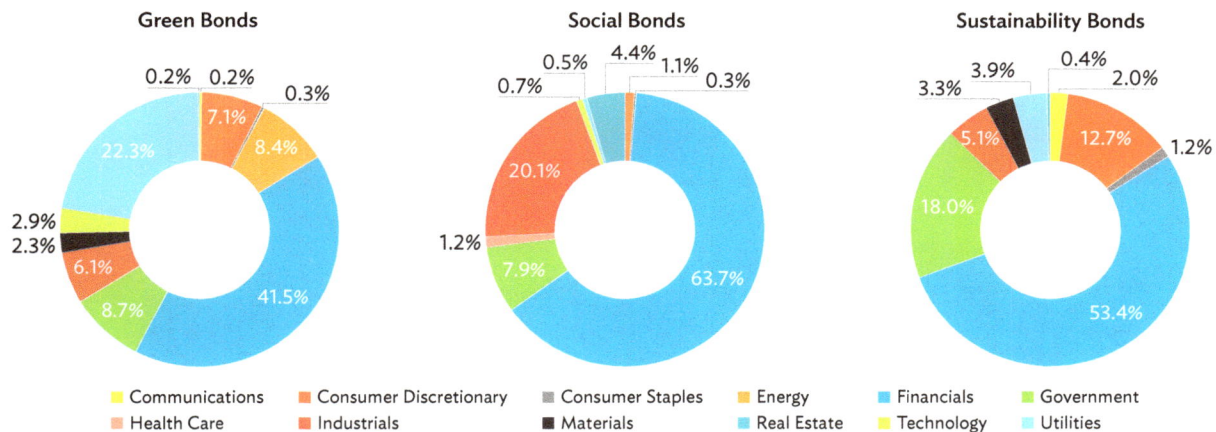

ASEAN = Association of Southeast Asian Nations.
Notes:
1. ASEAN includes the markets of Indonesia, Malaysia, the Philippines, Singapore, Thailand, and Viet Nam.
2. ASEAN+3 includes ASEAN members plus the People's Republic of China; Hong Kong, China; Japan; and the Republic of Korea.
3. Data for green, social, and sustainability bonds as of the end of September 2021 and include both local currency and foreign currency issues.
Source: *AsianBondsOnline* computations based on Bloomberg LP data.

Figure 22: Outstanding Green, Social, and Sustainability Bonds in ASEAN+3 by Type of Currency (share of total)

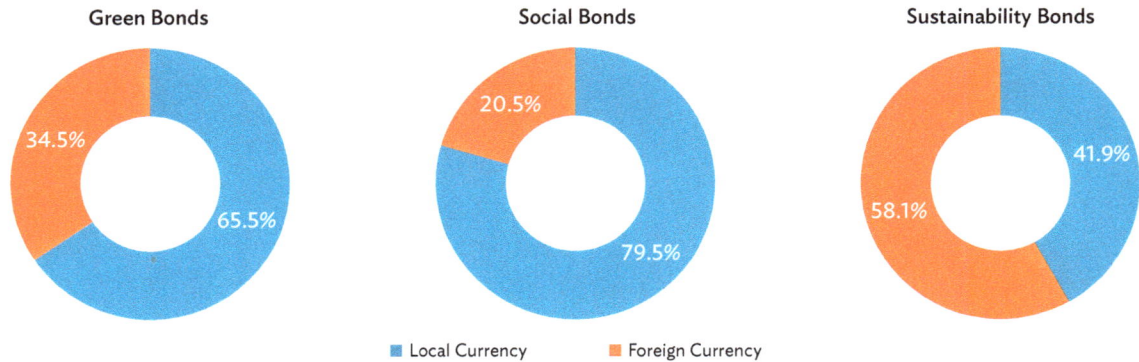

Green Bonds — 34.5% / 65.5%

Social Bonds — 20.5% / 79.5%

Sustainability Bonds — 41.9% / 58.1%

■ Local Currency   ■ Foreign Currency

ASEAN = Association of Southeast Asian Nations.
Notes:
1. ASEAN includes the markets of Indonesia, Malaysia, the Philippines, Singapore, Thailand, and Viet Nam.
2. ASEAN+3 includes ASEAN members plus the People's Republic of China; Hong Kong, China; Japan; and the Republic of Korea.
3. Data for green, social, and sustainability bonds as of the end of September 2021 and include both local currency and foreign currency issues.
Source: *AsianBondsOnline* computations based on Bloomberg LP data.

Figure 23: Outstanding Green, Social, and Sustainability Bonds in ASEAN+3 by Credit Ratings

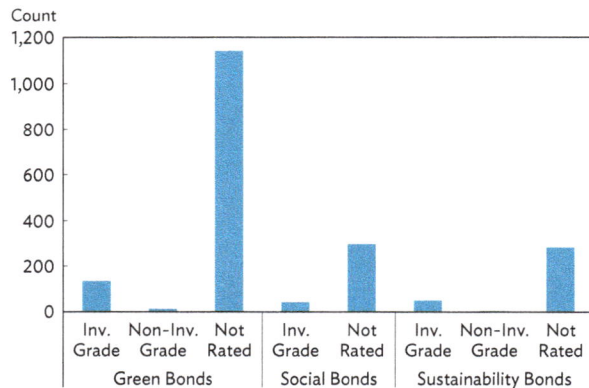

ASEAN = Association of Southeast Asian Nations, Inv. = Investment.
Notes:
1. ASEAN includes the markets of Indonesia, Malaysia, the Philippines, Singapore, Thailand, and Viet Nam.
2. ASEAN+3 includes ASEAN members plus the People's Republic of China; Hong Kong, China; Japan; and the Republic of Korea.
3. Data for green, social, and sustainability bonds as of the end of September 2021 and include both local currency and foreign currency issues.
4. Data is based on ratings provided by S&P Global.
Source: *AsianBondsOnline* computations based on Bloomberg LP data.

Policy and Regulatory Developments

People's Republic of China

Southbound Trading of Bond Connect Launched

In September, the Hong Kong Monetary Authority (HKMA) and the People's Bank of China jointly announced the opening of the southbound leg of the Bond Connect scheme. This will allow residents in the People's Republic of China (PRC) to buy bonds in Hong Kong, China, thereby facilitating outward investment flows. The People's Bank of China said that total transactions reached CNY4 billion during the first day of the launch.

Tax Incentives for Foreign Investors Extended

In October, the PRC extended tax exemptions for foreign investors in the PRC's domestic bond market, which was set to expire in November. The incentives exempt foreign investors from corporate income taxes and value-added taxes on bond investments. Exemptions were extended until the end of 2025.

Hong Kong, China

Hong Kong Monetary Authority Increases Issuance of Exchange Fund Bills

To meet the rise in demand for Exchange Fund Bills (EFB) amid excess liquidity in the financial system, the HKMA increased its issuance of 91-day EFBs starting in September. The HKMA increased the planned issuance size of 91-day EFBs by HKD5 billion in each of the tenders scheduled from 7 September to 21 December. The HKMA will monitor market conditions during the period and maintain the flexibility of adjusting or not executing the increases if deemed necessary.

Indonesia

Tax Cuts on Bond Investments for Domestic Investors

On 30 August, the Government of Indonesia reduced the tax on interest income on bond investments for domestic investors. The tax rate was lowered to 10% from the previous 15% to align the tax rate with that of foreign investors. (In February, the government reduced the tax on interest income for foreign bond investors from 20% to 10%.) The move is expected to further deepen the local currency bond market, encourage greater participation from domestic investors, and enhance liquidity. The tax cut applies to investments in both government bonds and corporate bonds, including *sukuk*.

Parliament Approves 2022 State Budget

In September, the Indonesian Parliament approved the 2022 state budget, which programs a lower budget deficit equivalent to 4.9% of gross domestic product (GDP) versus 5.8% in the 2021 state budget. The 2022 state budget sets the state revenue at IDR1,846.1 trillion, while state spending is estimated at IDR2,714.2 trillion. Macroeconomic assumptions used for the 2022 state budget include (i) economic growth of 5.2%, (ii) average consumer price inflation of 3.0%, (iii) an exchange rate of IDR14,350.0 per USD1.0, (iv) an average 10-year bond yield of 6.8%, and (v) an Indonesian crude oil price of USD63.0 per barrel.

Republic of Korea

The Government of the Republic of Korea Passes 2022 Budget Proposal

On 3 September, the Government of the Republic of Korea passed for approval to the National Assembly its 2022 budget proposal of KRW604.4 trillion. The proposed budget is 8.3% higher than the original 2021 budget of KRW558.0 trillion, and almost at par with the revised KRW604.9 trillion budget that includes all supplementary budgets passed during the year. The budget aims to aid citizens and society in the recovery from the pandemic, promote inclusive growth, and prepare for a post-pandemic economy. The 2022 budget is also expected to reduce the fiscal deficit by KRW20.0 trillion as tax revenues are expected to improve on the back of the continued economic recovery. The fiscal deficit as a percentage of gross domestic product is forecast to decline to 2.6% in 2022 from 4.4% in 2021.

Malaysia

Bank Negara Malaysia Launches Malaysia Overnight Rate

On 24 September, Bank Negara Malaysia (BNM) announced that the Malaysia overnight rate (MYOR) will be the new alternative reference rate for Malaysia. MYOR will be based on transactions in liquid markets, reflecting accurately Malaysia's financial environment. BNM clarified that the Kuala Lumpur interbank offered rate (KLIBOR) will still be used for other financial transactions. Periodic reviews will be conducted, however, to ensure that MYOR and KLIBOR are reflective of current market conditions. These benchmarks allow consumers to have the flexibility of choosing whichever rate suits their needs. The introduction of MYOR also broadens investors' risk management strategies. BNM also announced the discontinuation of the 2-month and 12-month KLIBOR starting 1 January 2023, as these rates are not used much in the financial market. Efforts are ongoing to develop a new Islamic benchmark rate to replace the Kuala Lumpur Islamic Reference Rate by the first half of 2022.

Philippines

Bureau of the Treasury Sets Borrowing Program to PHP400 Billion in October and November

The Bureau of the Treasury (BTr) which sets its borrowing plan on a monthly basis, planned to borrow PHP200 billion each in the months of October and November. The monthly amount is lower compared with the borrowing program in September, which was set at PHP250 billion. The planned monthly debt sale is composed of PHP60 billion of Treasury bills and PHP140 billion of Treasury bonds. It remained focused on longer-term debt as the BTr wanted to extend the debt maturity profile.

Bureau of the Treasury Issues Its First Onshore Retail Dollar Bonds

On 15 September, the BTr launched its maiden issuance of Retail Dollar Bonds (RDBs). The BTr stated that the RDB offer aimed to further advance financial inclusion in the Philippines by diversifying the investor portfolio. At the same time, the RDBs also diversified the government's funding types and sources. The RDB issuance comprised 5-year and 10-year tenors with coupon rates of 1.375% and 2.250%, respectively. The BTr issued a total of USD1.59 billion: USD1.11 billion of 5-year bonds and USD0.48 billion of 10-year bonds. The last time the BTr issued onshore USD-denominated bonds was in December 2012, when they were offered to institutional investors only.

Singapore

Monetary Authority of Singapore Issues Cash Management Treasury Bills

On 3 November, Monetary Authority of Singapore (MAS) issued a 7-day Cash Management Treasury Bill (CMTB) under the Local Treasury Bills Act to test the operational preparedness of the issuance. CMTBs are MAS's new financial instruments that are Singapore Government Securities bills with tenors of less than 6 months. CMTBs will be issued as a cash management instrument to allow the government to manage its short-term cashflows. MAS will not adhere to a schedule for the issuance of CMTBs, which will be issued on an ad hoc basis.

Thailand

Thai Government Raises Debt Ceiling

On 20 September, the Government of Thailand increased the debt ceiling from 60% to 70% of GDP to allow the government to raise more funds for its economic recovery efforts. The government had earlier issued an emergency loan decree in 2020 that authorized the Ministry of Finance to borrow THB1 trillion for economic stimulus measures. A second decree was issued in June 2021 allowing the government to borrow an additional THB500 billion to fund relief measures to combat the impacts of the prolonged pandemic. Thailand's public debt-to-GDP ratio stood at 57% as of September 2021.

Thailand to Issue More Long-Term Government Bonds

On 1 October, Thailand's Public Debt Management Office announced its plan to increase the share of long-dated bonds to finance the government's economic stimulus programs. Government bonds will comprise 48%–56% of total borrowing in fiscal year 2021–2022. In the previous fiscal year, government bonds comprised 31% of total borrowing as the government relied more on short-term instruments such as promissory notes and Treasury bills. For fiscal year 2021–2022, Treasury bills will comprise 23% of total borrowing, while promissory notes will comprise a 16%–25% share. Savings bonds and bond switching will each account for a 6% share of the total borrowing.

Viet Nam

State Treasury Implements Multiple Price Auction for 5-Year Treasury Bonds

On 6 October, the State Treasury implemented a pilot auction using a multiple price method for 5-year Treasury bonds. In a multiple price auction, the successful bidders pay the price stated in their respective bids for the allotted quantity of securities. The expected offering volume for the 5-year Treasury bond auctions was VND1,000–VND2,000 billion per session. For the rest of the tenors, the auction followed the uniform price method.[7]

---

[7] *Vietnam Bond Market Association*. 2021. "The State Treasury to Implement Pilot Auctions of Government Bonds by Multi-Price Method." 21 September. https://vbma.org.vn/en/activities/kho-bac-nha-nuoc-thi-diem-trien-khai-phat-hanh-trai-phieu-chinh-phu-theo-phuong-thuc-dau-thau-da-gia.

Price Differences Between Labeled and Unlabeled Green Bonds

The Rapid Growth of the Global Green Bond Market

Green bonds refer to bonds that finance investments that can mitigate the adverse effects of economic activity on climate change.[8] As such, they are financing instruments that can contribute greatly to funding the huge amounts of investments that are needed to build an environmentally sustainable world. Global green bond markets have grown rapidly since the first green bonds were issued by the European Investment Bank in 2007 and the World Bank in 2008. Indeed, green bond markets are one of the fastest-growing components of the global financial system.

Green bonds consist of labeled green bonds and unlabeled green bonds. The proceeds from issuing both types of bonds are used for climate-aligned projects and initiatives, but only labeled green bonds receive formal third-party certification. As such, they are generally regarded as being more credible in terms of their greenness. Bolton (2017) offers a more precise definition of the two types of bonds. Labeled green bonds are officially certified as complying with the Green Bond Principles (GBP), which are voluntary best practice guidelines established by a consortium of investment banks in 2014. The GBP are widely viewed as the gold standard of greenness certification. Unlabeled green bonds do not comply with GBP.

The Climate Bonds Initiative estimates that the amount of climate-aligned bonds outstanding worldwide surpassed USD1 trillion in December 2020.[9] Of this amount, labeled and unlabeled bonds accounted for USD240 billion and USD760 billion, respectively. Thus, labeled bonds comprise 24% of the climate-aligned bond universe and unlabeled bonds, which are generally less investible although they also contribute to a low-carbon economy, comprise the remaining 76%.

As mentioned earlier, the green bond market is not only large, it is also fast-growing. Global green bond issuance more than doubled to USD228 billion during the first half of 2021 from USD92 billion during the first half of 2020, when issuance was notably impacted by the global spread of coronavirus disease (COVID-19).[10] The issuance total in the first 6 months of 2021 marked a record for a half-year period. The Climate Bonds Initiative forecasts that around USD500 billion will be issued during full-year 2021, which would be an annual record. Green bonds were initially issued primarily by advanced economies and select supranational institutions, but issuers now include 67 economies and multiple supranational institutions. Developing economies such as the People's Republic of China, which has the world's second-biggest green bond market after the United States, are now integral parts of the global market.

Unlabeled versus Labeled Green Bonds

Most unlabeled bonds are issued by pure-play companies focusing on one particular type of business or industry, such as a manufacturer of solar panels or electric cars. While the proceeds of these companies may eventually be used to fund environmentally beneficial projects, proceeds could also be used for routine business activities such as daily operating expenses, management bonuses, or dividend payments. Such bonds are not labeled as green because they do not meet the GBP, which stipulate that the use of proceeds should be linked directly to specific environmental projects.

In addition, clean energy bonds that are used to finance new renewable energy projects with a quantifiable

---

[8] Suk Hyun, Donghyun Park, and Shu Tian. 2021. "Pricing of Green Labeling: A Comparison of Labeled and Unlabeled Green Bonds." *Finance Research Letters* 41 (2021). https://doi.org/10.1016/j.frl.2020.101816.
[9] See https://www.climatebonds.net/2020/12/1trillion-mark-reached-global-cumulative-green-issuance-climate-bonds-data-intelligence.
[10] See https://www.climatebonds.net/resources/press-releases/2021/08/green-bonds-market-track-record-half-trillion-year-usd4961bn-issued.

mitigation impact on greenhouse gas emissions are not equivalent to green bonds whose proceeds are used to maintain existing transportation or water infrastructure, or to finance a variety of climate projects with an unclearly defined environmental impact. Therefore, besides the issue of whether a bond is green or not, another fundamental issue is the validity of the green labeling. While a bond may be labeled as green, it may in fact be part of a portfolio for a company that produces coal energy and photovoltaic panels simultaneously.

Even in the presence of global standards such as the GBP, some economies have developed their own green bond guidelines. Since more economies are entering the global green bond market, the incompatibility of different national guidelines looms as a major problem. The overarching concern is that national or regional standards are less rigorous than international standards in their assessment of the greenness of a bond. This can reduce the credibility of labeling via national or regional standards relative to labeling via global standards. More broadly, rigorous third-party certification supported by well-defined and systematic evaluation of the environmental benefits of the investments financed by green bonds is vital for inspiring the confidence of investors in green bond markets.

Price Differences Between Labeled and Unlabeled Green Bonds

Most existing studies that delve into the yields, and thus prices, of green bonds focus on yield differences between green bonds and conventional bonds with similar characteristics. This literature not only empirically analyzes the yield differences between green versus conventional bonds but also the determinants of yield differences. That is, these studies seek to answer the question of whether the yields of green bonds differ significantly from the yields of conventional bonds and if so, why? While this literature is valuable in that it helps to identify differences between green bonds and conventional bonds, it implicitly assumes that all green bonds are equal. But there is, in fact, a great deal of heterogeneity among green bonds. Put simply, some green bonds are greener than others.

In particular, some green bonds are labeled while others are not. Labels matter to investors because labeling reduces the environmental risk of green bonds. In

conventional bond markets, a credit rating signals the level of the issuer's credit risk. A good rating signals that the issuer's credit risk is low whereas a poor credit rating signals that the issuer's credit risk is high. By the same token, labeled green bonds have a lower environmental risk than unlabeled green bonds. This is because labeling requires third-party certification that is supported by external review of the greenness of the projects financed by the bond's proceeds. Such an external assessment reduces the information costs of investors, who can rely on the label rather than undertake costly due diligence. The label is thus a source of valuable information for investors.

Hyun, Park, and Tian (forthcoming) address the gap in the literature by empirically analyzing the yield and thus price differences between labeled and unlabeled green bonds. The study's basic premise is that the price that investors are willing to pay may differ between labeled and unlabeled green bonds because the former is more credible in terms of their greenness. Intuitively, green labels such as those certifying compliance with the GBP are valuable for investors because they lower information costs and environmental risks. The analysis of the study empirically confirms that investors value green labels and are willing to pay for them.

Data, Methodology, and Empirical Results

Bloomberg Energy Finance (2015) classifies a bond as a green bond if the issuer (i) self-labels its bond as green or (ii) identifies the bond as oriented toward environmental sustainability objectives with clear statements about its commitment to use the proceeds for investments in compliance with the GBP. All proceeds must be used for green activities that are consistent with the GBP. Hyun, Park, and Tian (forthcoming) compiled Bloomberg data for 3,578 green bonds issued between January 2014 and December 2017. Of the green bond total, 282 were unlabeled and 3,296 were labeled. The GBP were launched in 2014, which is why that year was chosen as the beginning of the review period.

Table 6 shows the key statistical features of labeled and unlabeled green bonds after propensity score matching, which refers to a statistical technique to construct an artificial control group by matching each treated unit (i.e., labeled green bond) with a nontreated

Table 6: Summary Statistics of Labeled and Unlabeled Green Bonds

Variables	Unlabeled Green Bonds	Labeled Green Bonds	t-value
Yield (bps)	3.359	3.218	1.186
Tenor	3.516	3.565	−2.713***
Issue Amount	6.024	6.746	−9.768***
Liquidity	0.198	0.253	−1.443

Notes:
1. Yield is the yield to maturity in basis points (bps) of the bonds during the sample period.
2. Tenor is the logarithm of bond maturity measured in number of days on bond issuance.
3. Issuance amount is the logarithm of funds raised by each bond issuance (USD million).
4. Liquidity is the bid–ask spread for each green bond. ***, **, and * denote statistical significance at the 1%, 5%, and 10% levels, respectively.
Source: Hyun, Park, and Tian (forthcoming).

Table 7: Effects of Green Label on Green Bond Yield

	Model 1	Model 2
Green Label	−0.240***	−0.355***
	(−5.690)	(−4.941)
Tenor	1.915***	2.066***
	(20.216)	(10.408)
Issue Amount	0.087***	−0.070
	(2.978)	(−0.988)
Liquidity	0.618***	1.632***
	(12.006)	(3.722)
Adjusted R^2	0.43	0.37

Notes:
1. The dependent variable is the bid yield of a green bond.
2. Green label is a dummy variable indicating whether a green bond has a green label or not.
3. Tenor is the logarithm of bond maturity measured in number of days on bond issuance.
4. Issuance amount is the logarithm of funds raised by each bond issuance (USD million).
5. Liquidity is the bid–ask spread for each green bond. ***, **, and * denote statistical significance at the 1%, 5%, and 10% levels, respectively.
Source: Hyun, Park, and Tian (forthcoming).

unit (i.e., green bond) with similar characteristics. The technique allows for a more accurate assessment of the impact of an intervention (i.e., labeling). Table 6 shows that relative to unlabeled green bonds, labeled green bonds are characterized by lower yields, longer tenors, larger issue amounts, and less liquidity.

Table 7 reports the results of the econometric analysis of the impact of labeling on green bond yields. The analysis, which controls for factors other than green labels that affect yields, is based on matching a labeled green bond with an unlabeled green bond with similar characteristics. Models 1 and 2 refer to different ways of matching the two bonds. The results strongly confirm our conjecture that green labels have a visible effect on the yields of green bonds. More precisely, the yields of labeled green bonds are 24–36 basis points lower than the yields of unlabeled green bonds with similar attributes. The results are highly statistically significant at the 1% level and robustly consistent across both models. Bond yield is positively associated with tenor, issue amount, and liquidity.

Conclusion

Green bonds are not a homogeneous asset class. In particular, labeled green bonds differ substantively from unlabeled green bonds. The former undergo external review and assessment to receive formal certification of greenness, such as compliance with the GBP, whereas the latter do not. From the investor's perspective, a green label is valuable because it lowers information costs and environmental risks. From the issuer's perspective, a green label reduces financing costs. In light of such theoretical effects, there is reason to believe that green labels have

an impact on the yields and hence pricing of green bonds. Hyun, Park, and Tian (forthcoming) empirically analyze this possibility. Their analysis strongly confirms a statistically significant effect of green labels on the yield of green bonds: the yields of labeled green bonds are 24–36 basis points lower than the yields of unlabeled green bonds with similar characteristics. The salient implication for policymakers is that it is helpful to introduce widely accepted international labels of greenness that benefit both investors and issuers. In addition, educating issuers about the benefits of green labels, along with guidance on obtaining them, would promote greater use of green labels.

References

Bloomberg Energy Finance. 2015. Guide to Green Bonds on the Bloomberg Terminal.

Bolton, Ross. 2017. *Green Bonds: A Decade of Progress*. Boston: State Street Global Advisors.

Hyun, Suk, Donghyun Park, and Shu Tian. Forthcoming. "Price of Green Labeling: A Comparison of Labeled and Unlabeled Green Bonds." *Finance Research Letters*.

Market Summaries

People's Republic of China

Yield Movements

The People's Republic of China's (PRC) yield curve shifted upward for all tenors except the 3-month tenor, which fell 8 basis points (bps), between 31 August and 15 October (**Figure 1**). The remaining tenors rose an average of 9 bps, with the steepest increases seen for the 5-year tenor at 17 bps and for the 9-year to 30-year tenors, which rose between 13 and 15 bps. As a result of the rise in yields, particularly for the longer-dated maturities, the 2-year versus 10-year yield spread rose 8 bps from the end of August to 15 October.

The PRC's yield curve rose despite economic indicators showing that the domestic economy was slowing down. The PRC's gross domestic product growth fell to 4.9% year-on-year (y-o-y) in the third quarter (Q3) of 2021 from 7.9% y-o-y in the second (Q2) quarter. Economic growth fell largely due to a deceleration in the secondary sector, where growth declined from 7.5% in Q2 2021 to 3.6% in Q3 2021, and in the tertiary sector, in which growth fell from 8.3% to 5.4%. The growth rate in the primary sector fell to 7.1% from 7.5% in the same period.

The growth rate of industrial production has also been steadily declining from a high of 35.1% y-o-y in the first 2 months of 2021 to 3.1% y-o-y in September. Consumer demand, as measured by retail sales, also weakened with double-digit growth rates posted from January through June before falling to 8.5% in July and 2.5% in August, and rising to 4.4% in September.

Several reasons abound for the rise in yields despite softening growth. Following the reserve requirement rate reduction by the People's Bank of China (PBOC) in July, markets expected either a reduction in its loan prime rate or additional reserve requirement rate cuts. However, the PBOC so far has done neither, disappointing market expectations. In addition, despite economic weakness and turmoil in the property sector with several real estate companies at the brink of default, the Government of the PRC has not strongly shifted from its risk control focus.

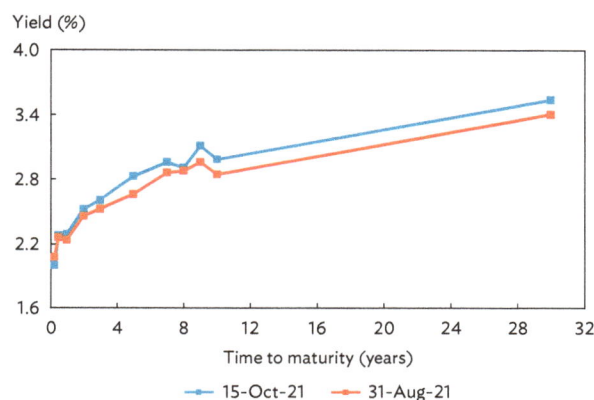

Figure 1: The People's Republic of China's Benchmark Yield Curve—Local Currency Government Bonds

Source: Based on data from Bloomberg LP.

Inflationary concerns also manifest. While consumer price inflation has been tame, with the inflation rate trending downward from 1.3% y-o-y in May to 0.7% y-o-y in September, producer price inflation has been rising strongly. September producer price inflation rose to 10.7% y-o-y from 9.5% y-o-y in August. The inflation rate was at 0.3% y-o-y in January. There are concerns that high producer prices will eventually make their way to consumer prices as the cost increases get passed on.

Size and Composition

Growth in the PRC's local currency (LCY) bond market accelerated to 3.8% quarter-on-quarter (q-o-q) in Q3 2021 from 3.0% q-o-q in Q2 2021, with bonds outstanding at the end of September reaching CNY110.6 trillion (USD17.2 trillion) (**Table 1**). However, the growth rate fell on a y-o-y basis to 12.6% in Q3 2021 from 14.4% in the preceding quarter.

Government bonds. Government bonds outstanding in the PRC grew 4.0% q-o-q to CNY71.1 trillion, accelerating from a 3.3% q-o-q gain in the previous quarter. Treasury and other government bonds and bank bonds all showed

Table 1: Size and Composition of the Local Currency Bond Market in the People's Republic of China

| | Outstanding Amount (billion) | | | | | | Growth Rates (%) | | | |
| | Q3 2020 | | Q2 2021 | | Q3 2021 | | Q3 2020 | | Q3 2021 | |
	CNY	USD	CNY	USD	CNY	USD	q-o-q	y-o-y	q-o-q	y-o-y
Total	98,178	14,457	106,590	16,507	110,589	17,159	5.4	19.9	3.8	12.6
Government	62,747	9,240	68,384	10,591	71,129	11,037	6.6	18.6	4.0	13.4
Treasury Bonds and Other Government Bonds	19,327	2,846	21,548	3,337	22,342	3,467	8.7	21.1	3.7	15.6
Central Bank Bonds	15	2	15	2	15	2	0.0	0.0	0.0	0.0
Policy Bank Bonds	17,489	2,575	18,658	2,890	19,253	2,987	5.0	13.2	3.2	10.1
Local Government Bonds	25,915	3,816	28,163	4,362	29,519	4,580	6.1	20.6	4.8	13.9
Corporate	35,432	5,217	38,207	5,917	39,460	6,123	3.2	22.2	3.3	11.4

CNY = Chinese yuan, q-o-q = quarter-on-quarter, Q2 = second quarter, Q3 = third quarter, USD = United States dollar, y-o-y = year-on-year.
Notes:
1. Calculated using data from national sources.
2. Treasury bonds include savings bonds and local government bonds.
3. Bloomberg LP end-of-period local currency–USD rates are used.
4. Growth rates are calculated from local currency base and do not include currency effects.
Sources: CEIC Data Company and Bloomberg LP.

an acceleration in growth rates, while the outstanding amount of central bank bonds remained unchanged.

The outstanding local government bonds growth rate dipped slightly to 4.8% q-o-q in Q3 2021 from 5.2% q-o-q in Q2 2021 due to base effects. After tepid issuance in the first quarter of 2021, local government bond issuance rose 173.5% q-o-q in Q2 2021 as local governments sought to complete their bond quotas. Local government bond issuance dipped slightly in Q3 2021, falling 7.0% q-o-q. Local government bond issuance is still expected to remain strong for the year, as net issuance for the first 9 months was only 61.0% of the allotted quota for 2021.

Growth in Treasury and other bonds outstanding accelerated to 3.7% q-o-q, to reach CNY22.3 trillion, from 2.5% q-o-q in the previous quarter, driven by a 37.6% q-o-q jump in issuance. Policy bank bonds also gained 3.2% q-o-q to reach CNY19.3 trillion, up from 1.5% q-o-q growth in Q2 2021. However, issuance of policy bank bonds in Q3 2021 was roughly comparable to Q2 2021.

Corporate bonds. The PRC's corporate bonds outstanding rose 3.3% q-o-q to CNY39.5 trillion after gaining 2.3% q-o-q in the previous quarter. While overall corporate bond growth accelerated, corporate bond issuance was significantly higher in Q3 2021, rising 17.1% q-o-q as a number of companies issued bonds to refinance maturing obligations.

Growth in outstanding corporate bonds was mainly from financial bonds, with a number of financial institutions issuing tier 2 bonds to raise capital, resulting in a

5.1% q-o-q gain in financial bonds outstanding (**Table 2**). Regulators have encouraged financial institutions to bolster their capital bases in the wake of a potential economic slowdown as well as rising corporate bond defaults. Asset-backed securities were the second-biggest gainer, with such bonds expanding 4.9% q-o-q. Demand for listed corporate bonds only gained 3.2% q-o-q but grew 17.9% y-o-y. Given rising interest rates, interest in commercial paper waned; while commercial paper outstanding gained 2.4% q-o-q, it declined 13.4% y-o-y.

Issuance amounts of financial bonds remained strong with levels in Q3 2021 similar to Q2 2021 (**Figure 2**). Issuance of commercial paper showed an increase as companies rolled over their existing maturities. Issuance of listed corporate bonds was the highest among all the major bond categories, driving the overall increase in the y-o-y growth rate of corporate bonds outstanding.

The top 30 issuers' share of total LCY corporate bonds outstanding stood at 28.3% at end of September (**Table 3**). The total amount of the top 30 was at CNY11.1 trillion and the 10 largest issuers accounted for CNY7.3 trillion. China Railway remained the largest issuer, accounting for 24.5% of the total bonds outstanding of the top 30 issuers. Due to capital-raising efforts, 14 banks were among the top 30 list of top issuers.

Table 4 lists the largest corporate bond issuances in Q3 2021. Of the five top issuers, four were financial institutions that sought to bolster their capital bases. China State Railway Group was the sole nonfinancial issuer among the top five issuances for Q3 2021.

Table 2: Corporate Bonds Outstanding in Key Categories

| | Amount (CNY billion) | | | Growth Rate (%) | | | |
| | | | | Q3 2020 | | Q3 2021 | |
	Q3 2020	Q2 2021	Q3 2021	q-o-q	y-o-y	q-o-q	y-o-y
Financial Bonds	7,166	8,038	8,447	1.1	30.2	5.1	17.9
Enterprise Bonds	3,826	3,808	3,876	1.0	(0.3)	1.8	1.3
Listed Corporate Bonds	9,619	10,986	11,341	1.1	32.7	3.2	17.9
Commercial Paper	2,694	2,279	2,334	1.0	25.2	2.4	(13.4)
Medium-Term Notes	7,351	7,457	7,623	1.0	19.7	2.2	3.7
Asset-Backed Securities	2,519	3,075	3,225	1.0	21.1	4.9	28.1

( ) = negative, CNY = Chinese yuan, q-o-q = quarter-on-quarter, Q2 = second quarter, Q3 = third quarter, y-o-y = year-on-year.
Source: CEIC Data Company.

Figure 2: Corporate Bond Issuance in Key Sectors

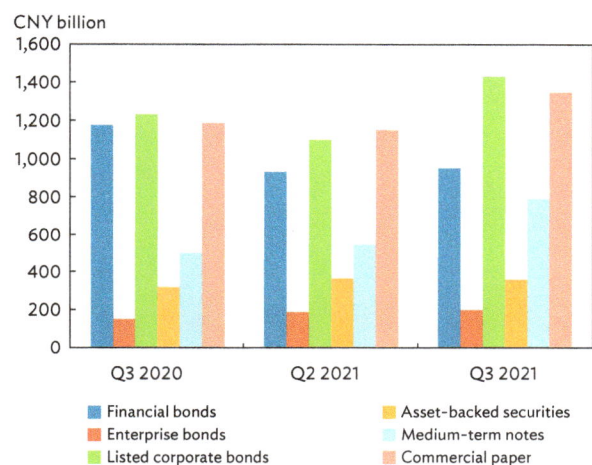

CNY = Chinese yuan, Q2 = second quarter, Q3 = third quarter.
Source: ChinaBond.

Investor Profile

Government bonds. Commercial banks were still the dominant investor group in government bonds in Q3 2021, but their share of outstanding bonds declined from a year earlier (**Figure 3**). However, banks still have an overwhelming presence in the local government bond market with a share of 86.9%.

Banks are still the major holders of Treasury bonds, with a 65.2% share in Q3 2021. But continued foreign investor interest has led to rapid gains in their share of Treasury bonds, which rose from 9.7% in Q2 2021 to 11.4% in Q3 2021. Foreign investors have also made significant inroads in policy bank bonds, with the foreign investor share rising to 5.5% from 4.8% in the same period.

Liquidity

The volume of interest rate swaps fell 4.6% q-o-q in Q3 2021 (**Table 5**). The 7-day repo rate was the most active instrument, while repo transactions exclusive to banks and other deposit taking institutions have fallen.

Policy, Institutional, and Regulatory Developments

Southbound Trading of Bond Connect Launched

In September, the Hong Kong Monetary Authority and the PBOC jointly announced the opening of the southbound leg of the Bond Connect scheme. This will allow residents in the PRC to buy bonds in Hong Kong, China, thereby facilitating outward investment flows. The PBOC said that total transactions reached CNY4 billion during the first day of the launch.

Tax Incentives for Foreign Investors Extended

In October, the PRC extended tax exemptions for foreign investors in the PRC's domestic bond market, which was set to expire in November. The incentives exempt foreign investors from corporate income taxes and value-added taxes on bond investments. Exemptions were extended until the end of 2025.

Table 3: Top 30 Issuers of Local Currency Corporate Bonds in the People's Republic of China

	Issuers	Outstanding Amount		State-Owned	Listed Company	Type of Industry
		LCY Bonds (CNY billion)	LCY Bonds (USD billion)			
1.	China Railway	2,735.5	424.45	Yes	No	Transportation
2.	Industrial and Commercial Bank of China	721.4	111.93	Yes	Yes	Banking
3.	Bank of China	688.1	106.77	Yes	Yes	Banking
4.	Agricultural Bank of China	650.3	100.90	Yes	Yes	Banking
5.	Bank of Communications	575.7	89.33	No	Yes	Banking
6.	Shanghai Pudong Development Bank	470.6	73.02	Yes	Yes	Banking
7.	China Construction Bank	468.1	72.62	Yes	Yes	Banking
8.	Central Huijin Investment	416.0	64.55	Yes	No	Asset Management
9.	China CITIC Bank	315.0	48.88	No	Yes	Banking
10.	Industrial Bank	286.2	44.41	No	Yes	Banking
11.	China Minsheng Bank	270.0	41.89	No	Yes	Banking
12.	China National Petroleum	269.9	41.88	Yes	No	Energy
13.	State Grid Corporation of China	262.5	40.73	Yes	No	Public Utilities
14.	State Power Investment	256.5	39.81	Yes	No	Power
15.	China Securities Finance	242.0	37.55	Yes	No	Finance
16.	Postal Savings Bank of China	220.0	34.14	Yes	Yes	Banking
17.	China Everbright Bank	215.9	33.50	No	Yes	Banking
18.	China Merchants Bank	209.2	32.46	No	Yes	Banking
19.	Ping An Bank	185.0	28.71	No	Yes	Banking
20.	CITIC Securities	181.5	28.16	Yes	Yes	Brokerage
21.	Huaxia Bank	180.0	27.93	No	Yes	Banking
22.	China Southern Power Grid	165.6	25.70	Yes	No	Public Utilities
23.	Huatai Securities	163.2	25.32	No	Yes	Brokerage
24.	Tianjin Infrastructure Investment Group	157.5	24.44	Yes	No	Capital Goods
25.	China Merchants Securities	155.8	24.17	No	No	Brokerage
26.	Shaanxi Coal and Chemical Industry Group	155.0	24.05	Yes	Yes	Coal
27.	Shenwan Hongyuan Securities	139.0	21.57	No	No	Brokerage
28.	GF Securities	134.0	20.79	No	Yes	Brokerage
29.	Guotai Junan Securities	131.1	20.35	Yes	Yes	Brokerage
30.	Haitong Securities	128.3	19.91	No	Yes	Brokerage
	Total Top 30 LCY Corporate Issuers	**11,149.0**	**1,729.9**			
	Total LCY Corporate Bonds	**39,459.6**	**6,122.7**			
	Top 30 as % of Total LCY Corporate Bonds	**28.3%**	**28.3%**			

CNY = Chinese yuan, LCY = local currency, USD = United States dollar.
Notes:
1. Data as of 30 September 2021.
2. State-owned firms are defined as those in which the government has more than a 50% ownership stake.
Source: *AsianBondsOnline* calculations based on Bloomberg LP data.

Table 4: Notable Local Currency Corporate Bond Issuances in the Third Quarter of 2021

Corporate Issuers	Coupon Rate (%)	Issued Amount (CNY billion)
Postal Savings Bank of China		
1-year bond	4.06	41.5
10-year bond	3.44	50.0
China Construction Bank[a]		
1-year bond	3.93	20.0
1-year bond	3.87	20.0
10-year bond	3.45	6.0
15-year bond	3.80	15.0
China State Railway Group		
5-year bond	316.00	15.0
10-year bond	3.30	20.0
30-year bond	3.78	5.0
Guotai Junan Securities[a]		
1-year bond	2.75	2.0
3-year bond	3.01	2.8
3-year bond	3.09	4.4
3-year bond	3.13	1.9
5-year bond	3.35	4.2
5-year bond	3.48	6.1
10-year bond	3.77	3.0
10-year bond	3.80	3.4
20-year bond	3.80	5.0
20-year bond	3.80	5.0
Shenwan Hongyuan Securities[a]		
2-year bond	2.95	2.3
3-year bond	3.04	2.8
3-year bond	3.13	2.0
3-year bond	3.02	3.0
3-year bond	3.05	4.8
3-year bond	3.10	2.3
5-year bond	3.40	1.0
5-year bond	3.38	4.2
10-year bond	3.77	3.0
10-year bond	3.75	3.0
Perpetual bond	3.70	3.3

CNY = Chinese yuan.
[a] Multiple issuance of the same tenor indicates issuance on different dates.
Source: Based on data from Bloomberg LP.

Figure 3: Local Currency Treasury Bonds and Policy Bank Bonds Investor Profile

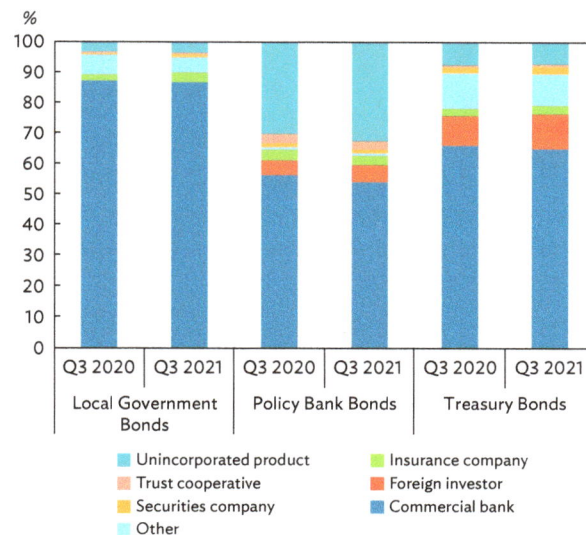

Q3 = third quarter.
Source: CEIC Data Company.

Table 5: Notional Values of the People's Republic of China's Interest Rate Swap Market in the Third Quarter of 2021

Interest Rate Swap Benchmarks	Notional Amount (CNY billion)	Share of Total Notional Amount (%)	Growth Rate (%)
	Q3 2021		q-o-q
7-Day Repo Rate	4,692.1	86.5	(3.2)
Overnight SHIBOR	7.2	0.1	(29.8)
3-Month SHIBOR	688.3	12.7	(14.0)
1-Year Lending Rate	20.8	0.4	73.7
5-Year Lending Rate	1.5	0.03	(20.5)
10-Year Treasury Yield	5.5	0.1	3.8
China Development Bank 10-Year Bond Yield	5.9	0.1	22.9
10-Year Corporate and Government Bond Yield	5.5	0.1	22.2
Total	5,426.8	100.0	(4.6)

( ) = negative, CNY = Chinese yuan, q-o-q = quarter-on-quarter, Q3 = third quarter, Repo = repurchase agreement, SHIBOR = Shanghai Interbank Offered Rate.
Note: Growth rate computed based on notional amounts.
Sources: *AsianBondsOnline* and *ChinaMoney*.

Hong Kong, China

Yield Movements

Between 31 August and 15 October, the local currency (LCY) government bond yield curve in Hong Kong, China remained unchanged at the shorter-end but shifted upward for tenors longer than 1 year (**Figure 1**). Yields for bonds with maturities of 1 year or less held steady, while yields for those with maturities longer than 1 year gained an average of 20 basis points (bps). The 10-year and 15-year tenors showed the most gain in yields, with both climbing 29 bps. The spread between the 2-year and the 10-year bond yields widened to 124 bps on 15 October from 101 bps on 31 August.

Hong Kong, China's LCY bond yield movements largely tracked the rate movements of United States (US) Treasuries during the review period as the Hong Kong dollar is pegged to the US dollar. The US bond yield curve shifted upward during the review period, with yields rising an average of 16 bps across all tenors. The rise was driven by inflation fears as supply chain bottlenecks generated upward pressure on prices. As widely expected, the US Federal Reserve announced that they will begin to taper bond purchases in November.

Hong Kong, China's consumer price inflation remained moderate, rising 1.4% year-on-year (y-o-y) in September after a 1.6% y-o-y increase in August. The underlying inflation rate, which nets out the effects of the government's relief measures on prices, also eased to 1.0% in September from 1.2% in August. The Census and Statistics Department expects that inflationary pressures would rise in the near term as the economic recovery continues but projects the underlying consumer inflation to remain modest if economic activities continue to fall short of pre-pandemic levels.

Hong Kong, China's gross domestic product rose 5.4% y-o-y in the third quarter (Q3) of 2021, following 7.6% y-o-y growth in the second quarter (Q2). The growth moderation in Q3 2021 was largely due to base effects and the stronger-than-expected economic expansion in the first half of the year. Robust external and domestic demand underpinned the growth in Q3 2021, with merchandise exports rising 14.2% y-o-y

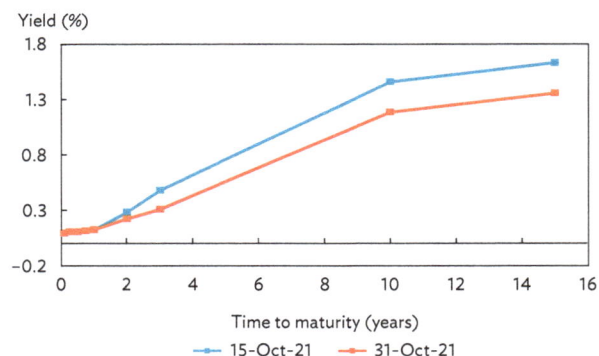

Figure 1: Hong Kong, China's Benchmark Yield Curve—Exchange Fund Bills and Notes

Source: Based on data from Bloomberg LP.

and private consumption expanding 7.1% y-o-y. Hong Kong, China's growth outlook continues to face several risk factors, including uncertainties over the track of major central banks' monetary policies and the continuing geopolitical tensions between the US and the People's Republic of China (PRC).

Size and Composition

Hong Kong, China's outstanding LCY bonds amounted to HKD2,428.6 billion (USD311.9 billion) at the end of September (**Table 1**). The LCY bond market posted a 0.1% quarter-on-quarter (q-o-q) rise in Q3 2021 after an 0.8% q-o-q drop in Q2 2021. The tepid growth in Hong Kong, China's LCY bond market in Q3 2021 was driven by a contraction in the corporate bond segment. On an annual basis, the LCY bond market expanded 6.1% y-o-y in Q3 2021, down from 7.0% y-o-y in the previous quarter. Hong Kong, China's LCY bond market was split almost evenly between government and corporate bonds, with government bonds comprising 51.6% of the total at the end of September.

Government bonds. LCY government bonds outstanding totaled HKD1,252.2 billion at the end of September on growth of 3.0% q-o-q and 8.2% y-o-y. The q-o-q growth in Q3 2021 was driven by expansions in the outstanding stock of Exchange Fund Bills (EFBs) and Hong Kong

Table 1: Size and Composition of the Local Currency Bond Market in Hong Kong, China

| | Outstanding Amount (billion) | | | | | | Growth Rate (%) | | | |
| | Q3 2020 | | Q2 2021 | | Q3 2021 | | Q3 2020 | | Q3 2021 | |
	HKD	USD	HKD	USD	HKD	USD	q-o-q	y-o-y	q-o-q	y-o-y
Total	2,288	295	2,427	313	2,429	312	0.9	1.0	0.1	6.1
Government	1,158	149	1,216	157	1,252	161	0.1	(1.1)	3.0	8.2
Exchange Fund Bills	1,042	134	1,044	134	1,064	137	0.03	(0.6)	1.9	2.1
Exchange Fund Notes	26	3	24	3	24	3	0.0	(9.2)	0.0	(6.2)
HKSAR Bonds	90	12	147	19	164	21	1.1	(4.4)	11.1	82.8
Corporate	1,130	146	1,211	156	1,176	151	1.6	3.3	(2.9)	4.1

( ) = negative, HKD = Hong Kong dollar, HKSAR = Hong Kong Special Administrative Region, q-o-q = quarter-on-quarter, Q2 = second quarter, Q3 = third quarter, USD = United States dollar, y-o-y = year-on-year.
Notes:
1. Calculated using data from national sources.
2. Bloomberg LP end-of-period local currency–USD rates are used.
3. Growth rates are calculated from local currency base and do not include currency effects.
Source: Hong Kong Monetary Authority.

Special Administrative Region (HKSAR) bonds, as the stock of Exchange Fund Notes (EFNs) remained steady during the quarter.

Issuance of government bonds amounted to HKD882.7 billion in Q3 2021 with growth easing to 3.2% q-o-q in Q3 2021 from 4.5% q-o-q in the prior quarter. The growth in issuance of LCY government bonds in Q3 2021 stemmed largely from strong issuance of EFBs.

Exchange Fund Bills. EFBs outstanding totaled HKD1,064.3 billion at the end of September on growth of 1.9% q-o-q and 2.1% y-o-y. EFBs accounted for 85.0% of total LCY government bonds at the end of September. Issuance of EFBs reached HKD850.5 billion in Q3 2021. Issuance growth more than doubled, rising 3.0% q-o-q in Q3 2021 from 1.4% q-o-q in Q2 2021. To absorb excess liquidity in the financial system, the Hong Kong Monetary Authority (HKMA) increased the issuance size of 91-day EFBs in September by a total of HKD20.0 million during the quarter.

Exchange Fund Notes. Outstanding EFNs amounted to HKD24.2 billion at the end of September. Since 2015, the HKMA has limited its issuance of EFNs to 2-year tenors. In August, the HKMA issued 2-year EFNs worth HKD1.2 billion. Due to maturities, outstanding EFNs posted zero q-o-q growth in Q3 2021. On a y-o-y basis, outstanding EFNs contracted 6.2% in Q3 2021. EFNs comprised 1.9% of total LCY government bonds at the end of September.

HKSAR bonds. HKSAR bonds outstanding reached HKD163.7 billion at the end of September on growth of 11.1% q-o-q and 82.8% y-o-y due to strong issuance. HKSAR bond issuance rose 9.9% q-o-q in Q3 2021. In August, the government issued HKD30.0 billion worth of 3-year Silver Bonds, which are bonds intended for senior citizens. The issuance received strong demand as the eligible age for subscription was lowered to 60 from 65. The government also issued HKD1.0 billion worth of 15-year HKSAR bonds in September. Outstanding HKSAR bonds accounted for 13.1% of total LCY government bonds at the end of Q3 2021.

Corporate bonds. Corporate bonds outstanding amounted to HKD1,176.4 billion at the end of September after a 2.9% q-o-q contraction in Q3 2021 due to maturities and a drop in issuance. On an annual basis, growth in LCY corporate bonds outstanding moderated to 4.1% y-o-y in Q3 2021 from 8.9% y-o-y in Q2 2021.

LCY bonds outstanding of Hong Kong, China's top 30 nonbank issuers totaled HKD300.6 billion at the end of Q3 2021, accounting for 25.6% of the total LCY corporate bond market (**Table 2**). Hong Kong Mortgage Corporation, Sung Hung Kai & Co., and The Hong Kong and China Gas Company continued to top the list, with outstanding bonds of HKD69.9 billion, HKD20.9 billion, and HKD18.0 billion, respectively. The top 30 issuers were predominantly finance and real estate companies. Finance firms' outstanding bonds accounted for 44.9% of the total bonds outstanding of the top 30 nonbank issuers, while real estate firms represented a 21.3% share. Among the

Table 2: Top 30 Nonbank Corporate Issuers of Local Currency Corporate Bonds in Hong Kong, China

	Issuers	Outstanding Amount		State-Owned	Listed Company	Type of Industry
		LCY Bonds (HKD billion)	LCY Bonds (USD billion)			
1.	Hong Kong Mortgage Corporation	69.9	9.0	Yes	No	Finance
2.	Sun Hung Kai & Co.	20.9	2.7	No	Yes	Finance
3.	The Hong Kong and China Gas Company	18.0	2.3	No	Yes	Utilities
4.	New World Development	16.0	2.0	No	Yes	Diversified
5.	Hang Lung Properties	13.2	1.7	No	Yes	Real Estate
6.	Hong Kong Land	12.9	1.7	No	No	Real Estate
7.	Link Holdings	12.7	1.6	No	Yes	Finance
8.	MTR	12.3	1.6	Yes	Yes	Transportation
9.	Henderson Land Development	12.0	1.5	No	Yes	Real Estate
10.	Swire Pacific	10.3	1.3	No	Yes	Diversified
11.	CK Asset Holdings	10.0	1.3	No	Yes	Real Estate
12.	The Wharf Holdings	9.7	1.2	No	Yes	Finance
13.	Guotai Junan International Holdings	9.1	1.2	No	Yes	Finance
14.	Cathay Pacific	9.0	1.1	No	Yes	Transportation
15.	Airport Authority	8.9	1.1	Yes	No	Transportation
16.	Hongkong Electric	8.5	1.1	No	No	Utilities
17.	CLP Power Hong Kong Financing	7.4	1.0	No	No	Finance
18.	Swire Properties	7.3	0.9	No	Yes	Diversified
19.	Hysan Development Corporation	6.1	0.8	No	Yes	Real Estate
20.	Future Days	4.2	0.5	No	No	Transportation
21.	Haitong International	3.3	0.4	No	Yes	Finance
22.	Lerthai Group	3.0	0.4	No	Yes	Real Estate
23.	AIA Group	2.4	0.3	No	Yes	Insurance
24.	Ev Dynamics Holdings	2.4	0.3	No	Yes	Diversified
25.	Champion REIT	2.3	0.3	No	Yes	Real Estate
26.	South Shore Holdings	2.2	0.3	No	Yes	Industrial
27.	IFC Development	2.0	0.3	No	No	Finance
28.	Nan Fung	1.8	0.2	No	No	Real Estate
29.	Wheelock and Company	1.5	0.2	No	Yes	Real Estate
30.	Emperor International Holdings	1.4	0.2	No	Yes	Real Estate
Total Top 30 Nonbank LCY Corporate Issuers		**300.6**	**38.6**			
Total LCY Corporate Bonds		**1,176.4**	**151.1**			
Top 30 as % of Total LCY Corporate Bonds		**25.6%**	**25.6%**			

HKD = Hong Kong dollar, LCY = local currency, REIT = real estate investment trust, USD = United States dollar.
Notes:
1. Data as of 30 September 2021.
2. State-owned firms are defined as those in which the government has more than a 50% ownership stake.
Source: *AsianBondsOnline* calculations based on Bloomberg LP data.

top 30 issuers, only three were government-owned while a majority were listed on the Hong Kong Stock Exchange.

Issuance of corporate debt amounted to HKD196.7 billion at the end of September. Issuance contracted 15.8% q-o-q in Q3 2021 as uncertainties regarding the trajectory of the pandemic and economic recovery continued to dampen demand for corporate debt.

Table 3 shows the largest corporate issuers in Q3 2021. Hong Kong Mortgage Corporation was the largest issuer with an aggregate HKD12.5 billion from 36 issuances, including a 1-year bond worth HKD1.0 billion. The longest tenor issued by Hong Kong Mortgage Corporation was a 7-year bond with a 0.40% coupon worth HKD0.2 billion. The next largest issuer was Haitong International, which raised HKD3.2 billion from seven issuances of bonds with maturities ranging from 3 months to 1 year. The next largest issuers during the quarter were Guotai Junan International, Sun Hung Kai & Co., and Henderson Land. Hong Kong Land's 10-year bond with a 1.96% coupon worth HKD0.4 billion was the longest tenor issued during the quarter.

Table 3: Notable Local Currency Corporate Bond Issuances in the Third Quarter of 2021

Corporate Issuers	Coupon Rate (%)	Issued Amount (HKD billion)
Hong Kong Mortgage Corporation		
1-year bond	0.29	1.00
2-year bond	0.42	0.26
3-year bond	0.71	0.48
7-year bond	0.40	0.20
Haitong International		
3-month bond	0.40	0.30
6-month bond	0.60	0.80
1-year bond	0.70	0.25
Guotai Junan International Holdings		
6-month bond	0.50	0.80
1-year bond	0.85	0.50
Sun Hung Kai & Co.		
3-year bond	0.82	0.60
7-year bond	1.87	0.39
Henderson Land		
2-year bond	1.00	0.30
3-year bond	1.20	0.40
Hong Kong Land		
10-year bond	1.96	0.38

HKD = Hong Kong dollar.
Source: Bloomberg LP.

Policy, Institutional, and Regulatory Developments

People's Bank of China and Hong Kong Monetary Authority Launch Southbound Bond Connect

On 24 September, the People's Bank of China and the HKMA announced the launch of southbound trading under the Bond Connect platform. The arrangement allows financial institutions in the PRC to invest in Hong Kong, China's bond market. The scheme followed the launch of Northbound Bond Connect 4 years earlier, which provided overseas investors access to the PRC's bond market. Southbound Connect featured an initial daily quota of CNY20 billion (HKD24 billion) and an annual quota of CNY500 billion (HKD600 billion). All bonds traded in Hong Kong, China's bond market were included in the scheme. The HKMA noted that Southbound Bond Connect will help drive the development of Hong Kong, China's bond market and enhance the connection between the financial infrastructures of the PRC and Hong Kong, China.

Hong Kong Monetary Authority Increases Issuance of Exchange Fund Bills

To meet the rise in demand for EFBs amid excess liquidity in the financial system, the HKMA increased its issuance of 91-day EFBs starting in September. The HKMA increased the planned issuance size of 91-day EFBs by HKD5 billion in each of the tenders scheduled from 7 September to 21 December. The HKMA will monitor market conditions during the period and maintain the flexibility of adjusting or not executing the increases if deemed necessary.

Hong Kong Monetary Authority Holds Countercyclical Capital Buffer Ratio at 1.0%

On 28 October, the HKMA held the countercyclical capital buffer ratio (CCyB) at 1.0%. The HKMA noted that despite its nascent recovery, the domestic economy still faces significant risks due to the global pandemic. The latest economic data as of Q2 2021 signaled a CCyB of 2.25%, but the HKMA decided to hold a lower CCyB at 1.0% to support economic recovery amid lingering uncertainties. The CCyB is an integral part of the Basel III regulatory capital framework intended to improve the resilience of the banking sector.

Indonesia

Yield Movements

Local currency (LCY) government bond yield curve in Indonesia shifted upward between 31 August and 15 October. Yields for all maturities that gained rose an average of 7 basis points (bps), while the 3-year, 4-year, 6-year, and 9-year bonds shed 38 bps, 17 bps, 8 bps, and 6 bps, respectively (**Figure 1**). Bond yields gained the most for the 13-year (24 bps) and 18-year (21 bps) tenors during the review period. The yield spread between the 2-year and 10-year maturities was barely changed at 203 bps on 15 October from 204 bps on 31 August.

Rising yields across the curve largely tracked movements in yields in advanced and regional markets amid rising inflationary concerns and an earlier-than-expected unwinding of asset purchases by the United States (US) Federal Reserve. A shift in monetary stance by the Federal Reserve caused an exodus of funds from the Indonesian government bond market, leading to a continued decline in the foreign holdings share. At the end of September, offshore holdings of government bonds comprised 21.6% of the government bond stock, a decline from 22.8% at the end of June and 27.0% from the same period a year earlier.

The increase in yields was also buoyed by a slew of positive developments pointing to a much improved economic outlook after mobility restrictions were eased in September. Indonesia is expected to log a narrower budget deficit this year as the finance minister estimates the budget gap will be the equivalent of 5.3%–5.4% of gross domestic product (GDP) in 2021 versus an earlier estimate of 5.8%.[11] The budget deficit forecast is fueled by optimism in the economic recovery and rising commodity prices. In addition, a strong export performance is expected to lead to an improvement in the current account balance for the year. Indonesia has enjoyed strong global demand for coal and palm oil amid rising energy prices.

Further fueling the growth outlook is the new tax law passed in October, which is expected to boost tax

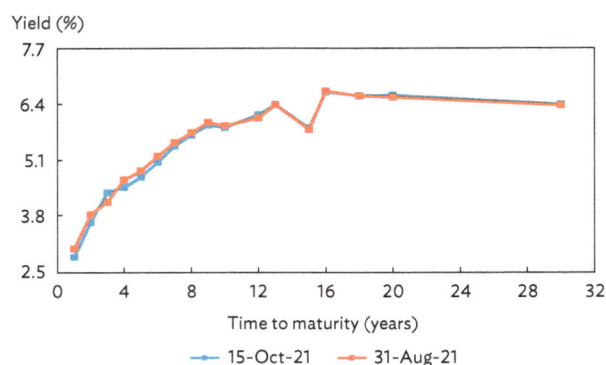

Figure 1: Indonesia's Benchmark Yield Curve—Local Currency Government Bonds

Source: Based on data from Bloomberg LP.

collection by about 9%–18% from 2022 to 2025.[12] This will provide additional fiscal space for the economy.

To bolster the economic recovery, Bank Indonesia, in its meeting held on 18–19 October, left its 7-day reverse repurchase rate unchanged at 3.50%, the deposit facility rate at 2.75%, and the lending facility rate at 4.25%. Bank Indonesia also continues to work with the government to propel economic recovery. As of 15 October, the central bank purchased a total of IDR142.5 trillion of government bonds and injected liquidity through quantitative easing into the banking industry.

Despite improving optimism in the economic recovery, inflation has remained low. Consumer prices rose 1.6% year-on-year (y-o-y) in September and 1.7% y-o-y in October, both lower than the inflation target of between 2.0% and 4.0% for full-year 2020. Bank Indonesia estimates inflation for 2021 to fall below the midpoint of its target range for the year.

Mobility restrictions imposed from July through August dragged down the economic performance for the third quarter (Q3) of 2021, with real GDP growth moderating to 3.5% y-o-y from 7.1% y-o-y in the second quarter

---

[11] *Bloomberg.* 2021. "Indonesia's Indrawati Sees Smaller-Than-Expected Budget Deficit." https://www.bloomberg.com/news/articles/2021-10-17/indonesia-s-indrawati-sees-smaller-than-expected-budget-deficit.

[12] *The Jakarta Post.* 2021. "New Tax Law Expected To Raise Tax Revenue by at Least 9%." https://www.thejakartapost.com/news/2021/10/11/new-tax-law-hoped-to-raise-tax-revenue-by-at-least-9.html.

(Q2) 2021. Domestic consumption, which accounts for a large share of GDP, eased to growth of 1.0% y-o-y after rising 6.0% y-o-y in Q2 2021. Growth in government spending also decelerated to 0.7% y-o-y in Q3 2021 from 8.0% y-o-y in Q2 2021, while growth in investments fell to 3.7% y-o-y from 7.5% y-o-y in the same period. Exports contributed the majority of Q3 2021 GDP growth, expanding 29.2% y-o-y, although this was slightly down from the 32.0% y-o-y hike in the prior quarter.

Size and Composition

The size of Indonesia's LCY bond market reached IDR5,089.5 trillion (USD355.6 billion) at the end of September (**Table 1**). Overall growth inched up to 3.6% quarter-on-quarter (q-o-q) in the third quarter (Q3) of 2021 from 2.4% q-o-q in Q2 2021. The higher growth was largely driven by government bonds, particularly Treasury bills and bonds, following increased issuance during the quarter. The stock of central bank bills also contributed to the growth but only to a minimal extent. On the other hand, both the stocks of nontradable bonds and corporate bonds continued to post q-o-q contractions in Q3 2021. Compared with the same period a year earlier, LCY bond market growth in Indonesia rose 23.9% y-o-y, moderating from a 30.6% y-o-y hike in Q2 2021. Indonesia remained the fastest-growing LCY bond market in emerging East Asia on a y-o-y basis.

Government bonds continued to dominate Indonesia's LCY bond stock at the end of September, accounting for 91.7% of its bond total. Compared with other emerging East Asian markets, the share of government bonds to total bonds outstanding is the largest in Indonesia. The Indonesian bond market also has the region's smallest share of corporate bonds relative to total bonds outstanding at 8.3%. This highlights the importance of LCY borrowing for the government in supporting economic development. It also reflects the vast potential of the corporate bond segment to further develop.

In the same period, Indonesia's bond market largely comprised conventional bonds, representing a share of 81.1% of the total bonds outstanding at the end of September. *Sukuk* (Islamic bonds) only accounted for 18.9% of the total bond stock at the end of September, representing an increase from a share of 17.6% at the end of June and 17.7% in the same period a year earlier.

Government bonds. Total government bonds outstanding climbed to IDR4,667.5 trillion at the end of September from IDR4,489.5 trillion at the end of June. Growth in the government bond segment quickened to 4.0% q-o-q in Q3 2021 from 2.8% q-o-q in Q2 2021. On a y-o-y basis, however, growth moderated to 27.3% from 34.8% in Q2 2021.

Table 1: Size and Composition of the Local Currency Bond Market in Indonesia

| | Outstanding Amount (billion) | | | | | | Growth Rate (%) | | | |
| | Q3 2020 | | Q2 2021 | | Q3 2021 | | Q3 2020 | | Q3 2021 | |
	IDR	USD	IDR	USD	IDR	USD	q-o-q	y-o-y	q-o-q	y-o-y
Total	4,108,191	276	4,912,250	339	5,089,510	356	9.2	19.8	3.6	23.9
Government	3,667,452	246	4,489,539	310	4,667,501	326	10.1	22.6	4.0	27.3
Central Govt. Bonds	3,461,396	233	4,282,623	295	4,460,456	312	11.4	29.9	4.2	28.9
of which: *Sukuk*	617,771	42	740,172	51	834,323	58	6.6	35.2	12.7	35.1
Central Bank Bonds	38,416	3	58,670	4	60,712	4	(22.6)	(67.1)	3.5	58.0
of which: *Sukuk*	38,416	3	58,670	4	60,712	4	(22.6)	(67.1)	3.5	58.0
Nontradable Bonds	167,640	11	148,246	10	146,334	10	(4.8)	(20.1)	(1.3)	(12.7)
of which: *Sukuk*	38,256	3	33,106	2	31,161	2	2.6	(9.7)	(5.9)	(18.5)
Corporate	440,739	30	422,711	29	422,008	29	2.6	0.7	(0.2)	(4.2)
of which: *Sukuk*	30,915	2	31,672	2	36,143	3	5.2	0.9	14.1	16.9

( ) = negative, IDR = Indonesian rupiah, q-o-q = quarter-on-quarter, Q2 = second quarter, Q3 = third quarter, USD = United States dollar, y-o-y = year-on-year.
Notes:
1. Calculated using data from national sources.
2. Bloomberg LP end-of-period local currency–USD rates are used.
3. Growth rates are calculated from local currency base and do not include currency effects.
4. *Sukuk* refers to Islamic bonds.
Sources: Bank Indonesia; Directorate General of Budget Financing and Risk Management, Ministry of Finance; Indonesia Stock Exchange; and Bloomberg LP.

Central government bonds. At the end of September, the outstanding size of central government bonds reached IDR4,460.5 trillion, representing 95.6% of the government bond total. Growth in central government bonds inched up to 4.2% q-o-q in Q3 2021 from 3.1% q-o-q in Q2 2021, buoyed by strong issuance of Treasury instruments during the quarter. On an annual basis, the growth in the stock of central government bonds eased to 28.9% y-o-y in Q3 2021 from 37.9% y-o-y in the preceding quarter.

In Q3 2021, issuance of Treasury bills and Treasury bonds tallied IDR262.2 trillion, up from IDR231.4 trillion in the prior quarter. Growth in central government bond issuance rebounded during the quarter, expanding 13.3% q-o-q after contracting 24.6% q-o-q in Q2 2021. The government issued more bonds during the quarter to support the economy and provide relief measures as mobility restrictions were reimposed in July.

Central bank bonds. The outstanding stock of central bank bills and bonds totaled IDR60.7 trillion at the end of September. Growth rose a modest 3.5% q-o-q following a 6.8% q-o-q expansion in Q2 2021. While issuance climbed 26.2% q-o-q in Q3 2021, the outstanding stock of central bank bonds barely changed, owing to the short-term maturities of central bank instruments. In Q3 2021, only Sukuk Bank Indonesia were issued with maturities of 7 days, 14 days, 28 days, 3 months, 9 months, and 12 months.

Corporate bonds. At the end of September, the outstanding size of LCY corporate bonds had declined 0.2% q-o-q in Q3 2021 after contracting 2.4% q-o-q in Q2 2021. The total corporate bond stock reached IDR422.0 trillion at the end of September, down from IDR422.7 trillion at the end of June. The smaller corporate bond stock at the end of September stemmed from a high volume of maturities that exceeded new issuance during the quarter.

Table 2 presents the 32 largest corporate bond issuers in Indonesia at the end of September.[13] The total aggregate bond stock of the leading issuers tallied IDR304.7 trillion, down from IDR308.7 trillion (aggregate of 31 firms) at the end of June. The outstanding bonds of the 32 largest corporate issuers accounted for 72.2% of the total corporate bond stock at the end of September.

The largest corporate bond issuers in Indonesia were dominated by firms from the banking and financial industry. Firms from large capitalized industries were also included in the list, particularly those coming from energy, telecommunications, construction, and manufacturing. A total of 20 state-owned firms were included in the list, of which nine firms were ranked in the top 10. There were 17 firms who also tapped the equity market for funding, with their shares listed in the Indonesia Stock Exchange.

The five largest corporate bond issuers at the end of September maintained their position since the end of March. At the top spot was energy firm Perusahaan Listrik Negara with total bonds outstanding of IDR35.1 trillion, whose share of the total corporate bond stock during Q3 2021 was steady at 8.3%. Next was financing firm Indonesia Eximbank with outstanding bonds of IDR21.2 trillion and a 5.0% share of the corporate bond total at the end of September. At the third spot was finance company Sarana Multi Infrastruktur with bonds outstanding of IDR18.5 trillion and a 4.4% share of the corporate bond stock. Completing the top five largest corporate bond issuers were Bank Rakyat Indonesia and Sarana Multigriya Finansial with respective shares of 3.9% and 3.3% of the corporate bonds outstanding at the end of the period in review.

In Q3 2021, corporate bond issuance climbed to IDR32.7 trillion, rebounding strongly by 73.3% q-o-q after contracting 8.5% q-o-q in Q2 2021. Corporates tapped the bond market to take advantage of low borrowing costs and to refinance maturing debt obligations. There were 29 corporates that raised funds from the bond market in Q3 2021 compared with only 14 firms in Q2 2021. Some of those who issued bonds during the quarter also had maturing bonds.

A total of 90 bond series were added to the total corporate bond stock at the end of September, of which 31 series were structured as *sukuk*. Both *sukuk mudharabah* (Islamic bonds backed by a profit-sharing scheme from a business venture or partnership) and *sukuk ijarah* (Islamic bonds backed by lease agreements) were issued during the quarter. Among the new bonds issued during the quarter were one series of convertible bond issued by transport firm Adi Sarana Armada and two series of subordinated bonds issued by Bank KB Bukopin.

---

[13] Three firms tied for the number 30 spot on the list.

Table 2: Top 32 Issuers of Local Currency Corporate Bonds in Indonesia

	Issuers	Outstanding Amount		State-Owned	Listed Company	Type of Industry
		LCY Bonds (IDR billion)	LCY Bonds (USD billion)			
1.	Perusahaan Listrik Negara	35,121	2.45	Yes	No	Energy
2.	Indonesia Eximbank	21,230	1.48	Yes	No	Finance
3.	Sarana Multi Infrastruktur	18,542	1.30	Yes	No	Finance
4.	Bank Rakyat Indonesia	16,619	1.16	Yes	Yes	Banking
5.	Sarana Multigriya Finansial	13,741	0.96	Yes	No	Finance
6.	Bank Mandiri	12,900	0.90	Yes	Yes	Banking
7.	Bank Tabungan Negara	12,445	0.87	Yes	Yes	Banking
8.	Pegadaian	11,548	0.81	Yes	No	Finance
9.	Permodalan Nasional Madani	10,835	0.76	Yes	No	Finance
10.	Indosat	10,405	0.73	No	Yes	Telecommunications
11.	Bank Pan Indonesia	9,927	0.69	No	Yes	Banking
12.	Waskita Karya	9,514	0.66	Yes	Yes	Building Construction
13.	Pupuk Indonesia	9,046	0.63	Yes	No	Chemical Manufacturing
14.	Indah Kiat Pulp & Paper	8,579	0.60	No	Yes	Pulp and Paper
15.	Hutama Karya	8,000	0.56	Yes	No	Nonbuilding Construction
16.	Wijaya Karya	7,500	0.52	Yes	Yes	Building Construction
17.	Astra Sedaya Finance	7,179	0.50	No	No	Finance
18.	Tower Bersama Infrastructure	7,171	0.50	No	Yes	Telecommunications Infrastructure Provider
19.	Semen Indonesia	7,078	0.49	Yes	Yes	Cement Manufacturing
20.	Telkom Indonesia	7,000	0.49	Yes	Yes	Telecommunications
21.	Bank CIMB Niaga	6,347	0.44	No	Yes	Banking
22.	Adira Dinamika Multi Finance	5,983	0.42	No	Yes	Finance
23.	Mandiri Tunas Finance	5,599	0.39	No	No	Finance
24.	Chandra Asri Petrochemical	5,489	0.38	No	Yes	Petrochemicals
25.	Bank Pembangunan Daerah Jawa Barat Dan Banten	5,413	0.38	Yes	Yes	Banking
26.	Federal International Finance	5,412	0.38	No	No	Finance
27.	Adhi Karya	4,990	0.35	Yes	Yes	Building Construction
28.	Angkasa Pura I	4,612	0.32	Yes	No	Airport Management Services
29.	Sinar Mas Agro Resources and Technology	4,500	0.31	No	Yes	Food
30.	Angkasa Pura II	4,000	0.28	Yes	No	Airport Management Services
31.	Kereta Api Indonesia	4,000	0.28	Yes	No	Transportation
32.	OKI Pulp & Paper Mills	4,000	0.28	No	No	Pulp and Paper Manufacturing
Total Top 32 LCY Corporate Issuers		**304,725**	**21.29**			
Total LCY Corporate Bonds		**422,008**	**29.48**			
Top 31 as % of Total LCY Corporate Bonds		**72.2%**	**72.2%**			

IDR = Indonesian rupiah, LCY = local currency, USD = United States dollar.
Notes:
1. Data as of 30 September 2021.
2. State-owned firms are defined as those in which the government has more than a 50% ownership stake.
Source: *AsianBondsOnline* calculations based on Indonesia Stock Exchange data.

Most corporate bonds issued during the quarter carried maturities of 3 years (31 out of 90 new series), 5 years (24 out of 90 series), and 370 days (20 out of 90 series). The longest-dated bonds issued in Q3 2021 were 7 years with nine series and 10 years with two series.

The largest corporate bond issuers during the quarter are presented in **Table 3**. Leading the list was paper manufacturing firm OKI Pulp & Paper Mills, which issued a combined IDR4.0 trillion comprising three tranches of conventional bonds and three tranches of *sukuk mudharabah*. Next was state-owned building and construction firm Wijaya Karya with total issuance of IDR2.5 trillion in six tranches, including three tranches of *sukuk mudharabah*. The next largest issuances came from PT PP, Permodalan Nasional Madani, and Bank KB Bukopin, with aggregate issuance of IDR2.0 trillion each.

Investor Profile

Foreign funds flowed out of Indonesia's bond market in Q3 2021, driven by a shift in monetary stance by the US Federal Reserve. Foreign fund outflows were seen in July and September for a combined amount of USD1.1 billion, which more than exceeded the USD1.0 billion of inflows posted in August. As a result, the foreign holdings share of LCY government bonds further slipped to 21.6% at the end of September, down from 22.8% at the end of June and 27.0% at the end of September 2020 (**Figure 2**). In nominal terms, offshore

Table 3: Notable Local Currency Corporate Bond Issuances in the Third Quarter of 2021

Corporate Issuers	Coupon Rate (%)	Issued Amount (IDR billion)
OKI Pulp & Paper Mills		
370-day bond	7.25	1,315
370-day *sukuk mudharabah*	7.25	1,348
3-year bond	9.50	336
3-year *sukuk mudharabah*	9.50	700
5-year bond	10.25	235
5-year *sukuk mudharabah*	10.25	65
Wijaya Karya		
3-year bond	8.25	571
3-year *sukuk mudharabah*	8.25	197
5-year bond	8.55	982
5-year *sukuk mudharabah*	8.55	326
7-year bond	9.25	92
7-year *sukuk mudharabah*	9.25	333
PT PP		
3-year bond	8.50	850
3-year *sukuk mudharabah*	8.50	650
5-year bond	9.10	400
5-year *sukuk mudharabah*	9.10	100
Permodalan Nasional Madani		
370-day *sukuk mudharabah*	6.00	1,158
3-year *sukuk mudharabah*	7.00	515
5-year *sukuk mudharabah*	8.00	327
Bank KB Bukopin		
3- year bonds	6.25	1,000
5-year subordinated bonds	8.00	315
7-year subordinated bonds	8.90	685

IDR = Indonesian rupiah.
Note: *Sukuk mudharabah* are Islamic bonds backed by a profit-sharing scheme from a business venture or partnership.
Source: Indonesia Stock Exchange.

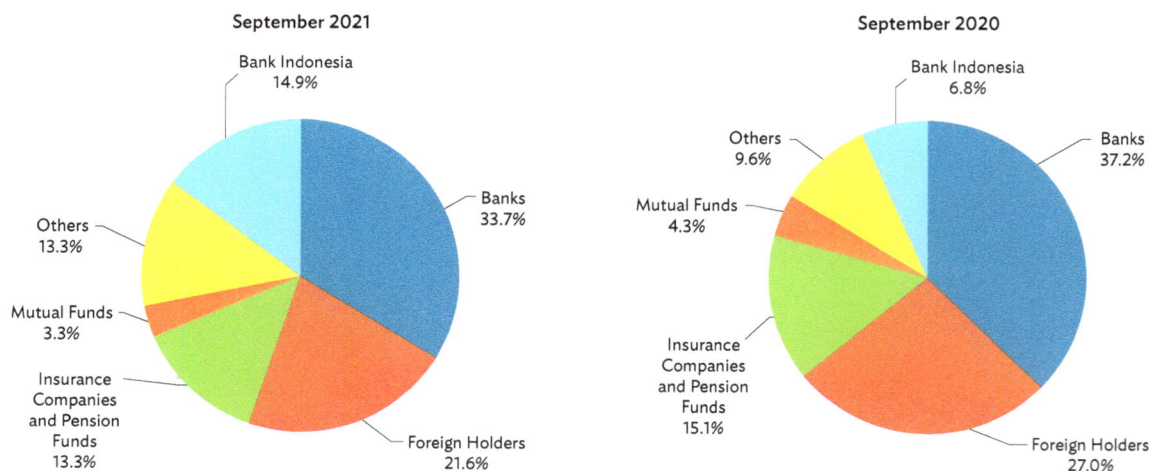

Figure 2: Local Currency Central Government Bonds Investor Profile

September 2021: Bank Indonesia 14.9%, Banks 33.7%, Foreign Holders 21.6%, Insurance Companies and Pension Funds 13.3%, Mutual Funds 3.3%, Others 13.3%.

September 2020: Bank Indonesia 6.8%, Banks 37.2%, Foreign Holders 27.0%, Insurance Companies and Pension Funds 15.1%, Mutual Funds 4.3%, Others 9.6%.

Source: Directorate General of Budget Financing and Risk Management, Ministry of Finance.

investor holdings of LCY government bonds totaled USD961.8 trillion at the end of September, up from USD933.1 trillion a year earlier.

Offshore investors holdings of bonds with maturities of 10 years or more stood at 28.8% of their total bond holdings at the end of September. However, this was lower compared with their 33.5% share at the end of December 2020 (**Figure 3**). The bond holdings of nonresidents for maturities of more than 1 year to 2 years, more than 2 years to 5 years, and more than 5 years to 10 years increased from the beginning of the year through the end of September. In contrast, bonds with maturities of less than 1 year accounted for 3.6% of total foreign holdings, down from 4.6% at the end of December.

Banking institutions remained the largest investor group in Indonesia's LCY government bond market at the end of September. However, their holdings declined to 33.7% at the end of September from 37.2% in the previous year. Insurance companies and pension funds and mutual funds also saw declines in their respective holdings of government bonds during the review period.

In contrast, only two investor groups recorded increases in their respective holdings of government bonds at the end of September, Bank Indonesia and other investors not elsewhere classified.

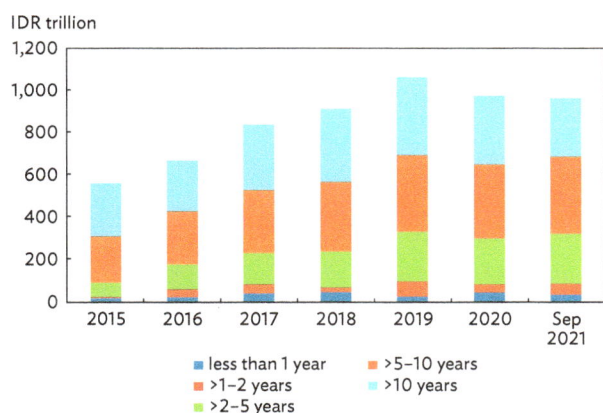

Figure 3: Foreign Holdings of Local Currency Central Government Bonds by Maturity

IDR = Indonesian rupiah.
Source: Directorate General of Budget Financing and Risk Management, Ministry of Finance.

Bank Indonesia continued to shore up its holdings of government bonds as part of synergistic endeavors with the government to support economic growth and recovery efforts. Holdings of government bonds more than doubled to a 14.9% share at the end of September from only 6.8% a year earlier. The central bank participated in primary auctions of government bonds and purchased bonds through green shoe options, in line with its burden-sharing agreement with the government. As of 15 October, Bank Indonesia had purchased a total of IDR142.5 trillion of government bonds.

Aggregate holdings of LCY government bonds by other investor group, which includes individuals, rose by 3.7 percentage points to 13.3% at the end of September from 9.6% in the same period a year earlier.

Policy, Institutional, and Regulatory Developments

Tax Cuts on Bond Investments for Domestic Investors

On 30 August, the Government of Indonesia reduced the tax on interest income on bond investments for domestic investors. The tax rate was lowered to 10% from the previous 15% to align the tax rate with that of foreign investors. (In February, the government reduced the tax on interest income for foreign bond investors from 20% to 10%.) The move is expected to further deepen the LCY bond market, encourage greater participation from domestic investors, and enhance liquidity. The tax cut applies to investments in both government bonds and corporate bonds, including *sukuk*.

Parliament Approves 2022 State Budget

In September, the Indonesian Parliament approved the 2022 state budget, which programs a lower budget deficit equivalent to 4.9% of GDP versus 5.8% in the 2021 state budget. The 2022 state budget sets the state revenue at IDR1,846.1 trillion, while state spending is estimated at IDR2,714.2 trillion. Macroeconomic assumptions used for the 2022 state budget include (i) economic growth of 5.2%, (ii) average consumer price inflation of 3.0%, (iii) an exchange rate of IDR14,350.0 per USD1.0, (iv) an average 10-year bond yield of 6.8%, and (v) an Indonesian crude oil price of USD63.0 per barrel.

Republic of Korea

Yield Movements

The Republic of Korea's local currency (LCY) government bond yields surged for most tenors between 31 August and 15 October (**Figure 1**). Yields for the 3-month and 6-month paper were mostly unchanged, while the 1-year bond yield increased 7 basis points (bps). Yields for tenors between 2 years and 50 years surged 38 bps on average, with the 5-year and 10-year bonds posting the largest increases at 46 bps and 45 bps, respectively. The yield spread between the 2-year and 10-year tenors rose to 75 bps from 67 bps during the review period.

Short-term government bond yields remained range-bound during the review period, following a spike in yields the week before the Bank of Korea's monetary policy meeting on 26 August, when the central bank raised its base rate to 0.75%. Yields barely moved thereafter given expectations that the central bank would maintain its policy rate at its October monetary policy meeting. On 12 October, as expected, the Bank of Korea kept the base rate steady.

The rise in yields for tenors of 2 years and longer continued throughout the review period on heightened expectations of another rate hike by the Bank of Korea in November, its last monetary policy meeting for the year. Subsequently on 25 November, the Bank of Korea raised the base rate by 25 bps to 1.00%. The domestic economy is forecast to continue its recovery supported by an improvement in consumption, exports, and investment. The growth forecast for 2021 was maintained at 4.0%. Meanwhile, inflation is expected to be well above the 2.0% level, with the central bank raising its forecast for 2021 to 2.3% from its August projection of 2.1%. The central bank also stated that it will assess when to further adjust the degree of monetary policy accommodation given sound economic growth and inflation running above the target level, driving expectations of further rate hikes in 2022.

Moreover, domestic yields tracked the rise in global yields as the United States (US) Federal Reserve is expected to announce tapering measures as early as at its November meeting. In addition, foreign selling of Korea Treasury Bond futures also contributed to the rise in domestic yields. This was driven by the weakening of the Korean won that resulted in smaller capital gains,

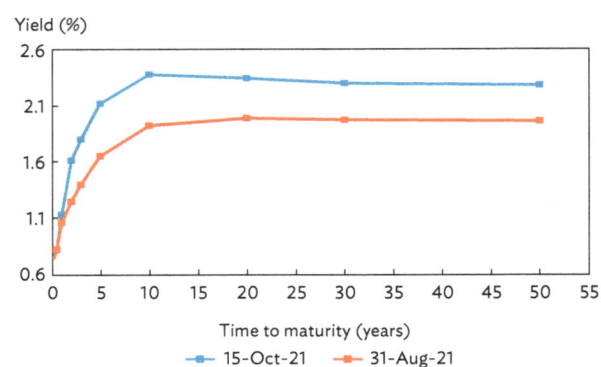

Figure 1: The Republic of Korea's Benchmark Yield Curve—Local Currency Government Bonds

Source: Based on data from Bloomberg LP.

making the instrument less attractive to foreign investors. The domestic currency depreciated 1.9% during the review period to KRW1,182.3 per USD1.0 on 15 October, and reaching a low of KRW1,198.9 per USD1.0 on 12 October due to the continued strengthening of the US dollar and foreign outflows from the equities market.

On 3 September, the government submitted its 2022 budget proposal to the National Assembly for approval. The budget amounts to KRW604.4 trillion, a 13.7% increase from the original 2021 budget and an 8.3% increase when including all supplementary budgets passed in 2021. The budget is also expected to result in lesser issuance of deficit-financing bonds in 2022 compared to 2021, easing bond oversupply concerns. However, this was not enough to drive down yields as the rise in global yields weighed more on the domestic bond market.

The Republic of Korea's economic growth moderated to 4.0% year-on-year (y-o-y) in the third quarter (Q3) of 2021 from 6.0% y-o-y in the second quarter (Q2), based on advance estimates by the Bank of Korea. The slower growth was driven by the lower annual increase in private consumption of 3.2% y-o-y from 3.7% y-o-y in Q2 2021 due to stricter social distancing measures imposed during the quarter. Gross fixed capital formation growth slowed in Q3 2021 to 1.8% y-o-y from 3.8% y-o-y. Export growth also slumped to 6.9% y-o-y from a surge of 22.4% y-o-y in Q2 2021. Meanwhile, government spending posted accelerated growth of 6.3% y-o-y from 5.3% y-o-y. Consumer price inflation in the Republic of Korea remained high at 2.6% y-o-y in both July and August, slightly easing to 2.5% y-o-y in September. In October, inflation surged to 3.2% y-o-y, the highest since January 2012, mainly driven by accelerated annual increases in the prices of utilities, transport, and communication.

Foreign demand for the Republic of Korea's LCY bonds remained strong in the month of July, with registered net inflows of KRW9,290 billion. However, inflows dropped in August to KRW1,689 billion as foreign investors sold domestic bonds due to the rise in short-term yields leading up to the Bank of Korea's rate hike on 26 August. Foreign inflows recovered in September to KRW5,172 billion, however, inflows were capped due to increased expectations of further tightening measures by the central bank and the possibility of tapering by the US Federal Reserve as early as November. Subsequently on its 2–3 November meeting, the Federal Reserve announced that it would begin tapering its asset purchases starting in November.

Size and Composition

The Republic of Korea's LCY bond market grew 1.6% quarter-on-quarter (q-o-q) to reach a size of KRW2,799.9 trillion (USD2,364.6 billion) at the end of Q3 2021 (**Table 1**). This was slower than the 2.3% q-o-q expansion posted in the previous quarter. The growth was largely driven by the government bond market as the corporate segment grew at a slower pace. From the same period in 2020, the Republic of Korea's bond market rose 7.6% y-o-y, slower than the 7.9% y-o-y growth posted in Q2 2021.

Government bonds. The Republic of Korea's LCY government bond market rose 1.9% q-o-q in Q3 2021 to KRW1,179.7 trillion (USD996.3 billion). However, this was lower than the 3.2% q-o-q growth posted in the previous quarter. Growth continued to stem from the rise in the stock of central government bonds, which expanded 3.0% q-o-q to KRW831.7 trillion. Meanwhile, the outstanding size of Monetary Stabilization Bonds issued by the Bank of Korea declined 2.1% q-o-q to KRW151.1 trillion. The outstanding bonds issued by other government-owned entities inched up 0.3% q-o-q to KRW197.0 trillion.

Issuance of government bonds dropped 19.0% q-o-q to KRW92.5 trillion in Q3 2021, as both issuance of central government bonds (–29.0% q-o-q) and central bank bonds (–9.1% q-o-q) bonds declined during the quarter. The lower issuance of central government bonds during the quarter was due to a high base in Q2 2021 in line with the government's frontloading policy in the first half of the year. Bonds issued by other government owned-entities also fell 6.8% q-o-q.

Foreign Exchange Stabilization Bonds. The Republic of Korea issued USD1.3 billion worth of Foreign Exchange Stabilization Bonds on 7 October. These bonds are issued to promote foreign exchange market stability through accumulation of foreign exchange reserves, and the resulting rates will also serve as a guide for prospective companies planning to issue bonds offshore. The bond offer was conducted via a dual-tranche issuance comprising USD500.0 million worth of 10-year bonds priced at 1.796% (25-bps spread over

Table 1: Size and Composition of the Local Currency Bond Market in the Republic of Korea

| | Outstanding Amount (billion) | | | | | | Growth Rate (%) | | | |
| | Q3 2020 | | Q2 2021 | | Q3 2021 | | Q3 2020 | | Q3 2021 | |
	KRW	USD	KRW	USD	KRW	USD	q-o-q	y-o-y	q-o-q	y-o-y
Total	2,602,081	2,224	2,756,445	2,447	2,799,920	2,365	1.9	9.8	1.6	7.6
Government	1,069,062	914	1,158,252	1,028	1,179,746	996	3.0	12.1	1.9	10.4
Central Government Bonds	707,681	605	807,725	717	831,745	702	4.2	16.6	3.0	17.5
Central Bank Bonds	166,750	143	154,230	137	151,050	128	(1.3)	(2.5)	(2.1)	(9.4)
Others	194,631	166	196,297	174	196,951	166	2.3	10.7	0.3	1.2
Corporate	1,533,019	1,310	1,598,193	1,419	1,620,174	1,368	1.1	8.2	1.4	5.7

( ) = negative, KRW = Korean won, q-o-q = quarter-on-quarter, Q2 = second quarter, Q3 = third quarter, USD = United States dollar, y-o-y = year-on-year.
Notes:
1. Calculated using data from national sources.
2. Bloomberg LP end-of-period local currency–USD rates are used.
3. Growth rates are calculated from local currency base and do not include currency effects.
4. "Others" comprise Korea Development Bank Bonds, National Housing Bonds, and Seoul Metro Bonds.
5. Corporate bonds include equity-linked securities and derivatives-linked securities.
Sources: The Bank of Korea and KG Zeroin Corporation.

the 10-year US Treasury) and EUR700.0 million worth of 5-year bonds priced at −0.053% (13 bps spread over the 5-year benchmark euro mid-swap). The euro tranche was also a green bond issuance listed on the Frankfurt Stock Exchange and, eventually, on the London Stock Exchange.

Corporate bonds. The outstanding size of the Republic of Korea's LCY corporate bond market inched up 1.4% q-o-q to KRW1,620.2 trillion (USD1,368.3 billion), with growth slightly lower than the 1.6% q-o-q increase posted in the previous quarter. **Table 2** lists the top 30 LCY corporate bond issuers in the Republic of Korea, with aggregate

Table 2: Top 30 Issuers of Local Currency Corporate Bonds in the Republic of Korea

	Issuers	Outstanding Amount LCY Bonds (KRW billion)	LCY Bonds (USD billion)	State-Owned	Listed on KOSPI	KOSDAQ	Type of Industry
1.	Korea Housing Finance Corporation	153,269	129.4	Yes	No	No	Housing Finance
2.	Industrial Bank of Korea	70,250	59.3	Yes	Yes	No	Banking
3.	Mirae Asset Securities Co.	60,133	50.8	No	Yes	No	Securities
4.	Korea Investment and Securities	56,780	48.0	No	No	No	Securities
5.	Hana Financial Investment	50,209	42.4	No	No	No	Securities
6.	KB Securities	49,620	41.9	No	No	No	Securities
7.	Shinhan Investment Corporation	40,377	34.1	No	No	No	Securities
8.	NH Investment & Securities	34,075	28.8	Yes	Yes	No	Securities
9.	Korea Electric Power Corporation	30,610	25.9	Yes	Yes	No	Electricity, Energy, and Power
10.	Korea Land & Housing Corporation	30,533	25.8	Yes	No	No	Real Estate
11.	Samsung Securities	30,341	25.6	No	Yes	No	Securities
12.	Meritz Securities Co.	29,079	24.6	No	Yes	No	Securities
13.	Shinhan Bank	28,992	24.5	No	No	No	Banking
14.	Korea Expressway	25,670	21.7	Yes	No	No	Transport Infrastructure
15.	The Export-Import Bank of Korea	23,630	20.0	Yes	No	No	Banking
16.	Woori Bank	22,520	19.0	Yes	Yes	No	Banking
17.	Kookmin Bank	21,704	18.3	No	No	No	Banking
18.	KEB Hana Bank	20,815	17.6	No	No	No	Banking
19.	NongHyup Bank	19,320	16.3	Yes	No	No	Banking
20.	Korea SMEs and Startups Agency	19,228	16.2	Yes	No	No	SME Development
21.	Korea National Railway	19,050	16.1	Yes	No	No	Transport Infrastructure
22.	Shinyoung Securities	17,784	15.0	No	Yes	No	Securities
23.	Hanwha Investment and Securities	17,378	14.7	No	No	No	Securities
24.	Shinhan Card	16,185	13.7	No	No	No	Credit Card
25.	KB Kookmin Bank Card	14,350	12.1	No	No	No	Consumer Finance
26.	Hyundai Capital Services	14,205	12.0	No	No	No	Consumer Finance
27.	Standard Chartered Bank Korea	13,760	11.6	No	No	No	Banking
28.	NongHyup	13,580	11.5	Yes	No	No	Banking
29.	Samsung Card Co.	12,088	10.2	No	Yes	No	Credit Card
30.	Shinhan Financial Group	10,865	9.2	No	Yes	No	Banking
	Total Top 30 LCY Corporate Issuers	**966,401**	**816**				
	Total LCY Corporate Bonds	**1,620,174**	**1,368.3**				
	Top 30 as % of Total LCY Corporate Bonds	**59.6%**	**59.6%**				

KOSDAQ = Korean Securities Dealers Automated Quotations, KOSPI = Korea Composite Stock Price Index, KRW = Korean won, LCY = local currency, SMEs = small and medium-sized enterprises, USD = United States dollar.
Notes:
1. Data as of 30 September 2021.
2. State-owned firms are defined as those in which the government has more than a 50% ownership stake.
3. Corporate bonds include equity-linked securities and derivatives-linked securities.
Sources: *AsianBondsOnline* calculations based on Bloomberg LP and KG Zeroin Corporation data.

bonds outstanding of KRW966.4 trillion at the end of September, accounting for 59.6% of the total LCY corporate bond market. Financial institutions, particularly banks and securities and investment firms, continued to comprise a majority of the list and had a collective share of 65.3% of the total volume. Korea Housing Finance Corporation, a government-related institution providing financial assistance for social housing, remained the largest single-largest corporate bond issuer with outstanding bonds of KRW153.3 trillion. Industrial Bank of Korea and Mirae Asset Securities followed with total bonds outstanding of KRW70.2 trillion and KRW60.1 trillion, respectively.

The slower q-o-q growth in the Republic of Korea's corporate bond market was driven by the decline in issuance of 19.9% q-o-q to KRW120.6 trillion from KRW150.5 trillion in the previous quarter. All categories—special public entities, financial debentures, and private companies—posted q-o-q decreases. Firms borrowed less during the quarter, particularly in the month of August, due to the spike in yields leading up to the Bank of Korea rate hike. **Table 3** lists the notable corporate bond issuances in Q2 2021. Financial firms such as Kookmin Bank, Woori Bank, and NongHyup Bank had the largest issuances during the quarter.

Investor Profile

Insurance companies and pension funds remained the top holders of the Republic of Korea's LCY government bonds with a market share of 34.1% at the end of June 2021, almost at par with 34.2% in June 2020 (**Figure 2**). Banks were the second-largest investor group with a share of 19.1%, up from 16.7% in Q2 2020. The shares of general government and other financial institutions fell in Q2 2021 to 16.2% and 14.6%, respectively, from 16.5% and 16.0% in the same period in 2020. Foreign holdings of LCY government bonds rose to 15.4% at the end June 2021 from 13.0% in the previous year, as high levels of foreign inflows were registered in the first half of 2021.

In Q2 2021, other financial institutions continued to surpass insurance companies and pension funds as the largest investor group of the Republic of Korea's LCY corporate bond market (**Figure 3**). The share of other financial institutions jumped to 40.2% from 37.4% in the same period in 2020, while the share of insurance companies and pension funds fell to 35.5% from 37.2%. The respective shares of the general government and banks increased to 14.3% and 9.5%. Meanwhile, the share of foreign holders remained negligible at 0.1%.

Table 3: Notable Local Currency Corporate Bond Issuances in the Third Quarter of 2021

Corporate Issuers	Coupon Rate (%)	Issued Amount (KRW billion)	Corporate Issuers	Coupon Rate (%)	Issued Amount (KRW billion)
Kookmin Bank[a]			NongHyup Bank[a]		
1-year bond	1.14	530	1-year bond	1.11	700
1-year bond	1.10	400	1-year bond	1.14	550
1-year bond	1.11	400	1-year bond	1.23	480
1-year bond	1.12	380	1-year bond	0.13	340
1-year bond	1.07	380	1-year bond	1.09	300
1-year bond	1.14	370	Sinbo Securitization Specialty[a]		
1-year bond	1.10	350	3-year bond	1.77	609
1-year bond	1.10	300	3-year bond	2.01	326
1-year bond	1.15	270	Shinhan Bank[a]		
1-year bond	1.15	250	1-year bond	1.17	480
Woori Bank[a]			1-year bond	1.11	240
1-year bond	1.10	590	1-year bond	1.14	200
1-year bond	1.10	500	Kyobo Life Insurance		
1-year bond	1.15	300	30-year bond	3.72	470
1-year bond	1.10	300	Cube Banpo Securitization		
1-year bond	1.55	280	4-year bond	1.88	400
1-year bond	0.13	280	Samsung Biologics		
1-year bond	1.13	250	3-year bond	1.89	380
1-year bond	1.12	250			
3-year bond	1.58	300			

KRW = Korean won.
[a] Multiple issuance of the same tenor indicates issuance on different dates.
Source: Based on data from Bloomberg LP.

Figure 2: Local Currency Government Bonds Investor Profile

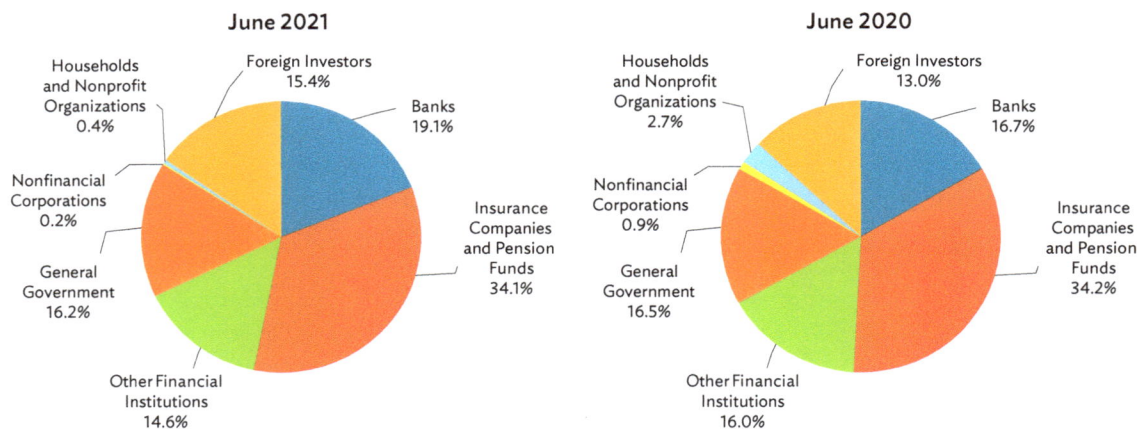

June 2021

- Foreign Investors 15.4%
- Banks 19.1%
- Insurance Companies and Pension Funds 34.1%
- Other Financial Institutions 14.6%
- General Government 16.2%
- Nonfinancial Corporations 0.2%
- Households and Nonprofit Organizations 0.4%

June 2020

- Foreign Investors 13.0%
- Banks 16.7%
- Insurance Companies and Pension Funds 34.2%
- Other Financial Institutions 16.0%
- General Government 16.5%
- Nonfinancial Corporations 0.9%
- Households and Nonprofit Organizations 2.7%

Source: *AsianBondsOnline* and The Bank of Korea.

Figure 3: Local Currency Corporate Bonds Investor Profile

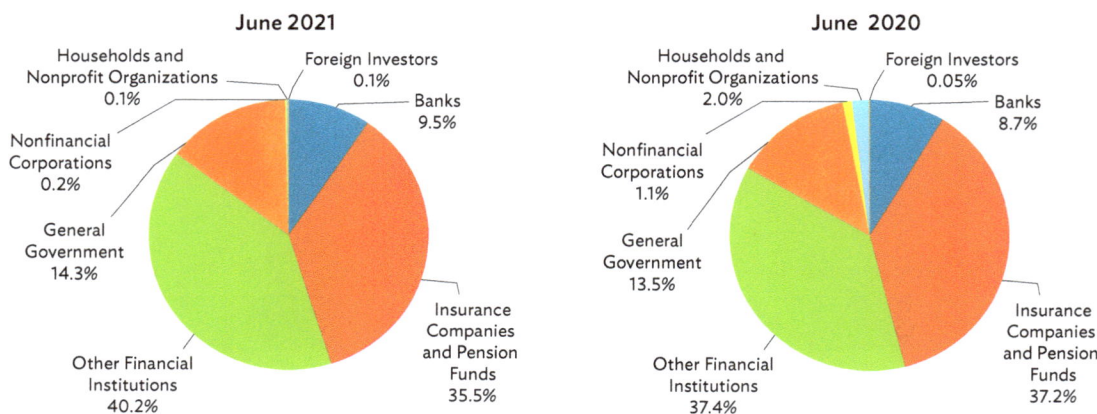

June 2021

- Households and Nonprofit Organizations 0.1%
- Foreign Investors 0.1%
- Banks 9.5%
- Nonfinancial Corporations 0.2%
- Insurance Companies and Pension Funds 35.5%
- General Government 14.3%
- Other Financial Institutions 40.2%

June 2020

- Households and Nonprofit Organizations 2.0%
- Foreign Investors 0.05%
- Banks 8.7%
- Nonfinancial Corporations 1.1%
- Insurance Companies and Pension Funds 37.2%
- General Government 13.5%
- Other Financial Institutions 37.4%

Source: *AsianBondsOnline* and The Bank of Korea.

Net foreign inflows into the Republic of Korea's LCY bond market remained high in July with another record volume of KRW9,290 billion, the second-highest level for the year (**Figure 4**). However, net inflows fell to KRW1,689 billion in August as net foreign purchases of longer-tenor bonds were offset by the net outflows from short-term bonds (**Figure 5**). Foreign investors sold Korean LCY bonds, particularly those with tenors of less than 1 year, amid a surge in short-term yields leading up to the rate hike by the Bank of Korea in its 26 August monetary policy meeting. Foreign inflows recovered in September to KRW5,172 billion. However, this was capped by the continued outflows from the short-term bond segment, which were driven by expectations of another rate hike by the Bank of Korea before the year ends and the Federal Reserve announcement of possible tightening measures beginning as early as November.

Figure 4: Net Foreign Investment in Local Currency Bonds in the Republic of Korea

KRW billion

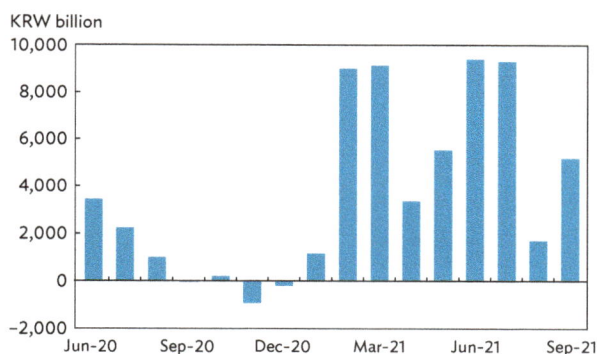

KRW = Korean won.
Source: Financial Supervisory Service.

Figure 5: Net Foreign Investment in Local Currency Bonds in the Republic of Korea by Remaining Maturity

KRW billion

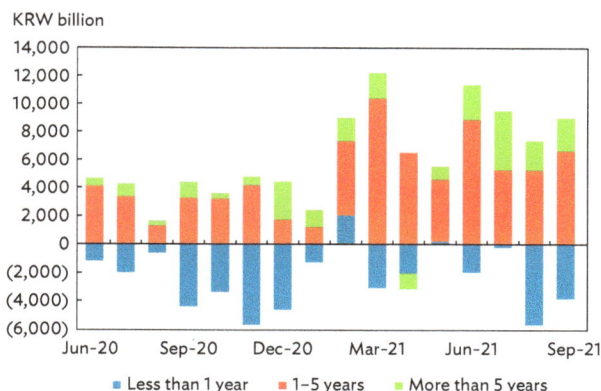

■ Less than 1 year   ■ 1–5 years   ■ More than 5 years

KRW = Korean won.
Source: Financial Supervisory Service.

Policy, Institutional, and Regulatory Developments

The Government of the Republic of Korea Passes 2022 Budget Proposal

On 3 September, the Government of the Republic of Korea passed for approval to the National Assembly its 2022 budget proposal of KRW604.4 trillion. The proposed budget is 8.3% higher than the original 2021 budget of KRW558.0 trillion, and almost at par with the revised KRW604.9 trillion budget that includes all supplementary budgets passed during the year. The budget aims to aid citizens and society in the recovery from the pandemic, promote inclusive growth, and prepare for a post-pandemic economy. The 2022 budget is also expected to reduce the fiscal deficit by KRW20.0 trillion as tax revenues are expected to improve on the back of the continued economic recovery. The fiscal deficit as a percentage of gross domestic product is forecast to decline to 2.6% in 2022 from 4.4% in 2021.

Malaysia

Yield Movements

Local currency (LCY) government bond yields in Malaysia increased for all tenors between 31 August and 15 October (**Figure 1**). Yields for short-term tenors (1 month to 1 year) jumped an average of 3 basis points (bps), while bonds with 4-year to 15-year tenors soared an average of 36 bps. Yields of 1-month and 3-month tenors jumped the least at 1 bp each, while the 5-year yield rose the most among all tenors with a 44-bps gain during the review period. The yield spread between 2-year and 10-year government bonds expanded from 126 bps to 146 bps during the review period.

Investors flocked to safe-haven assets, leading to low demand for Malaysian government bonds. Net capital inflows in the third quarter (Q3) of 2021 were just MYR3.0 billion, a contraction of 67.1% quarter-on-quarter (q-o-q) from MYR9.0 billion in the previous quarter. Investors moved their investments to safe-haven assets in Q3 2021 to take advantage of the the prospect of the United States (US) Federal Reserve's earlier-than-expected normalization of interest rates.

Developments on the domestic political front also contributed to this guarded stance as investors observed how the new administration would tackle the economic challenges Malaysia is facing. The less-than-enthusiastic reception for government securities may also be attributed to short-term bond supply concerns amid an increased number of auctions in October and the anticipation of the 2022 budget announcement. Malaysia continued to have a low-interest-rate environment as Bank Negara Malaysia (BNM) kept its overnight policy rate unchanged in September.

On 9 September, the monetary policy committee of BNM maintained its policy rate at 1.75%. The committee is optimistic that the global and domestic economies are still on track to their path to recovery. Even as movement restrictions dampened Malaysia's economic growth in the second quarter (Q2) of 2021, the gradual reopening of the economy and policy support mitigated the impact. The year-to-date consumer price inflation of 2.3% was still within the range of 2.0%–3.0% expected by BNM for full-year 2021.

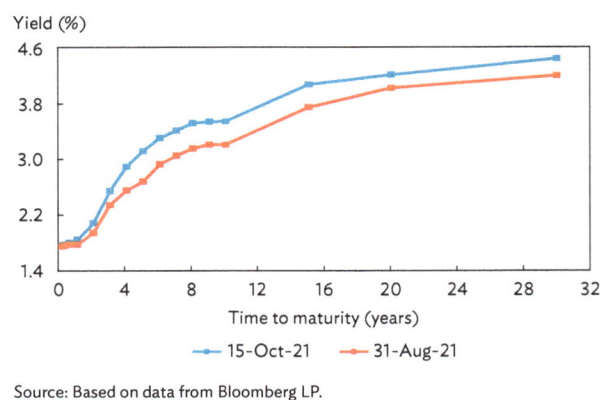

Figure 1: Malaysia's Benchmark Yield Curve—Local Currency Government Bonds

Source: Based on data from Bloomberg LP.

A lack of major developments on the financial front during the review period could be seen in the performance of Malaysia's currency. The Malaysian ringgit slightly weakened 0.1% against the US dollar during the review period to close at MYR4.1575 per USD1.0 dollar on 15 October.

Malaysia's economy contracted 4.5% year-on-year (y-o-y) in Q3 2021, after contracting 16.1% y-o-y in Q2 2021, due to coronavirus disease (COVID-19)-induced restrictions imposed in July affecting all major economic sectors. BNM expects Malaysia's full-year 2021 economic growth to fall in the range of 3.0%–4.0%.

The increase in prices of basic goods and services in Malaysia was largely unchanged during Q3 2021. Coming from a high level of 3.4% y-o-y in June, consumer price inflation decelerated in July and August, recording inflation of 2.2% y-o-y and 2.0% y-o-y, respectively. Inflation picked up slightly to 2.2% y-o-y in September, back to its July level, as prices of food and nonalcoholic beverages increased.

As part of the Government of Malaysia's National Recovery Plan, which is an exit strategy from the COVID-19 crisis, states have been classified according to four phases based on various thresholds, with Phase 1 having the strictest restrictions. As of 18 October, no state was in Phases 1 and 2, nine states were in Phase 3, while seven states were in Phase 4. As of 18 October,

70.2% of Malaysia's adult population had been fully vaccinated.

Size and Composition

Malaysia's LCY bond market grew 1.5% q-o-q in Q3 2021, reaching a size of MYR1,718.8 billion (USD410.6 billion) at the end of the quarter, up from MYR1,693.3 billion at the end of the prior quarter (**Table 1**). The expansion in Q3 2021 was slower than the 2.7% q-o-q growth logged in Q2 2021. On a y-o-y basis, the LCY bond market expanded 8.5% y-o-y, a moderation from the 8.9% y-o-y growth posted in Q2 2021. The growth may be attributed to increases in both LCY government and corporate bonds, which accounted for 54.6% and 45.4%, respectively, of total LCY bonds outstanding at the end of Q3 2021. Total outstanding *sukuk* (Islamic bonds) reached MYR1,096.7 billion at the end of September on growth of 3.0% q-o-q. This rise was supported by increased stocks of government and corporate *sukuk*.

LCY bonds issued in Q3 2021 declined 14.2% q-o-q to MYR86.8 billion from MYR101.2 billion in Q2 2021 as government and corporate bond issuances both decreased.

Government bonds. At the end of Q3 2021, Malaysia's LCY government bond market expanded 1.5% q-o-q to a size of MYR938.4 billion from MYR924.1 billion at the

end of June. The growth was slower than the increase of 3.9% q-o-q in the prior quarter. The LCY government bond market's growth was driven by the 1.6% q-o-q growth in outstanding central government bonds, which comprised 97.4% of total outstanding LCY government bonds at the end of September. No outstanding central bank bills were recorded at the end of Q3 2021, while the amount of outstanding Sukuk Perumahan Kerajaan, which comprised 2.6% of total outstanding LCY government bonds at the end of September, was unchanged from Q2 2021.

Issuance of LCY government bonds in Q3 2021 contracted 13.4% q-o-q to MYR48.5 billion from MYR56.0 billion in Q2 2021. The decline was due to a drop in issuances of Treasury bills. Total Malaysian Government Securities (conventional bonds) issued during the quarter declined, while Government Investment Issues increased in Q3 2021 compared to Q2 2021 at MYR24.1 billion.

Corporate bonds. LCY corporate bonds outstanding jumped 1.4% q-o-q to MYR780.4 billion at the end of September from MYR769.2 billion at the end of June. This growth was faster than the 1.3% q-o-q expansion recorded in Q2 2021. The amount of outstanding corporate *sukuk* expanded 1.9% q-o-q to MYR638.0 billion in Q3 2021 from MYR626.4 billion in Q2 2021, with growth easing from 2.0% q-o-q in the prior quarter.

Table 1: Size and Composition of the Local Currency Bond Market in Malaysia

	Outstanding Amount (billion)						Growth Rate (%)			
	Q3 2020		Q2 2021		Q3 2021		Q3 2020		Q3 2021	
	MYR	USD	MYR	USD	MYR	USD	q-o-q	y-o-y	q-o-q	y-o-y
Total	1,584	381	1,693	408	1,719	411	1.9	6.1	1.5	8.5
Government	848	204	924	223	938	224	2.3	8.0	1.5	10.6
Central Government Bonds	820	197	900	217	914	218	2.9	9.6	1.6	11.5
of which: *Sukuk*	377	91	415	100	435	104	2.7	13.8	4.8	15.2
Central Bank Bills	4	1	0	0	0	0	(20.0)	(60.8)	–	(100.0)
of which: *Sukuk*	0	0	0	0	0	0	–	(100.0)	–	–
Sukuk Perumahan Kerajaan	24	6	24	6	24	6	(10.1)	(10.1)	0.0	0.0
Corporate	735	177	769	185	780	186	1.3	3.9	1.4	6.1
of which: *Sukuk*	592	142	626	151	638	152	1.7	6.0	1.9	7.8

( ) = negative, – = not applicable, MYR = Malaysian ringgit, q-o-q = quarter-on-quarter, Q2 = second quarter, Q3 = third quarter, USD = United States dollar, y-o-y = year-on-year.
Notes:
1. Calculated using data from national sources.
2. Bloomberg LP end-of-period local currency–USD rates are used.
3. Growth rates are calculated from local currency base and do not include currency effects.
4. *Sukuk* refers to Islamic bonds.
5. Sukuk Perumahan Kerajaan are Islamic bonds issued by the Government of Malaysia to refinance funding for housing loans to government employees and to extend new housing loans.
Sources: Bank Negara Malaysia Fully Automated System for Issuing/Tendering and Bloomberg LP.

The top 30 corporate bond issuers in Malaysia comprised MYR462.8 billion of LCY corporate bonds outstanding at the end of September, representing 59.3% of the total LCY corporate bond market (**Table 2**). Government institution Danainfra Nasional led all issuers with outstanding LCY corporate bonds totaling MYR74.9 billion. The largest share among all sectors in the top 30 list belonged to financial institutions (51.8%) with MYR239.7 billion of outstanding LCY corporate bonds at the end of September.

Issuances of LCY corporate bonds in Q3 2021 declined 15.3% q-o-q to MYR38.3 billion from MYR45.2 billion in Q2 2021. The contraction was a reversal from the growth of 4.7% q-o-q posted in the previous quarter due to slow issuance activities in July and August.

In September, Lembaga Pembiayaan Perumahan Sektor Awam, Malaysia's statutory body in charge of handling public housing financing services, issued eight tranches of Islamic bond totaling MYR4.0 billion with tenors ranging from 7 years to 30 years and coupon rates from 3.34% to 4.58% (**Table 3**). Guaranteed by the Government of Malaysia, the bond was drawn from the company's Islamic Commercial Paper and Medium-Term Note Programme. In July, another government agency, Malaysia Rail Link, issued a six-tranche *sukuk* totaling MYR3.0 billion. The tenors of the tranches ranged from 5 years to 25 years and the periodic distribution rate came as low as 2.88% and as high as 4.48%. Proceeds from the issuance will be used for the East Coast Rail Link project. In August, Cagamas, the National Mortgage Corporation of Malaysia, had a double issuance of a 3-year ASEAN sustainability sukuk and 3-year conventional ASEAN sustainability bond totaling MYR300.0 million. In the same month, Cagamas raised MYR200.0 million from a 1-year floating rate conventional note, MYR85.0 million from a 1-year conventional medium-term note, and MYR25.0 million from a 1-year Islamic bond. Funds raised from these issuances will be used to purchase Islamic financing and affordable housing loans. In September, Cagamas continued its fundraising efforts, successfully issuing MYR550.0 million of 2-year conventional bonds and a total of MYR1.5 billion from a triple-tranche *sukuk* with tenors of 1 year, 2 years, and 3 years. Proceeds from the September fundraising efforts will be used to fund the purchase of housing loans and other eligible assets from Malaysia's financial system.

Investor Profile

In the Malaysian market, foreign holdings of LCY government bonds slightly fell in July, with holdings of foreign investors amounting to MYR230.1 billion worth of LCY government bonds from MYR233.8 billion in June. Foreign holdings increased in both August and September to MYR236.5 billion and MYR236.8 billion, respectively (**Figure 2**). Net capital outflows from the bond market were recorded in July totaling MYR3.7 billion, offseting some of the inflows of MYR6.4 billion and MYR0.3 billion in the succeeding 2 months. The pullback in July can be attributed to persistently high COVID-19 cases and political uncertainties in Malaysia. The positive sentiment from foreign investors in August, on the other hand, was due to positive progress in the government's National Recovery Plan and the National Immunization Programme, leading to the gradual reopening of the economy. The selling pressure in September was due to the US Federal Reserve's shift in monetary stance allowing the possibility of policy rate normalization in 2022, which would be earlier than previously expected by investors. Foreign holdings as a share of LCY government bonds declined from 26.0% at the end of June to 25.5% at the end of July before recovering to 26.0% in August and slightly falling by the end of September to 25.9%.

At the end of June 2021, financial institutions and social security institutions led all investors in LCY government bonds with holdings equivalent to 34.7% and 27.2% of the total market, respectively (**Figure 3**). The holdings of financial institutions and social security institutions each declined compared to the same month in 2020. The foreign holders' share expanded to 25.7% during the review period from 22.6% in the previous year. The holdings of insurance companies and BNM grew to 4.8% and 1.9%, respectively, from 4.5% and 1.5% between June 2020 and June 2021.

Table 2: Top 30 Issuers of Local Currency Corporate Bonds in Malaysia

	Issuers	Outstanding Amount		State-Owned	Listed Company	Type of Industry
		LCY Bonds (MYR billion)	LCY Bonds (USD billion)			
1.	Danainfra Nasional	74.9	17.9	Yes	No	Finance
2.	Prasarana	38.7	9.2	Yes	No	Transport, Storage, and Communications
3.	Lembaga Pembiayaan Perumahan Sektor Awam	37.6	9.0	Yes	No	Property and Real Estate
4.	Cagamas	31.9	7.6	Yes	No	Finance
5.	Project Lebuhraya Usahasama	28.9	6.9	No	No	Transport, Storage, and Communications
6.	Urusharta Jamaah	27.3	6.5	Yes	No	Finance
7.	Perbadanan Tabung Pendidikan Tinggi Nasional	23.8	5.7	Yes	No	Finance
8.	Pengurusan Air	18.5	4.4	Yes	No	Energy, Gas, and Water
9.	Malayan Banking	14.6	3.5	No	Yes	Banking
10.	Maybank Islamic	13.0	3.1	No	Yes	Banking
11.	Sarawak Energy	12.0	2.9	Yes	No	Energy, Gas, and Water
12.	Khazanah	11.9	2.8	Yes	No	Finance
13.	CIMB Bank	11.9	2.8	Yes	No	Finance
14.	CIMB Group Holdings	11.6	2.8	Yes	No	Finance
15.	Tenaga Nasional	10.3	2.4	No	Yes	Energy, Gas, and Water
16.	Danga Capital	10.0	2.4	Yes	No	Finance
17.	Jimah East Power	8.9	2.1	Yes	No	Energy, Gas, and Water
18.	Danum Capital	8.4	2.0	No	No	Finance
19.	Public Bank	6.9	1.6	No	No	Banking
20.	Sapura TMC	6.4	1.5	No	No	Finance
21.	YTL Power International	6.1	1.5	No	Yes	Energy, Gas, and Water
22.	Bank Pembangunan Malaysia	6.1	1.4	Yes	No	Banking
23.	Malaysia Rail Link	5.8	1.4	Yes	No	Construction
24.	Infracap Resources	5.8	1.4	Yes	No	Finance
25.	GOVCO Holdings	5.7	1.4	Yes	No	Finance
26.	Bakun Hydro Power Generation	5.5	1.3	No	No	Energy, Gas, and Water
27.	Turus Pesawat	5.3	1.3	Yes	No	Transport, Storage, and Communications
28.	GENM Capital	5.3	1.3	No	No	Finance
29.	EDRA Energy	5.1	1.2	No	Yes	Energy, Gas, and Water
30.	1Malaysia Development	5.0	1.2	Yes	No	Finance
	Total Top 30 LCY Corporate Issuers	**462.8**	**110.6**			
	Total LCY Corporate Bonds	**780.4**	**186.4**			
	Top 30 as % of Total LCY Corporate Bonds	**59.3%**	**59.3%**			

LCY = local currency, MYR = Malaysian ringgit, USD = United States dollar.
Notes:
1. Data as of 30 September 2021.
2. State-owned firms are defined as those in which the government has more than a 50% ownership stake.
Source: *AsianBondsOnline* calculations based on Bank Negara Malaysia Fully Automated System for Issuing/Tendering data.

Table 3: Notable Local Currency Corporate Bond Issuances in the Second Quarter of 2021

Corporate Issuers	Coupon Rate (%)	Issued Amount (MYR million)
Lembaga Pembiayaan Perumahan Sektor Awam		
7-year *sukuk murabahah*	3.34	235.0
8-year *sukuk murabahah*	3.44	785.0
13-year *sukuk murabahah*	3.86	600.0
14-year *sukuk murabahah*	4.00	600.0
18-year *sukuk murabahah*	4.27	900.0
19-year *sukuk murabahah*	4.33	200.0
24-year *sukuk murabahah*	4.48	100.0
30-year *sukuk murabahah*	4.58	580.0
Malaysia Rail Link[a]		
5-year *sukuk murabahah*	2.88	400.0
7-year *sukuk murabahah*	3.33	465.0
15-year *sukuk murabahah*	4.12	635.0
15-year *sukuk murabahah*	4.06	500.0
20-year *sukuk murabahah*	4.41	500.0
25-year *sukuk murabahah*	4.48	500.0
Cagamas[a]		
1-year Islamic MTN	2.15	25.0
1-year Islamic MTN	2.18	200.0
1-year MTN	Floating	200.0
1-year MTN	2.15	85.0
2-year Islamic MTN	2.40	150.0
2-year MTN	2.37	300.0
2-year MTN	2.40	250.0
3-year ASEAN Sustainability Sukuk	2.67	100.0
3-year ASEAN Sustainability Bond	2.67	200.0
3-year Islamic MTN	2.78	1,150.0

MTN = medium-term note, MYR = Malaysian ringgit.
Note: *Sukuk murabahah* are Islamic bonds in which bondholders are entitled to a share of the revenues generated by the assets.
[a] Multiple issuance of the same tenor indicates issuance on different dates.
Source: Bank Negara Malaysia Bond Info Hub.

Figure 2: Foreign Holdings and Capital Flows in the Malaysian Local Currency Government Bond Market

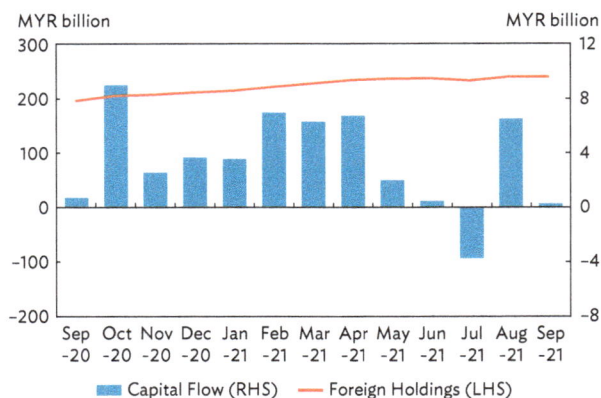

LHS = left-hand side, MYR = Malaysian ringgit, RHS = right-hand side.
Notes:
1. Figures exclude foreign holdings of Bank Negara Malaysia bills.
2. Month-on-month changes in foreign holdings of local currency government bonds were used as a proxy for bond flows.
Source: Bank Negara Malaysia Monthly Statistical Bulletin.

Figure 3: Local Currency Government Bonds Investor Profile

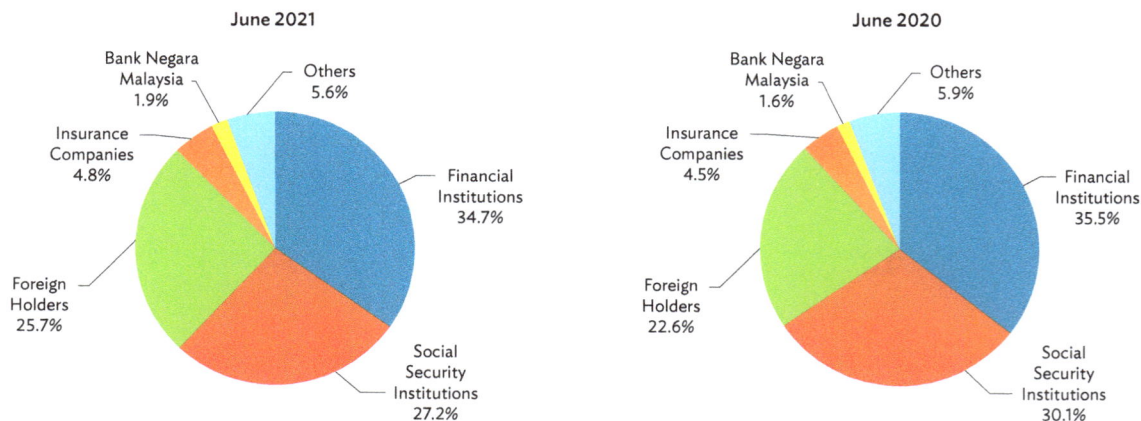

Note: "Others" include statutory bodies, nominees and trustee companies, and cooperatives and unclassified items.
Source: Bank Negara Malaysia.

Policy, Institutional, and Regulatory Developments

Bank Negara Malaysia Launches Malaysia Overnight Rate

On 24 September, BNM announced that the Malaysia overnight rate (MYOR) will be the new alternative reference rate for Malaysia. MYOR will be based on transactions in liquid markets, reflecting accurately Malaysia's financial environment. BNM clarified that the Kuala Lumpur interbank offered rate (KLIBOR) will still be used for other financial transactions. Periodic reviews will be conducted, however, to ensure that MYOR and KLIBOR are reflective of current market conditions. These benchmarks allow consumers to have the flexibility of choosing whichever rate suits their needs. The introduction of MYOR also broadens investors' risk management strategies. BNM also announced the discontinuation of the 2-month and 12-month KLIBOR starting 1 January 2023, as these rates are not used much in the financial market. Efforts are ongoing to develop a new Islamic benchmark rate to replace the Kuala Lumpur Islamic Reference Rate by the first half of 2022.

Malaysian Banks to Stop Issuing London Interbank Offered Rate-Referenced Contracts

On 22 October, BNM announced that by 31 December banks under its supervision must stop issuing new contracts referencing the London interbank offered rate (LIBOR). This is in line with global developments wherein other benchmark rates for major currencies will be replacing LIBOR starting January 2022. BNM set the fourth quarter of 2021 as a period when banks must ensure that contracts currently referencing the USD-denominated LIBOR and maturing after June 2023 have a fallback provision (i.e., a procedure for replacing LIBOR as a benchmark rate). Banks must also make sure that their systems and procedures are ready for the transition from LIBOR. In recent months, BNM has been preparing for the discontinuation of LIBOR by developing an alternative reference rate that will be used in parallel with the existing KLIBOR.

Philippines

Yield Movements

The yields of local currency (LCY) government bonds in the Philippines increased for all tenors between 31 August and 15 October except for 1-year bonds (**Figure 1**). Yields on the shorter end of the curve (1-month to 6-month tenors) climbed 4 basis points (bps) on average, while those at the longer end of the curve (20-year and 25-year tenors) increased an average of 5 bps. Much larger increases were seen for the yields of bonds with 2-year to 10-year maturities, which rose by 64 bps on average. The largest was for 10-year bonds with an 84-bps increase. In contrast, the yield fell 2 bps for 1-year bonds. The yield spread between the 2-year and 10-year tenors widened during the review period from 215 bps to 269 bps.

Inflation concerns and the impending winding down of the United States (US) Federal Reserve's monetary stimulus largely caused the upward movement of the yield curve.

Inflation remained elevated even as it slowed to 4.6% year-on-year (y-o-y) in October from 4.8% y-o-y in September and from a 32-month high of 4.9% y-o-y in August. The slower rate of consumer price inflation was primarily due to lower food prices. The October inflation reading and the resulting year-to-date average of 4.5% y-o-y were above the Bangko Sentral ng Pilipinas' (BSP) target of 2.0%–4.0% for 2021. Inflation has been above the BSP's annual target every month since January, except in July when it was at 4.0%. In November, the BSP lowered its 2021 inflation forecast to 4.3% from 4.4% in September. Its 2022 and 2023 forecasts were unchanged at 3.3% and 3.2%, respectively.

The increase in yields may have also been due to some uncertainty in the domestic economic recovery, resulting in investors requiring a premium for the associated risks. For example, persistently high inflation might temper the recovery by discouraging consumer spending on the back of a weak labor market. In addition, while its vaccination rate is improving, the Philippines remained among the lowest in the region in terms of the percentage of the population vaccinated, making it vulnerable to economic setbacks. Nonetheless, the Philippine economy grew 7.1% y-o-y in the third quarter (Q3) of 2021 despite the tighter restrictions on movements imposed in August.

Figure 1: Philippines' Benchmark Yield Curve— Local Currency Government Bonds

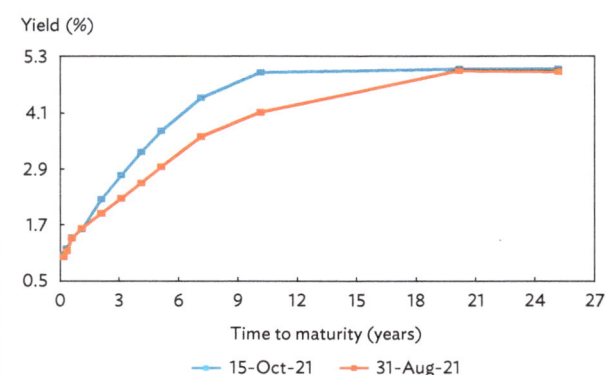

Source: Based on data from Bloomberg LP.

To an extent, the growth was magnified by a base effect, owing to the economic contraction a year earlier. On the supply side, the industrial and services sectors posted expansions, while the primary sector contracted. On the demand side, all components posted positive y-o-y growth. Year-to-date through the end of September, gross domestic product grew 4.9% y-o-y, which was at the upper end of the government's growth target for full-year 2021 of 4.0%–5.0%.

Meanwhile, yield increases in short-tenor bonds were anchored by the BSP's dovish monetary policy signals. The central bank stated that there will be no policy setting adjustment until the end of the year, stressing that tightening monetary policy prematurely could harm the economy's recovery. The BSP maintained the policy rate at 2.00% in its 18 November policy meeting to allow the economic recovery to gain more ground, while also saying that elevated inflation is transitory in nature and remained manageable.

The Philippine peso traded at PHP50.7 per USD1.0 on 15 October, weakening by 1.9% from 31 August. The domestic currency's depreciation versus the US dollar was largely due to the shift in the Federal Reserve's monetary policy stance. In November, the Federal Reserve announced that it will start reducing its bond purchase program during the month. Soaring global oil prices and an improvement in the Philippines' import prospects as the economy reopened contributed to increased demand for US dollars.

Size and Composition

The Philippine LCY bond market expanded 4.4% quarter-on-quarter (q-o-q) in Q3 2021 to reach a size of PHP9,761.7 billion (USD191.4 billion) at the end of September, which was faster than the growth of 2.5% q-o-q in the second quarter (Q2) of 2021 (**Table 1**). The quarterly growth was driven solely by the government segment as the corporate segment contracted during the quarter. On an annual basis, the size of the LCY bond market increased 20.0% y-o-y. Government bonds accounted for 85.3% of the total bond market at the end of September, while corporate bonds accounted for 14.7%.

Government bonds. Total LCY government bonds outstanding amounted to PHP8,322.0 billion at the end of Q3 2021, with growth accelerating to 6.2% q-o-q from 3.9% q-o-q in the previous quarter. The market expansion was driven by Treasury bonds and BSP bills.

Treasury bonds outstanding increased 8.3% q-o-q to PHP6,879.6 billion in Q3 2021, more than doubling the growth of 3.6% q-o-q in Q2 2021, on the back of higher bond offer volume and sales during the quarter. On the other hand, outstanding Treasury bills fell to PHP942.5 billion in Q3 2021 on an accelerated decline

of 7.9% q-o-q, following a 2.5% q-o-q contraction in Q2 2021, due to a drop in short-term security issuance.

The BSP also added to the expansion in the government bond market's size with its outstanding securities increasing 10.0% q-o-q to PHP440.0 billion at the end of September. Outstanding debt from government-related entities barely changed during quarter.

Total government securities issuances increased 4.5% q-o-q to PHP2,099.8 billion in Q3 2021, following a decline of 3.5% q-o-q in Q2 2021. The increase was mainly propelled by Treasury bonds and supplemented by BSP securities. On the other hand, the drop in the sale of Treasury bills restrained issuance growth in the government segment.

Debt raised via Treasury bonds in Q3 2021 amounted to PHP487.8 billion, increasing 46.9% q-o-q. The Bureau of the Treasury (BTr) increased the offer volume for Treasury bonds during the quarter as it wanted to extend its debt maturity profile to take advantage of favorable interest rates. Despite having one auction with partial awards and one unsuccessful auction, the resulting total debt sales in Q3 2021 were still up significantly from the previous quarter as the BTr opened its tap facility on several occasions.

Issuance of Treasury bills declined by 36.4% q-o-q to PHP272.0 billion in Q3 2021 after posting an increase of 14.7% q-o-q in the previous quarter. Even though all

Table 1: Size and Composition of the Local Currency Bond Market in the Philippines

| | Outstanding Amount (billion) | | | | | | Growth Rate (%) | | | |
| | Q3 2020 | | Q2 2021 | | Q3 2021 | | Q3 2020 | | Q3 2021 | |
	PHP	USD	PHP	USD	PHP	USD	q-o-q	y-o-y	q-o-q	y-o-y
Total	8,136	168	9,351	192	9,762	191	8.8	21.5	4.4	20.0
Government	6,503	134	7,834	160	8,322	163	10.1	23.8	6.2	28.0
Treasury Bills	876	18	1,023	21	943	18	10.0	58.5	(7.9)	7.5
Treasury Bonds	5,537	114	6,351	130	6,880	135	9.3	18.4	8.3	24.3
Central Bank Securities	50	1	400	8	440	9	–	–	10.0	780.0
Others	40	0.8	60	1	60	1	(0.02)	83.3	(0.01)	50.2
Corporate	1,633	34	1,517	31	1,440	28	3.8	12.9	(5.1)	(11.9)

( ) = negative, – = not applicable, PHP = Philippine peso, q-o-q = quarter-on-quarter, Q2 = second quarter, Q3 = third quarter, USD = United States dollar, y-o-y = year-on-year.
Notes:
1. Calculated using data from national sources.
2. Bloomberg end-of-period local currency–USD rates are used.
3. Growth rates are calculated from local currency base and do not include currency effects.
4. "Others" comprise bonds issued by government agencies, entities, and corporations for which repayment is guaranteed by the Government of the Philippines. This includes bonds issued by Power Sector Assets and Liabilities Management and the National Food Authority, among others.
5. Peso Global Bonds (PHP-denominated bonds payable in USD) are not included.
Sources: Bloomberg LP and Bureau of the Treasury.

auctions for Treasury bills were successful, the BTr's move to adjust its borrowing program in favor of longer-term securities caused the quarterly decline.

Following the successful issuance of EUR- and JPY-denominated bonds in Q2 2021, the Philippines tapped again the international bond market with its two-tranche sale of USD-denominated bonds. In July, it raised USD3.0 billion comprising 10.5-year bonds amounting to USD750.0 million (1.95% coupon) and 25-year bonds amounting USD2,250.0 million (3.20% coupon). The international issuance reflected investor confidence in Philippine debt remaining intact despite the adverse effect of the coronavirus disease (COVID-19) pandemic to the economy.

The issuance of BSP bills climbed 7.2% q-o-q to PHP1,340.0 billion in Q3 2021, underpinned by higher volumes offered during the quarter. All issuances were met with strong demand, which was indicative of market liquidity remaining abundant. Meanwhile, there was no securities issuance from government-related entities during the quarter.

The government plans to borrow a total of PHP3.0 trillion in 2021 to fund its widening budget gap in response to COVID-19 relief measures and associated economic recovery plans.

Corporate bonds. Debt outstanding in the corporate sector registered a faster decline of 5.1% q-o-q in Q3 2021 compared with a 3.9% q-o-q dip in the previous quarter. The corporate bond market contracted to PHP1,439.7 billion on the back of the maturation of bonds amid low issuance volume during the quarter.

The banking sector remained the largest segment of the LCY corporate bond market with a share of 38.6% at the end of September, albeit this represented a decline from 41.7% from a year earlier (**Figure 2**). Property companies remained in the second spot with a share of 25.1%, up from 23.8% in September 2020. Holding firms came next in terms of corporate bonds outstanding with their market share rising to 16.9% at the end of September, overtaking utilities firms whose share dipped to 13.4%. Transport and telecommunications firms each saw lower market shares in September 2021 versus a year earlier, while the share of "others" went up.

The top 30 corporate issuers had aggregate debt outstanding of PHP1,278.3 billion at the end of September, which comprised 88.8% of the total corporate bond market (**Table 2**). The banking sector continued to have the largest share at 41.4% (PHP529.5 billion), followed by holdings firms with a share of 24.0% (PHP307.4 billion) and property firms with a share of 18.0% (PHP229.7 billion). BDO Unibank had the

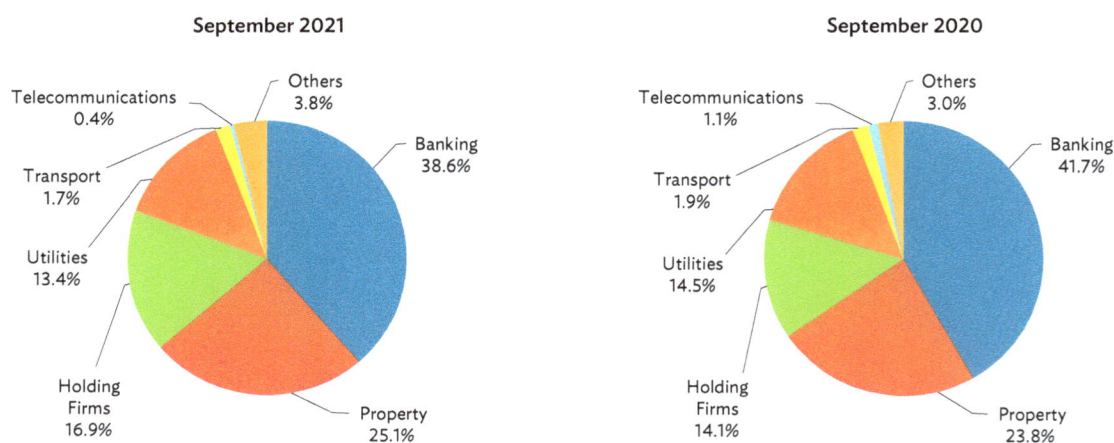

Figure 2: Local Currency Corporate Bonds Outstanding by Sector

Source: Based on data from Bloomberg LP.

Table 2: Top 30 Issuers of Local Currency Corporate Bonds in the Philippines

	Issuers	Outstanding Amount		State-Owned	Listed Company	Type of Industry
		LCY Bonds (PHP billion)	LCY Bonds (USD billion)			
1.	BDO Unibank	109.9	2.2	No	Yes	Banking
2.	Ayala Land	108.9	2.1	No	Yes	Property
3.	Metropolitan Bank	100.1	2.0	No	Yes	Banking
4.	SM Prime Holdings	93.3	1.8	No	Yes	Holding Firms
5.	San Miguel	90.0	1.8	No	Yes	Holding Firms
6.	SMC Global Power	73.8	1.4	No	No	Electricity, Energy, and Power
7.	China Bank	61.2	1.2	No	Yes	Banking
8.	Rizal Commercial Banking Corporation	55.1	1.1	No	Yes	Banking
9.	Bank of the Philippine Islands	52.2	1.0	No	Yes	Banking
10.	Security Bank	48.3	0.9	No	Yes	Banking
11.	SM Investments	43.3	0.8	No	Yes	Holding Firms
12.	Petron	42.9	0.8	No	Yes	Electricity, Energy, and Power
13.	Vista Land	42.8	0.8	No	Yes	Property
14.	Ayala Corporation	40.0	0.8	No	Yes	Holding Firms
15.	Aboitiz Power	38.0	0.7	No	Yes	Electricity, Energy, and Power
16.	Philippine National Bank	31.8	0.6	No	Yes	Banking
17.	Aboitiz Equity Ventures	29.4	0.6	No	Yes	Holding Firms
18.	Filinvest Land	25.8	0.5	No	Yes	Property
19.	Robinsons Land	25.2	0.5	No	Yes	Property
20.	Union Bank of the Philippines	24.6	0.5	No	Yes	Banking
21.	Philippine Savings Bank	19.1	0.4	No	Yes	Banking
22.	Maynilad	18.5	0.4	No	No	Water
23.	East West Banking	16.2	0.3	No	Yes	Banking
24.	Doubledragon	15.0	0.3	No	Yes	Property
25.	San Miguel Food and Beverage	15.0	0.3	No	Yes	Food and Beverage
26.	Megaworld	12.0	0.2	No	Yes	Property
27.	Puregold	12.0	0.2	No	Yes	Whole and Retail Trading
28.	MTD Manila Expressway	11.5	0.2	No	No	Infrastructure
29.	Metro Pacific Investments	11.4	0.2	No	Yes	Holding Firms
30.	Robinsons Bank	11.0	0.2	No	No	Banking
	Total Top 30 LCY Corporate Issuers	**1,278.3**	**25.1**			
	Total LCY Corporate Bonds	**1,439.7**	**28.2**			
	Top 30 as % of Total LCY Corporate Bonds	**88.8%**	**88.8%**			

LCY = local currency, PHP = Philippine peso, USD = United States dollar.
Notes:
1. Data as of 30 September 2021.
2. State-owned firms are defined as those in which the government has more than a 50% ownership stake.
Source: *AsianBondsOnline* calculations based on Bloomberg LP data.

most corporate bonds outstanding among all issuers, followed by Ayala Land and Metropolitan Bank. Each had outstanding debt of over PHP100 billion at the end of September.

Issuance activity in the corporate sector improved in Q3 2021 following three consecutive quarters of q-o-q declines. Debt sales from firms rose 5.1% q-o-q to PHP49.4 billion during the quarter. Proceeds will mainly be used for general corporate purposes, with its decision to tap the local bond market likely influenced by the optimism of the reopening of the economy. **Table 3** lists all issuances in Q3 2021. Notable debt sales included San Miguel Corporation's 6-year bond amounting to PHP30.0 billion, which will be used to redenominate existing USD-denominated obligations of the company. D&L Industries made its first bond issuance with a two-tranche sale comprising 3-year and 5-year bonds amounting to PHP3.0 billion and PHP2.0 billion, respectively.

Two firms turned to the international debt market to generate funds in Q3 2021. In September, AYC Finance Limited issued a USD-denominated perpetual bond amounting to USD400.0 million with a coupon rate of 3.9%. Proceeds will be used to refinance its outstanding

Table 3: Notable Local Currency Corporate Bond Issuances in the Third Quarter of 2021

Corporate Issuers	Coupon Rate (%)	Issued Amount (PHP billion)
San Miguel Corporation		
6-year bond	3.38	30.00
Aboitiz Equity Ventures		
4-year bond	3.30	5.00
7-year bond	4.10	5.00
D&L Industries		
3-year bond	2.79	3.00
5-year bond	3.60	2.00
PHINMA Corporation		
3-year bond	3.53	3.00
Alsons Consolidated Resources[a]		
1-year bond	zero coupon	1.14
1-year bond	zero coupon	0.27

PHP = Philippine peso.
[a] Multiple issuance of the same tenor indicates issuance on different dates.
Source: Based on data from Bloomberg LP.

USD-denominated obligations. In the same month, ACEN Finance Limited raised USD400.0 million from its sale of a perpetual green bond that carried a 4.0% coupon. Funds raised will be used to finance or refinance ACEN's renewable energy projects.

Figure 3: Local Currency Government Bonds Investor Profile

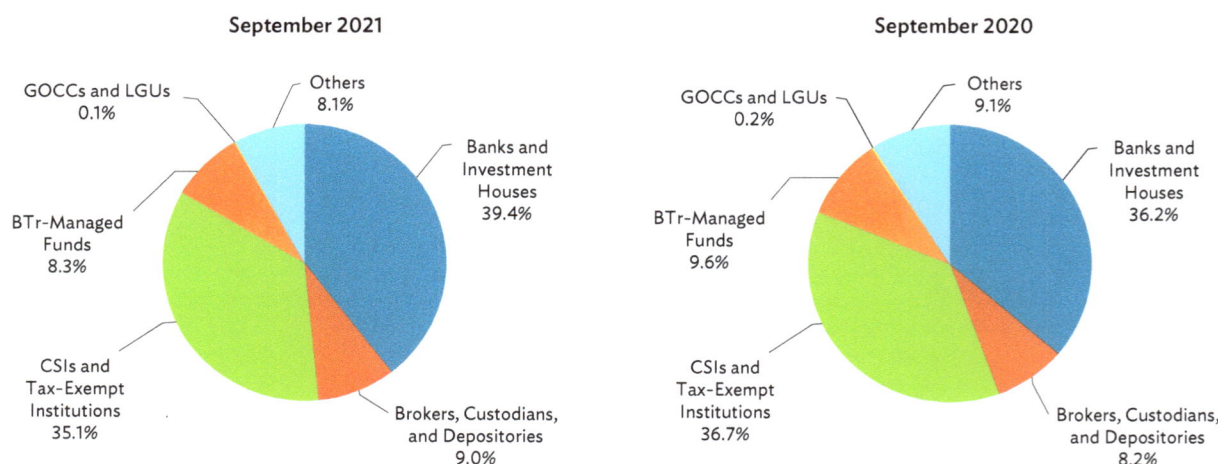

September 2021

GOCCs and LGUs 0.1%
Others 8.1%
Banks and Investment Houses 39.4%
BTr-Managed Funds 8.3%
CSIs and Tax-Exempt Institutions 35.1%
Brokers, Custodians, and Depositories 9.0%

September 2020

GOCCs and LGUs 0.2%
Others 9.1%
Banks and Investment Houses 36.2%
BTr-Managed Funds 9.6%
CSIs and Tax-Exempt Institutions 36.7%
Brokers, Custodians, and Depositories 8.2%

BTr = Bureau of the Treasury, CSI = contractual savings institution, GOCC = government-owned or -controlled corporation, LGU = local government unit.
Source: Bureau of the Treasury.

Investor Profile

Banks and investment houses were the largest investor group in LCY government bonds at the end of September, overtaking contractual savings and tax-exempt institutions (**Figure 3**). Banks and investment houses' market share climbed to 39.4% from 36.2% a year earlier, while that of contractual savings and tax-exempt institutions declined to 35.1% from 36.7%. Brokers, custodians, and depositories (9.0%) overtook BTr-managed funds (8.3%) in having the third-largest market share, with the former group posting an increase in their aggregate market share from September 2020 and the latter posting a decrease. The "others" investor group was the fifth largest by market share (8.1%), while government-owned or -controlled corporations and local government units remained the investor group with the smallest holdings of government bonds (0.1%).

Ratings Update

On 6 September, Japan Credit Rating Agency affirmed the Philippines sovereign credit rating of A– with a stable outlook. According to the ratings agency, the affirmation was due to the Philippines' high and sustainable economic growth performance backed by solid domestic demand, resilience to external shocks with its low external debt-to-gross domestic product ratio and ample foreign exchange reserves, solid fiscal position despite widening budget deficit, and sound banking sector. The stable outlook was further backed by strong remittance flows, which can help cushion the economy from external shocks.

Policy, Institutional, and Regulatory Developments

Bureau of the Treasury Sets Borrowing Program to PHP400 Billion in October and November

The BTr, which sets its borrowing plan on a monthly basis, planned to borrow PHP200 billion each in the months of October and November. The monthly amount is lower compared to the borrowing program in September, which was set at PHP250 billion. The planned monthly debt sale is composed of PHP60 billion of Treasury bills and PHP140 billion of Treasury bonds. It remained focused on longer-term debt as the BTr wanted to extend the debt maturity profile.

Bureau of the Treasury Issues Its First Onshore Retail Dollar Bonds

On 15 September, the BTr launched its maiden issuance of Retail Dollar Bonds (RDBs). The BTr stated that the RDB offer aimed to further advance financial inclusion in the Philippines by diversifying the investor portfolio. At the same time, the RDBs also diversified the government's funding types and sources. The RDB issuance comprised 5-year and 10-year tenors with coupon rates of 1.375% and 2.250%, respectively. The BTr issued a total of USD1.59 billion: USD1.11 billion of 5-year bonds and USD0.48 billion of 10-year bonds. The last time the BTr issued onshore USD-denominated bonds was in December 2012, when they were offered to institutional investors only.

Singapore

Yield Movements

Between 31 August and 15 October, the local currency (LCY) government bond yield curve of Singapore shifted upward with yields rising across all tenors (**Figure 1**). Short-term tenors (from 3 months to 1 year) jumped an average of 6 basis points (bps), while bonds with tenors of 2 years to 30 years soared an average of 27 bps. The smallest gain for the review period was recorded for the 3-month and 6-month yields, which rose 4 bps each. On the other hand, the highest jump was registered for the 15-year yield, which surged 34 bps. The yield spread between 2-year and 10-year government bonds slightly contracted from 105 bps to 104 bps during the review period.

The higher yields for Singapore government bonds was due to the decision by Monetary Authority of Singapore (MAS) to tighten its monetary policy to rein in the economy's consumer price inflation. Despite encouraging signs from the stock market, investors decided to remain cautiously optimistic as the economy recovers slowly from the coronavirus disease (COVID-19) pandemic.

On 14 October, MAS decided to slightly raise from zero the slope of its Singapore dollar nominal effective exchange rate policy band. The tightening of the monetary policy aims to ensure consumer price stability amid the accumulation of inflation pressures. The central bank expects Singapore's trade-dependent economy to continue its path to recovery as global and domestic economies gradually reopen.

During the review period, the Singapore dollar slightly weakened by 0.3% against the United States (US) dollar, closing at SGD1.3483 per USD1.0 dollar on 15 October, the day after MAS's monetary policy statement was released. On the other hand, the equity market, represented by the Straits Times Index, jumped 3.9% from 31 August, reaching a level of 3,173.9 on 15 October amid optimistic growth prospects for the Singapore economy.

Singapore's economy grew 7.1% year-on-year (y-o-y) in the third quarter (Q3) of 2021, extending the 15.2% y-o-y growth recorded in the second quarter (Q2). The slower expansion was due to restrained growth in the

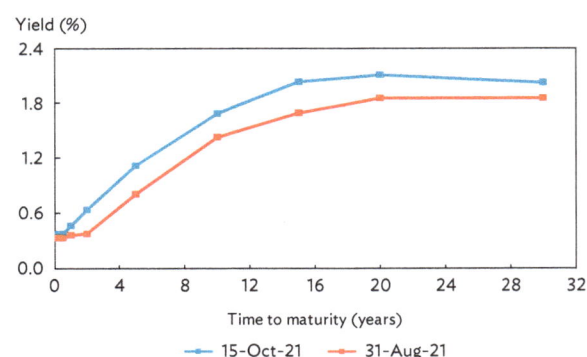

Figure 1: Singapore's Benchmark Yield Curve— Local Currency Government Bonds

Source: Based on data from Bloomberg LP.

performance of all sectors as businesses were affected by tightened restrictions aimed at slowing the spread of COVID-19 during the quarter. On a quarter-on-quarter (q-o-q) basis, Singapore's economy expanded 1.3% in Q3 2021, a reversal of the contraction of 1.4% q-o-q recorded in the previous quarter. On an annual basis, MAS expects Singapore's economic growth to be around 7.0% for full-year 2021.

Consumer price inflation in Singapore increased 2.5% y-o-y in September, the same level as in July after dipping a little to 2.4% y-o-y in August. In its September report, MAS noted that the supply–demand gap in some commodities and goods is expected to persist in the short term. Singapore's sluggish labor market is also expected to recover, leading to increased wages. Year-to-date, consumer price inflation in Singapore averaged 1.8% y-o-y. MAS expects the full-year 2021 inflation to be around 2.0% y-o-y due to rising imported and labor costs brought about by the normalization of domestic activities. Strengthening global demand and tight supply also contribute to the accumulation of inflationary pressures.

Singapore was placed under the less restrictive Preparatory Stage of Phase 2 (Safe Transition) starting 19 August after being under Phase 2 (Heightened Alert) in July. However, due to the rising number of cases straining Singapore's health-care system toward the end of August, tightened measures, such as limited social gatherings and stricter vaccination and testing requirements for entering establishments, were announced in September. The measures took effect from 27 September through 24 October to curb the community transmission of the virus. Under the city-state's national vaccination program, 84% of Singapore's population had been fully vaccinated as of 17 October.

Size and Composition

Singapore's LCY bond market grew 6.3% q-o-q in Q3 2021, increasing to a size of SGD590.0 billion (USD434.6 billion) at the end of September from SGD555.0 billion at the end of June 2021 (**Table 1**). This rate of expansion was the same as in the previous quarter. On a y-o-y basis, the LCY bond market expanded 21.9% y-o-y in Q3 2021, accelerating from the 17.1% y-o-y growth logged in Q2 2021. The growth of Singapore's LCY bond market was due to the growth in both LCY government and corporate bonds, which accounted for 67.0% and 33.0%, respectively, of total outstanding LCY bonds at the end of September.

Issuance of LCY bonds in Q3 2021 increased 6.7% q-o-q to SGD278.9 billion from SGD261.4 billion in the previous quarter due to the expansion of government bond issuances. The growth in issuance of government bonds was dampened by the decline in corporate bond issuance. The Q3 2021 growth was slower than the expansion of 15.3% q-o-q recorded in the previous quarter.

Government bonds. During the review period, LCY government bonds outstanding expanded 8.0% q-o-q to SGD395.3 billion from SGD365.9 billion in Q2 2021.

The bond growth in Q3 2021 was an acceleration from the growth of 4.8% q-o-q posted in the prior quarter. Outstanding Singapore Government Securities (SGS) bills and bonds, which comprised 54.5% of total LCY government bonds outstanding at the end of Q3 2021, jumped 4.3% q-o-q. MAS bills, which comprised 45.5% of all LCY government bonds outstanding, increased 12.9% q-o-q.

LCY government bond issuance expanded 8.9% q-o-q in Q3 2021. Central bank bills jumped 13.2% q-o-q due to higher issuance amounts granted to meet investor demand. In contrast, issuances of SGS bills and bonds declined 12.9% q-o-q due to low issuance in September, as MAS scaled down the issuance amount of 20-year SGS bonds to pave the way for the issuance of its first 30-year infrastructure bond in October.

Corporate bonds. LCY corporate bonds outstanding expanded 3.0% q-o-q to SGD194.7 billion in Q3 2021 from SGD189.1 billion in the prior quarter. The growth was an extension of the 9.3% q-o-q gain in Q2 2021, albeit smaller, as investors took advantage of the low-interest-rate environment.

The top 30 issuers of LCY corporate bonds in Singapore had total outstanding bonds of SGD104.0 billion, or 53.4% of the total LCY corporate bond market, at the end of Q3 2021 (**Table 2**). Government institution Housing & Development Board was the largest issuer during the quarter with outstanding LCY corporate bonds totaling SGD24.9 billion. Among the top 30 LCY corporate bonds issuers, the largest sectoral share came from

Table 1: Size and Composition of the Local Currency Bond Market in Singapore

| | Outstanding Amount (billion) | | | | | | Growth Rate (%) | | | |
| | Q3 2020 | | Q2 2021 | | Q3 2021 | | Q3 2020 | | Q3 2021 | |
	SGD	USD	SGD	USD	SGD	USD	q-o-q	y-o-y	q-o-q	y-o-y
Total	484	355	555	412	590	435	2.1	10.2	6.3	21.9
Government	313	229	366	272	395	291	2.4	13.0	8.0	26.3
SGS Bills and Bonds	191	140	207	154	216	159	(1.7)	17.7	4.3	12.7
MAS Bills	122	89	159	118	180	132	9.5	6.4	12.9	47.7
Corporate	171	125	189	141	195	143	1.6	5.5	3.0	13.8

( ) = negative, MAS = Monetary Authority of Singapore, q-o-q = quarter-on-quarter, Q2 = second quarter, Q3 = third quarter, SGD = Singapore dollar, SGS = Singapore Government Securities, USD = United States dollar, y-o-y = year-on-year.
Notes:
1. Government bonds are calculated using data from national sources. Corporate bonds are based on *AsianBondsOnline* estimates.
2. SGS bills and bonds do not include the special issue of SGS held by the Singapore Central Provident Fund.
3. Bloomberg LP end-of-period local currency–USD rates are used.
4. Growth rates are calculated from local currency base and do not include currency effects.
Sources: Bloomberg LP, Monetary Authority of Singapore, and Singapore Government Securities.

Table 2: Top 30 Issuers of Local Currency Corporate Bonds in Singapore

	Issuers	LCY Bonds (SGD billion)	LCY Bonds (USD billion)	State-Owned	Listed Company	Type of Industry
1.	Housing & Development Board	24.9	18.3	Yes	No	Real Estate
2.	Singapore Airlines	14.7	10.8	Yes	Yes	Transportation
3.	Land Transport Authority	9.5	7.0	Yes	No	Transportation
4.	CapitaLand	5.6	4.1	Yes	Yes	Real Estate
5.	Temasek Financial	4.6	3.4	Yes	No	Finance
6.	Frasers Property	4.0	3.0	No	Yes	Real Estate
7.	United Overseas Bank	4.0	2.9	No	Yes	Banking
8.	Mapletree Treasury Services	3.3	2.4	No	No	Finance
9.	Sembcorp Industries	3.3	2.4	No	Yes	Diversified
10.	DBS Bank	2.9	2.1	No	Yes	Banking
11.	Keppel Corporation	2.6	1.9	No	Yes	Diversified
12.	City Developments Limited	2.1	1.5	No	Yes	Real Estate
13.	CapitaLand Mall Trust	2.0	1.5	No	No	Finance
14.	Olam International	1.8	1.4	No	Yes	Consumer Goods
15.	Oversea-Chinese Banking Corporation	1.7	1.3	No	Yes	Banking
16.	National Environment Agency	1.7	1.2	Yes	No	Environmental Services
17.	Shangri-La Hotel	1.5	1.1	No	Yes	Real Estate
18.	Ascendas Real Estate Investment Trust	1.5	1.1	No	Yes	Finance
19.	NTUC Income	1.4	1.0	No	No	Finance
20.	Singtel Group Treasury	1.3	0.9	No	No	Finance
21.	Suntec Real Estate Investment Trust	1.2	0.9	No	Yes	Real Estate
22.	Singapore Technologies Telemedia	1.2	0.9	Yes	No	Utilities
23.	GuocoLand Limited IHT	1.1	0.8	No	No	Real Estate
24.	Public Utilities Board	1.0	0.7	Yes	No	Utilities
25.	Ascott Residence	1.0	0.7	No	Yes	Real Estate
26.	Singapore Press Holdings	1.0	0.7	No	Yes	Communications
27.	Keppel Real Estate Investment Trust	0.9	0.7	No	No	Real Estate
28.	StarHub	0.9	0.7	No	Yes	Diversified
29.	Keppel Land International	0.9	0.7	No	No	Real Estate
30.	Hyflux	0.9	0.7	No	Yes	Utilities
	Total Top 30 LCY Corporate Issuers	**104.0**	**76.6**			
	Total LCY Corporate Bonds	**194.7**	**143.4**			
	Top 30 as % of Total LCY Corporate Bonds	**53.4%**	**53.4%**			

LCY = local currency, SGD = Singapore dollar, USD = United States dollar.
Notes:
1. Data as of 30 September 2021.
2. State-owned firms are defined as those in which the government has more than a 50% ownership stake.
Source: *AsianBondsOnline* calculations based on Bloomberg LP data.

real estate companies (41.4%) with SGD43.1 billion of aggregate outstanding LCY corporate bonds at the end of September.

During the review period, LCY corporate bond issuance fell to SGD7.2 billion, a contraction of 39.8% q-o-q from SGD12.0 billion in the previous quarter. The decline in LCY corporate bond issuances was due to a high base after a huge issuance by flagship carrier Singapore Airlines in June. Without Singapore Airlines' issuance in the previous quarter, LCY corporate bond issuance would have recorded an expansion of 24.5% q-o-q in Q3 2021.

Singapore's National Environment Agency issued a dual-tranche green bond totaling SGD1.65 billion in September (**Table 3**). The bond had a 10-year and a 30-year tranche, and was the first green bond and the largest first issuance by a public agency in Singapore. Proceeds from the issuance will be used for projects under the agency's green bond framework. Temasek Financial issued a SGD1.5 billion 50-year bond in August. The bond had the longest tenor among nonperpetual bonds issued during the quarter. The 50-year tenor was the first such issuance from Temasek Financial, which aims to provide the company with funding flexibility and an expanded investor base. Proceeds from the issuance will be used for the ordinary course of business. Mapletree Treasury Services raised SGD600.0 million in August from Singapore's first subordinated fixed-for-life perpetual noncallable bond. The issuance was drawn from the company's Medium-Term Note Programme. In September, Keppel Corporation issued a SGD400.0 million perpetual bond with a coupon of 2.9%, the lowest coupon for a Singaporean corporate issuer outside the financial sector. Property developer Oxley Holdings raised SGD155.0 million in July from the reopening of its 3-year bond to fund its buyback of a part of its SGD150.0 million 5.7% notes due in 2022. The issuances also had the highest coupon during the review period.

Table 3: Notable Local Currency Corporate Bond Issuances in the Third Quarter of 2021

Corporate Issuers	Coupon Rate (%)	Issued Amount (SGD million)
National Environment Agency		
10-year bond	1.670	350.0
30-year bond	2.500	1,300.0
Temasek Financial		
50-year bond	2.800	1,500.0
Mapletree Treasury Services		
Perpetual bond	3.700	600.0
Keppel Corporation		
Perpetual bond	2.900	400.0
AIMS APAC Real Estate Investment Trust		
Perpetual bond	5.375	250.0
Oxley Holdings		
3-year bond	6.900	155.0
Aspial Treasury		
1-year bond	6.000	70.0

SGD = Singapore dollar.
Source: Bloomberg LP.

Policy, Institutional, and Regulatory Developments

Monetary Authority of Singapore Issues Cash Management Treasury Bills

On 3 November, MAS issued a 7-day Cash Management Treasury Bill (CMTB) under the Local Treasury Bills Act to test the operational preparedness of the issuance. CMTBs are MAS's new financial instruments that are SGS bills with tenors of less than 6 months. CMTBs will be issued as a cash management instrument to allow the government to manage its short-term cashflows. MAS will not adhere to a schedule for the issuance of CMTBs, which will be issued on an ad hoc basis.

Thailand

Yield Movements

Between 31 August and 15 October, Thailand's local currency (LCY) government bond yields rose across all tenors, shifting the yield curve upward (**Figure 1**). Yields jumped an average of 34 basis points (bps), with the 15-year tenor gaining the most at 52 bps. The yield on 2-year bonds rose 18 bps, while the yield on 10-year bonds jumped 40 bps. As a result, the spread between the 2-year and 10-year yields widened to 134 bps on 15 October from 111 bps on 31 August.

The rise in Thai LCY bond yields tracked the movements of other sovereign bond yields in the region, which rose in tandem with United States (US) Treasury yields. The uptick in yields was primarily due to inflation fears and uncertainties over the US Federal Reserve's plan to taper its quantitative easing measures starting in November. The Thai bond market saw net outflows of foreign funds in September amounting to THB36.7 billion, the biggest monthly net outflows since March 2020.

Domestic conditions also factored into the rise in Thai sovereign debt yields. In September, the Government of Thailand lifted the public debt ceiling from 60% to 70% of gross domestic product (GDP) to accommodate the additional borrowing needed to continue funding stimulus measures. Expectations of an increased supply of government bonds in the near to medium term put upward pressure on bonds yields.

The Thai economy contracted in the third quarter (Q3) of 2021 as mobility restrictions imposed to arrest the Delta variant-driven surge of infections capped consumption and investment. GDP dipped 0.3% year-on-year (y-o-y) in Q3 2021 after recording a 7.6% y-o-y expansion in the second quarter (Q2) of 2021. Private consumption and investment contracted 3.2% y-o-y and 0.4% y-o-y, respectively, after recording positive growth in the previous quarter. Growth in government consumption rose to 2.5% y-o-y in Q3 2021 from 1.0% y-o-y in the prior quarter.

Thailand's path to recovery remained clouded by risks brought about by the uncertain trajectory of the pandemic. In September, the Bank of Thailand (BOT)

Figure 1: Thailand's Benchmark Yield Curve— Local Currency Government Bonds

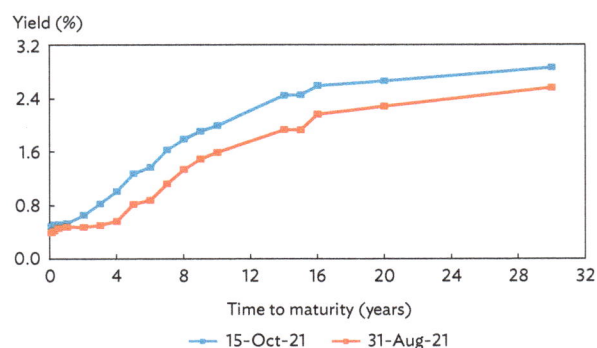

Sources: Based on data from Bloomberg LP and Thai Bond Market Association.

revised downward its GDP growth forecast for full-year 2021 to 0.7% from the 1.8% projection announced in June, but it maintained the growth forecast for 2022 at 3.9%. The BOT also lowered the projected foreign tourist arrivals for full-year 2021 to 200,000 from the previous estimate of 700,000. Estimated foreign tourist arrivals for 2022 were also reduced to 6 million from the June forecast of 10 million.

Thailand's consumer price inflation rose to 2.4% y-o-y in October from 1.7% y-o-y in September. The jump in headline inflation was primarily due to a hike in energy costs, as global oil prices increased and government subsidies on utilities ended. Thailand's core inflation, which excludes volatile food and energy prices, was steady at 0.2% y-o-y from September to October. The BOT expects headline inflation to rise temporarily owing to global supply shocks, but remain within its target range of 1.0%–3.0%.

On 10 November, the BOT's Monetary Policy Committee held the policy rate steady at 0.5%. The BOT assessed that the Thai economy has entered a recovery phase following the relaxation of restrictions and reopening of tourism, but decided to maintain an accommodative monetary policy to support continued recovery amid lingering uncertainties. In response to the pandemic, the BOT had earlier reduced the policy rate by 25 bps each in its February, March, and May 2020 meetings.

Size and Composition

Thailand's outstanding LCY bond stock amounted to THB14,479.7 billion (USD429.6 billion) at the end of September (**Table 1**). Overall growth eased to 1.9% quarter-on-quarter (q-o-q) in Q3 2021 from 2.6% q-o-q in the previous quarter, driven by weaker growth in the corporate bond segment. Annual growth also slowed to 3.3% y-o-y in Q3 2021 from 5.6% y-o-y in Q2 2021. Government bonds continued to dominate the Thai LCY bond market with a share of 72.9% of total bonds outstanding at the end of September.

Government bonds. The LCY government bond market reached a size of THB10,552.0 billion at the end of September. Growth in total government bonds outstanding rose to 2.2% q-o-q in Q3 2021 from 1.7% q-o-q in Q2 2021. The faster expansion was driven primarily by stronger growth in government bonds and Treasury bills, which rose 3.1% q-o-q in Q3 2021 versus 2.1% q-o-q in the previous quarter. Growth in BOT bonds outstanding remained negligible at 0.3% q-o-q in Q3 2021, similar to the 0.2% q-o-q growth posted in Q2 2021. Growth in the stock of state-owned enterprise and other bonds dropped to 2.4% q-o-q in Q3 2021 from 3.2% q-o-q in the prior quarter. On a y-o-y basis, the Thai LCY government bond market expanded 2.8% in Q2 2021, down from 6.1% in Q2 2021. At the end of September, outstanding government bonds and Treasury bills reached THB6,683.5 billion, accounting for the largest share of total outstanding LCY

government bonds at 63.3%. Outstanding BOT bonds (THB2,925.8 billion) and state-owned enterprise and other bonds (THB942.8 billion) comprised smaller shares at 27.7% and 8.9%, respectively.

The issuance of LCY government bonds totaled THB1,865.5 billion in Q3 2021. Issuance growth jumped to 7.8% q-o-q in Q3 2021 from 2.6% q-o-q in the previous quarter, driven mainly by a hike in the issuance of BOT bonds and a rebound in the issuance of state-owned enterprise and other bonds. Growth in issuance of BOT bonds rose to 10.8% q-o-q in Q3 2021 from 7.0% q-o-q in the previous quarter. Issuance of government bonds and Treasury bills posted modest growth of 0.7% q-o-q in Q3 2021 after contracting 3.7% q-o-q in the previous quarter. Issuance of state-owned enterprise and other bonds rebounded, rising 25.4% q-o-q in Q3 2021 after a 17.7% q-o-q drop in Q2 2021. On an annual basis, issuance of Thai LCY government bonds posted a steeper decline of 28.9% y-o-y in Q3 2021 after a 20.8% y-o-y drop in the previous quarter, due to a high base in both Q2 2020 and Q3 2020 at the height of government borrowing to fund pandemic relief measures.

Corporate bonds. Outstanding corporate bonds reached a size of THB3,927.6 billion at the end of September. Growth eased to 1.2% q-o-q in Q3 2021 from 5.1% in the previous quarter as the spread of the Delta variant dampened investor confidence. On a y-o-y basis, growth in the outstanding stock of LCY corporate bonds inched up to 4.5% in Q3 2021 from 4.4% in Q2 2021.

Table 1: Size and Composition of the Local Currency Bond Market in Thailand

| | Outstanding Amount (billion) | | | | | | Growth Rate (%) | | | |
| | Q3 2020 | | Q2 2021 | | Q3 2021 | | Q3 2020 | | Q3 2021 | |
	THB	USD	THB	USD	THB	USD	q-o-q	y-o-y	q-o-q	y-o-y
Total	14,018	444	14,203	443	14,480	430	4.2	8.3	1.9	3.3
Government	10,260	325	10,324	322	10,552	313	5.4	11.3	2.2	2.8
Government Bonds and Treasury Bills	5,735	182	6,485	202	6,683	198	8.1	18.8	3.1	16.5
Central Bank Bonds	3,702	117	2,917	91	2,926	87	1.9	1.8	0.3	(21.0)
State-Owned Enterprise and Other Bonds	823	26	921	29	943	28	3.9	8.7	2.4	14.5
Corporate	3,758	119	3,880	121	3,928	117	1.1	0.9	1.2	4.5

( ) = negative, q-o-q = quarter-on-quarter, Q2 = second quarter, Q3 = third quarter, THB = Thai baht, USD = United States dollar, y-o-y = year-on-year.
Notes:
1. Calculated using data from national sources.
2. Bloomberg LP end-of-period local currency–USD rates are used.
3. Growth rates are calculated from local currency base and do not include currency effects.
Source: Bank of Thailand.

At the end of September, the LCY bonds outstanding of the top 30 corporate issuers totaled THB2,338.6 billion, accounting for 59.5% of the Thai corporate bond market (**Table 2**). The top 30 issuers were dominated by companies in the following sectors: food and beverage, commerce, energy and utilities, and finance and securities. Only four of the top 30 were state-owned firms, while the majority were listed on the Stock Exchange of Thailand. CP ALL topped the list, with an outstanding bond stock amounting to THB246.5 billion. Thai Beverage and Siam Cement were the next largest issuers, with outstanding bond stocks of THB173.1 billion and THB165.0 billion, respectively. PTT and True Corp followed, with outstanding bond stocks of THB134.6 billion and THB134.3 billion, respectively.

Corporate bond issuance slipped to THB470.5 billion in Q3 2021 from THB477.2 billion in the previous quarter. Issuance of corporate debt contracted 1.4% q-o-q in Q3 2021, after strong growth of 61.9% q-o-q in Q2 2021, as the spread of the Delta variant restricted economic activities. Compared with a year prior, corporate debt issuance was still relatively robust as borrowing costs remained low. On an annual basis, corporate bond issuance expanded 45.0% y-o-y in Q3 2021 after rising 87.4% y-o-y in Q2 2021.

The top 3 corporate issuers in Q3 2021 were energy companies (**Table 3**). PTT, a state-owned and exchange-listed oil and gas company, was the top issuer, raising a total of THB43.0 billion from bonds with tenors of 3–10 years and carrying coupons ranging from 0.96% to 2.37%. Gulf Energy Development was the second-largest issuer, raising a total of THB30.0 billion from bonds with tenors of 3–10 years. Banpu, another energy company, was the next largest issuer with total issuance amounting to THB16.0 billion. CPF Thailand, a food and beverage company, was the fourth largest issuer in Q3 2021, with total issuance of THB15.0 from a triple-tranche issuance of bonds with tenors of 6–12 years.

Investor Profile

Central government bonds. Financial corporations continued to hold the largest share of Thai government bonds, although their share slipped to 38.1% in September 2021 from 39.9% in September 2020 (**Figure 2**). The second-largest holder of government bonds were other depository corporations with a 23.2% share in September 2021, up from 19.2% a year earlier. The share of the two largest holders of central government bonds increased to 61.2% in September 2021 from 59.1% a year earlier. The central government's holdings of government bonds decreased to 15.2% from 16.4% during the same period. Nonresidents' holdings of Thai government bonds inched down to 13.4% in September 2021 from 14.0% a year earlier. The BOT's holdings of government bonds dropped to 3.2% in September 2021 from 4.0% in September 2020, as the central bank eased its purchases of government debt during the review period.

Central bank bonds. Other depository corporations held the largest share of BOT bonds at 41.7% in September 2021, though their share dipped from 45.7% in September 2020 (**Figure 3**). Financial corporations had the second-largest holdings of BOT bonds, with their share inching up to 30.6% in September 2021 from 29.3% in September 2020. The combined shares of the two top holders amounted to 72.3% of total BOT bonds outstanding at the end of September 2021, down from 75.0% a year earlier. During the same period, the BOT's holdings of its own LCY bonds rose slightly to 13.6% from 12.7%. The central government's holdings of BOT bonds also increased to 9.9% from 8.8% during the review period. Nonresidents' holdings of BOT bonds held steady at 0.9% from September 2020 to September 2021.

Net inflows from foreign investors to the Thai LCY bond market fell to THB20.1 billion in Q3 2021 from THB83.7 billion in Q2 2021 (**Figure 4**). The Thai LCY bond market recorded net inflows in July (THB9.3 billion) and August (THB47.5 billion), but saw net outflows of THB36.7 billion in September as inflation expectations and fears that the Federal Reserve would start tapering its quantitative easing measures by November prompted global investors to sell emerging market bonds, including Thai LCY bonds. The net outflows of foreign investment from the Thai LCY bond market in September were the highest monthly net outflows recorded since March 2020.

Ratings Update

On 20 September, S&P Global Ratings held Thailand's long-term foreign currency issuer default rating at BBB+ with a stable outlook. The rating affirmation was based on Thailand's robust financial and external positions amid the ongoing global pandemic. S&P Global Ratings expects

Table 2: Top 30 Issuers of Local Currency Corporate Bonds in Thailand

	Issuers	Outstanding Amount		State-Owned	Listed Company	Type of Industry
		LCY Bonds (THB billion)	LCY Bonds (USD billion)			
1.	CP ALL	246.5	7.3	No	Yes	Commerce
2.	Thai Beverage	173.1	5.1	No	No	Food and Beverage
3.	Siam Cement	165.0	4.9	Yes	Yes	Construction Material
4.	PTT	134.6	4.0	Yes	Yes	Energy and Utilities
5.	True Corp	134.3	4.0	No	No	Communications
6.	Charoen Pokphand Foods	131.2	3.9	No	Yes	Food and Beverage
7.	Berli Jucker	117.6	3.5	No	Yes	Commerce
8.	True Move H Universal Communication	105.0	3.1	No	No	Communication
9.	Bank of Ayudhya	94.8	2.8	No	Yes	Banking
10.	CPF Thailand	79.1	2.3	No	No	Food and Beverage
11.	Toyota Leasing Thailand	73.6	2.2	No	No	Finance and Securities
12.	Minor International	68.1	2.0	No	Yes	Hospitality and Leisure
13.	Indorama Ventures	66.5	2.0	No	Yes	Petrochemicals and Chemicals
14.	Banpu	61.3	1.8	No	Yes	Energy and Utilities
15.	Bangkok Commercial Asset Management	59.2	1.8	No	Yes	Finance and Securities
16.	Frasers Property Thailand	49.3	1.5	No	Yes	Property and Construction
17.	Gulf Energy Development	47.5	1.4	No	Yes	Energy and Utilities
18.	Muangthai Capital	46.0	1.4	No	Yes	Finance and Securities
19.	BTS Group Holdings	45.1	1.3	No	Yes	Diversified
20.	Krung Thai Bank	44.0	1.3	Yes	Yes	Banking
21.	dtac TriNet	43.5	1.3	No	Yes	Communications
22.	Krungthai Card	42.6	1.3	Yes	Yes	Banking
23.	Global Power Synergy	41.5	1.2	No	Yes	Energy and Utilies
24.	Sansiri	40.5	1.2	No	Yes	Property and Construction
25.	Bangkok Expressway & Metro	40.1	1.2	No	Yes	Transportation and Logistics
26.	TPI Polene	39.5	1.2	No	Yes	Property and Construction
27.	ICBC Thai Leasing	38.5	1.1	No	No	Finance and Securities
28.	CH Karnchang	38.4	1.1	No	Yes	Property and Construction
29.	B Grimm	36.8	1.1	No	Yes	Energy and Utilities
30.	Land & Houses	35.6	1.1	No	Yes	Property and Construction
	Total Top 30 LCY Corporate Issuers	2,338.6	69.4			
	Total LCY Corporate Bonds	3,938.2	116.9			
	Top 30 as % of Total LCY Corporate Bonds	59.5%	59.5%			

LCY = local currency, THB = Thai baht, USD = United States dollar.
Notes:
1. Data as of 30 September 2021.
2. State-owned firms are defined as those in which the government has more than a 50% ownership stake.
Source: *AsianBondsOnline* calculations based on Bloomberg LP data.

Table 3: Notable Local Currency Corporate Bond Issuances in the Third Quarter of 2021

Corporate Issuers	Coupon Rate (%)	Issued Amount (THB billion)
PTT		
3-year bond	0.96	15.0
5-year bond	1.31	15.0
7-year bond	1.79	5.0
10-year bond	2.37	8.0
Gulf Energy Development		
3-year bond	1.74	12.0
5-year bond	2.48	6.0
7-year bond	3.01	3.0
10-year bond	3.40	9.0
Banpu		
3-year bond	1.58	2.0
5-year bond	2.90	3.9
7-year bond	3.30	4.0
10-year bond	3.80	6.0
CPF Thailand		
6-year bond	2.50	4.5
8-year bond	3.18	6.0
12 year bond	3.70	4.5

THB = Thai baht.
Source: Bloomberg LP.

the Thai economy to grow 1.1% in 2021. The ratings body also maintained Thailand's long-term local currency issuer default rating at A– with a stable outlook.

Policy, Institutional, and Regulatory Developments

Thai Government Raises Debt Ceiling

On 20 September, the Government of Thailand increased the debt ceiling from 60% to 70% of GDP to allow the government to raise more funds for its economic recovery efforts. The government had earlier issued an emergency loan decree in 2020 that authorized the Ministry of Finance to borrow THB1 trillion for economic stimulus measures. A second decree was issued in June 2021 allowing the government to borrow an additional THB500 billion to fund relief measures to combat the impacts of the prolonged pandemic. Thailand's public debt-to-GDP ratio stood at 57% as of September 2021.

Figure 2: Local Currency Government Bonds Investor Profile

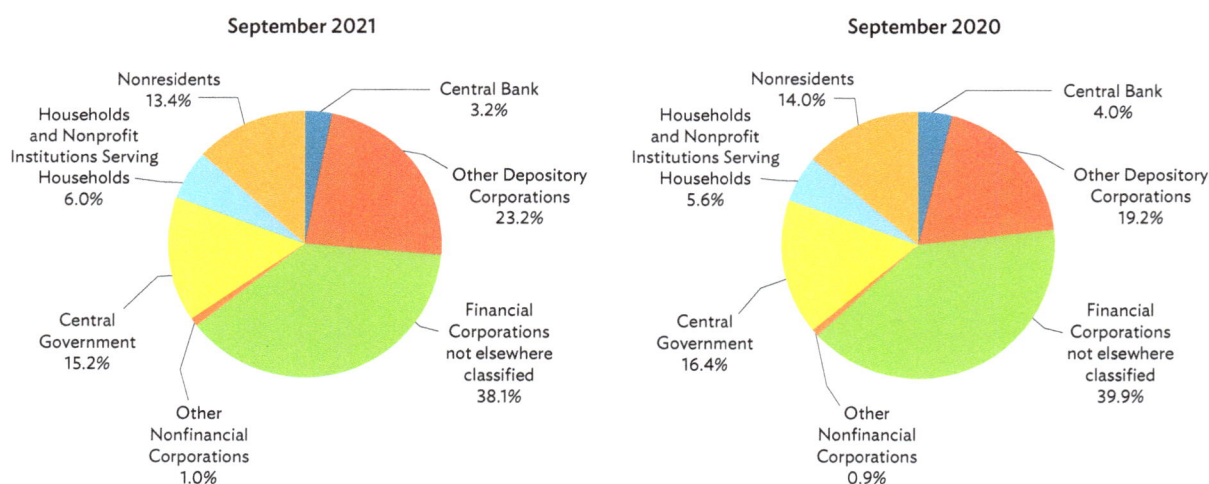

September 2021

- Nonresidents 13.4%
- Central Bank 3.2%
- Households and Nonprofit Institutions Serving Households 6.0%
- Other Depository Corporations 23.2%
- Central Government 15.2%
- Financial Corporations not elsewhere classified 38.1%
- Other Nonfinancial Corporations 1.0%

September 2020

- Nonresidents 14.0%
- Central Bank 4.0%
- Households and Nonprofit Institutions Serving Households 5.6%
- Other Depository Corporations 19.2%
- Central Government 16.4%
- Financial Corporations not elsewhere classified 39.9%
- Other Nonfinancial Corporations 0.9%

Note: Government bonds include Treasury bills and bonds.
Source: *AsianBondsOnline* and Bank of Thailand.

Figure 3: Local Currency Central Bank Securities Investor Profile

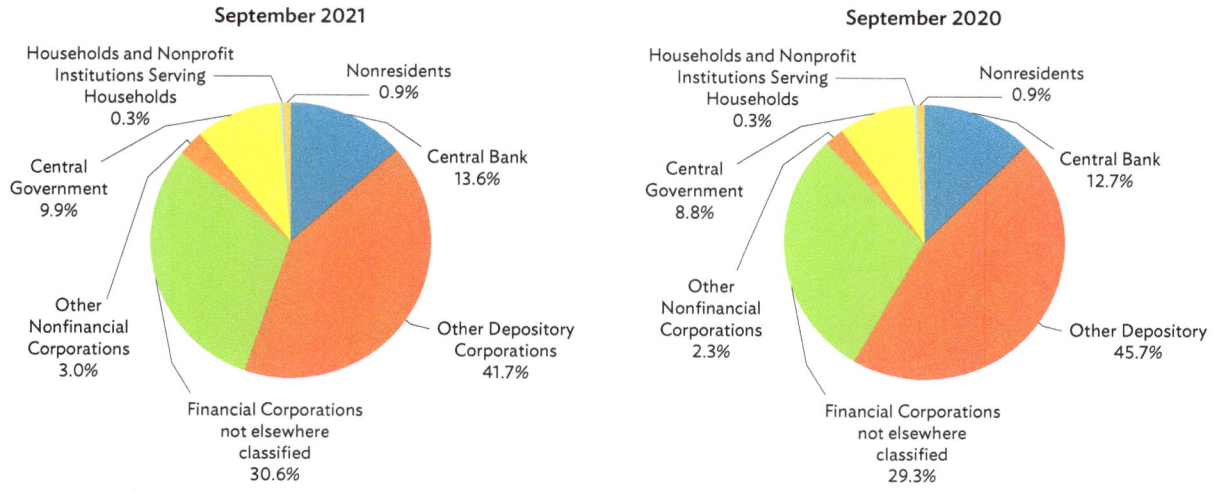

September 2021

Households and Nonprofit Institutions Serving Households 0.3%

Nonresidents 0.9%

Central Bank 13.6%

Central Government 9.9%

Other Nonfinancial Corporations 3.0%

Other Depository Corporations 41.7%

Financial Corporations not elsewhere classified 30.6%

September 2020

Households and Nonprofit Institutions Serving Households 0.3%

Nonresidents 0.9%

Central Bank 12.7%

Central Government 8.8%

Other Nonfinancial Corporations 2.3%

Other Depository Corporations 45.7%

Financial Corporations not elsewhere classified 29.3%

Source: Bank of Thailand.

Figure 4: Foreign Investor Net Trading of Local Currency Bonds in Thailand

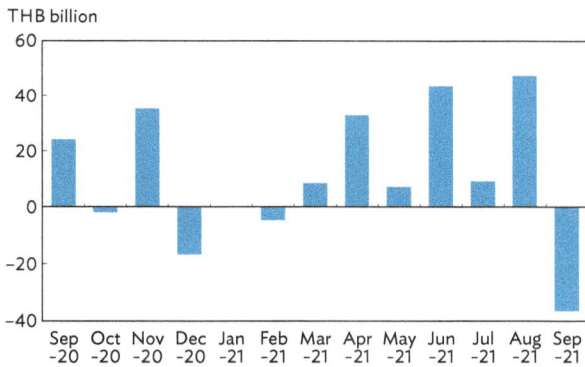

THB billion

THB = Thai baht.
Source: Thai Bond Market Association.

Thailand to Issue More Long-Term Government Bonds

On 1 October, Thailand's Public Debt Management Office announced its plan to increase the share of long-dated bonds to finance the government's economic stimulus programs. Government bonds will comprise 48%–56% of total borrowing in fiscal year 2021–2022. In the previous fiscal year, government bonds comprised 31% of total borrowing as the government relied more on short-term instruments such as promissory notes and Treasury bills. For fiscal year 2021–2022, Treasury bills will comprise 23% of total borrowing, while promissory notes will comprise a 16%–25% share. Savings bonds and bond switching will each account for a 6% share of the total borrowing.

Viet Nam

Yield Movements

The yield curve of local currency (LCY) government bonds in Viet Nam shifted upward, with rates increasing across the board between 31 August and 15 October (**Figure 1**). Yields increased 8 basis points (bps) on average for all tenors. The largest increase was seen for the 1-year tenor at 15 bps, while the smallest gain was for the 5-year and 7-year tenors at 5 bps each. The yield spread between the 2-year and 10-year tenors marginally widened during the review period from 143 bps to 144 bps.

The upward adjustment of the yield curve is in line with the regional trend of increasing bond yields in response to the shift in the monetary stance of the United States Federal Reserve of cutting back its asset purchases later in the year and the possibility of earlier rate hikes thereafter. Viet Nam's economic downturn in the third quarter (Q3) of 2021 also affected the rise in yields as it renewed uncertainty over recovery prospects, prompting investors to ask for higher returns for the risks. Nonetheless, the increases were not as high as in other regional markets as the central bank maintained its accommodative stance, inflation rate remained low, and liquidity was still abundant.

Viet Nam's economy contracted in Q3 2021 with its gross domestic product (GDP) declining 6.2% year-on-year (y-o-y) after posting 6.6% y-o-y growth in the second quarter (Q2) of 2021. It is the largest recorded drop since quarterly GDP was tracked in 2000. The domestic economy managed to sustain its positive growth since the start of the coronavirus disease (COVID-19) pandemic in early 2020. However, the fourth wave of COVID-19 had a deeply adverse impact on the economy as the imposition of quarantine restrictions disrupted production and consumption. In the first 3 quarters of 2021, the Vietnamese economy expanded 1.4% y-o-y. The government forecasts GDP growth of 3.0% y-o-y to 3.5% y-o-y for 2021.

The State Bank of Vietnam (SBV) announced in October that there would be no rate cuts for the year and it would be monitoring the developments on the COVID-19 situation and its impact on the economy and financial markets to appropriately manage rates. The key policy

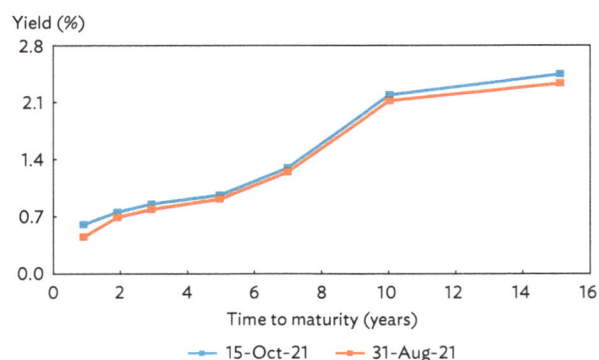

Figure 1: Viet Nam's Benchmark Yield Curve—Local Currency Government Bonds

Source: Based on data from Bloomberg LP.

rate remained at 4.00% after the central bank last reduced it by 50 bps in October 2020. In 2020, the SBV cut the policy rate by a total of 200 bps to support the economy from the impact of the COVID-19 pandemic.

The prices of consumer goods in Viet Nam inched up 1.8% y-o-y in October, easing from a 2.1% y-o-y gain in September. The downward adjustment in prices was attributed to lower goods prices as the COVID-19 situation improved, decreased utilities demand, and lower housing rentals. Year-to-date through the end of September, consumer price inflation was 1.8%. The government has put a ceiling of 4.0% for inflation in 2021.

The Vietnamese dong traded at VND22,749.0 per USD1.0 on 15 October, appreciating only 0.2% from its value on 31 August, reflecting the stability of the domestic currency. The strength of the dong, while subtle, is supported by net inflows from trade and foreign direct investment.

Size and Composition

Viet Nam's LCY bond market expanded 8.1% quarter-on-quarter (q-o-q) to VND1,902.1 trillion (USD83.6 billion) at the end of Q3 2021, on faster growth compared to the previous quarter's increase of 6.1% q-o-q (**Table 1**). The quarterly growth emanated from both the government and corporate segments as both posted quarterly

Table 1: Size and Composition of the Local Currency Bond Market in Viet Nam

	Outstanding Amount (billion)						Growth Rate (%)			
	Q3 2020		Q2 2021		Q3 2021		Q3 2020		Q3 2021	
	VND	USD	VND	USD	VND	USD	q-o-q	y-o-y	q-o-q	y-o-y
Total	1,540,040	66	1,758,977	76	1,902,088	84	11.6	17.1	8.1	23.5
Government	1,289,363	56	1,357,573	59	1,414,481	62	8.9	6.8	4.2	9.7
Treasury Bonds	1,149,375	50	1,221,237	53	1,276,988	56	10.6	17.8	4.6	11.1
Central Bank Bills	0	0	0	0	0	0	–	(100.0)	–	–
Government-Guaranteed and Municipal Bonds	139,988	6	136,337	6	137,494	6	(2.7)	(12.5)	0.8	(1.8)
Corporate	250,677	11	401,404	17	487,607	21	27.7	132.4	21.5	94.5

( ) = negative, – = not applicable, q-o-q = quarter-on-quarter, Q2 = second quarter, Q3 = third quarter, USD = United States dollar, VND = Vietnamese dong, y-o-y = year-on-year.
Notes:
1. Bloomberg LP end-of-period local currency–USD rates are used.
2. Growth rates are calculated from local currency base and do not include currency effects.
Sources: Bloomberg LP and Vietnam Bond Market Association.

increases. At the end of September, government bonds accounted for 74.4% of Viet Nam's bond market, while corporate bonds comprised 25.6%. On an annual basis, the bond market expanded 23.5% y-o-y in Q3 2021, slowing from 27.5% y-o-y growth in Q2 2021.

Government bonds. The government bond market increased 4.2% q-o-q in Q3 2021, reversing the slight contraction of 0.5% q-o-q in the previous quarter. The government's outstanding debt amounted to VND1,414.5 trillion, with increases across all government bond segments except for central bank bills, which remained at zero.

Treasury bonds outstanding increased 4.6% q-o-q to VND1,277.0 trillion in Q3 2021, accelerating from growth of 0.1% q-o-q in Q2 2021. The growth was supported by the issuance of Treasury bonds amounting to VND96.2 trillion during the quarter. Total debt sales were about 80% of the planned issuance of VND120.0 trillion for Q3 2021.

Outstanding government-guaranteed and municipal bonds also increased in Q3 2021, albeit slightly, by 0.8% q-o-q to VND137.5 trillion after declining by 5.3% q-o-q in the previous quarter. The rebound can be attributed to bond issuance during the quarter from the government-guaranteed Vietnam Bank for Social Policies totaling VND11.0 trillion, which offset the maturing debts. In Q2 2021, there was no issuance from the government segment, while there was a considerable amount of maturing securities.

Corporate bonds. The corporate bond market maintained its strong expansion at 21.5% q-o-q in Q3 2021, although this was slower compared to Q2 2021 growth of 36.6% q-o-q. Outstanding corporate bonds reached VND487.6 trillion at the end of September. The growth was underpinned by vibrant issuance activity in the corporate sector during the quarter.

The top 30 LCY corporate issuers had aggregate bonds outstanding of VND309.1 trillion at the end of September, comprising 63.4% of the total corporate bond market (**Table 2**). The outstanding bonds were largely from banks and property firms. Banks had the largest amount of outstanding bonds totaling VND217.2 trillion, or 70.3% of the top 30's total debt, and property firms had VND49.0 billion with a share of 15.8%. The Bank for Investment and Development of Vietnam remained the largest issuer at the end of Q3 2021 with outstanding debt of VND37.6 trillion, growing from VND25.9 trillion at the end of Q2 2021.

Issuance activity from the corporate sector remained fairly active in Q3 2021 with total debt sales of VND94.4 trillion. However, this was down 15.9% from total corporate bond issuance in Q2 2021, likely as a result of a fourth COVID-19 outbreak that hit economic centers and halted business activities during the most recent quarter.

Firms resorted to the bond market for funding as regulations from the SBV cautioned against lending to risky sectors. Despite the risk, corporate bonds,

Table 2: Top 30 Issuers of Local Currency Corporate Bonds in Viet Nam

	Issuers	Outstanding Amount		State-Owned	Listed Company	Type of Industry
		LCY Bonds (VND billion)	LCY Bonds (USD billion)			
1.	Bank for Investment and Development of Vietnam	37,590	1.65	Yes	Yes	Banking
2.	Asia Commercial Joint Stock Bank	20,400	0.90	No	Yes	Banking
3.	Ho Chi Minh City Development Joint Stock Commercial Bank	20,348	0.89	No	Yes	Banking
4.	Lien Viet Post Joint Stock Commercial Bank	20,100	0.88	No	Yes	Banking
5.	Vietnam Prosperity Joint Stock Commercial Bank	19,080	0.84	No	Yes	Banking
6.	Vietnam International Joint Stock Commercial Bank	17,150	0.75	No	Yes	Banking
7.	Masan Group	16,900	0.74	No	Yes	Finance
8.	Orient Commercial Joint Stock Bank	16,535	0.73	No	No	Banking
9.	Tien Phong Commercial Joint Stock Bank	15,649	0.69	No	Yes	Banking
10.	Vietnam Joint Stock Commercial Bank for Industry and Trade	13,339	0.59	Yes	Yes	Banking
11.	Vinhomes Joint Stock Company	8,890	0.39	No	Yes	Property
12.	Saigon - Ha Noi Commercial Joint Stock Bank	8,450	0.37	No	Yes	Banking
13.	Saigon Glory Company Limited	8,000	0.35	No	No	Property
14.	Sovico Group Joint Stock Company	7,550	0.33	No	Yes	Property
15.	An Binh Commercial Joint Stock Bank	7,000	0.31	No	No	Banking
16.	Vietnam Maritime Joint Stock Commercial Bank	6,699	0.29	No	Yes	Banking
17.	Bac A Commercial Joint Stock Bank	6,140	0.27	No	Yes	Banking
18.	Golden Hill Real Estate JSC	5,701	0.25	No	No	Property
19.	Vingroup	5,425	0.24	No	Yes	Property
20.	Mediterranean Revival Villas Company Limited	5,000	0.22	No	No	Property
21.	Vietnam Technological and Commercial Joint Stock Bank	5,000	0.22	No	Yes	Banking
22	Bong Sen JSC	4,800	0.21	No	No	Manufacturing
23.	Trung Nam Dak Lak 1 Wind Power JSC	4,500	0.20	No	No	Energy
24.	Phu My Hung Corporation	4,497	0.20	No	No	Property
25.	Truong Hai Auto Corp	4,400	0.19	No	Yes	Manufacturing
26.	Ho Chi Minh City Infrastructure Investment Joint Stock Company	4,370	0.19	No	Yes	Construction
27.	Nui Phao Mining and Processing Co., Ltd.	4,310	0.19	No	No	Mining
28.	NoVa Real Estate Investment Corporation JSC	3,907	0.17	No	Yes	Property
29.	Vietnam Bank for Agriculture and Rural Development	3,760	0.17	Yes	No	Banking
30.	VP Bank Finance Company Limited	3,600	0.16	No	No	Finance
	Total Top 30 LCY Corporate Issuers	**309,089**	**13.58**			
	Total LCY Corporate Bonds	**487,607**	**21.42**			
	Top 30 as % of Total LCY Corporate Bonds	**63.4%**	**63.4%**			

LCY = local currency, USD = United States dollar, VND = Vietnamese dong.
Notes:
1. Data as of 30 September 2021.
2. State-owned firms are defined as those in which the government has more than a 50% ownership stake.
Sources: *AsianBondsOnline* calculations based on Bloomberg LP and Vietnam Bond Market Association data.

particularly from property firms, remained attractive to investors as they offered higher rates.

Banks dominated the debt market, raising an aggregate VND46.7 trillion in Q3 2021, which accounted for about half of total issuance. The debt sales were down from VND64.9 trillion in Q2 2021. Property firms were second, raising VND28.6 trillion, which was up from VND26.5 trillion in the previous quarter. Large bond issuances during the quarter are listed in **Table 3**. Bong Sen JSC had the largest single issuance with a 1-year

bond worth VND4.3 trillion. In aggregate terms, the Bank for Investment and Development of Vietnam was the biggest debt issuer in Q3 2021 with VND10.9 trillion.

In Q3 2021, two firms tapped the international bond market to raise funds. In July, Novaland issued more USD-denominated debt amounting to USD300.0 million after it had successfully mobilized USD500.0 million in April. The recently issued bond has a 5-year maturity and a coupon of 5.25%. The capital will be allocated to land acquisition and project development. In September, Vinpearl issued world's first exchange sustainable bond amounting to USD425.0 million with a maturity of 5 years and a coupon of 3.25%.

Table 3: Notable Local Currency Corporate Bond Issuances in the Third Quarter of 2021

Corporate Issuers	Coupon Rate (%)	Issued Amount (VND billion)
Bank for Investment and Development of Vietnam[a]		
6-year bond	–	3,000
8-year bond	0.9% + average interest rate for 12-month deposit	3,000
8-year bond	–	2,000
Mediterranean Revival Villas Company Limited[a]		
1-year bond	–	2,500
1-year bond	–	2,500
Bong Sen JSC		
1-year bond	11.00	4,320
Asia Commercial Joint Stock Bank		
3-year bond	–	2,500

– = not available, VND = Vietnamese dong.
[a] Multiple issuance of the same tenor indicates issuance on different dates.
Source: Vietnam Bond Market Association.

Investor Profile

Government securities outstanding were held almost entirely by insurance firms and banks at the end of September, which together accounted for 99.1% of the total holdings. Insurance firms held 56.8% of government securities, up from 53.9% at the end of September 2020, while banks held 42.3%, down from 44.8% during the same period. The remaining outstanding bonds were held by securities companies, investment funds, offshore investors, and other investors. Foreign investors held 0.7% of government securities at the end of September, increasing from 0.6% a year earlier. Viet Nam's LCY bond market had the smallest foreign holdings share among emerging East Asian economies.

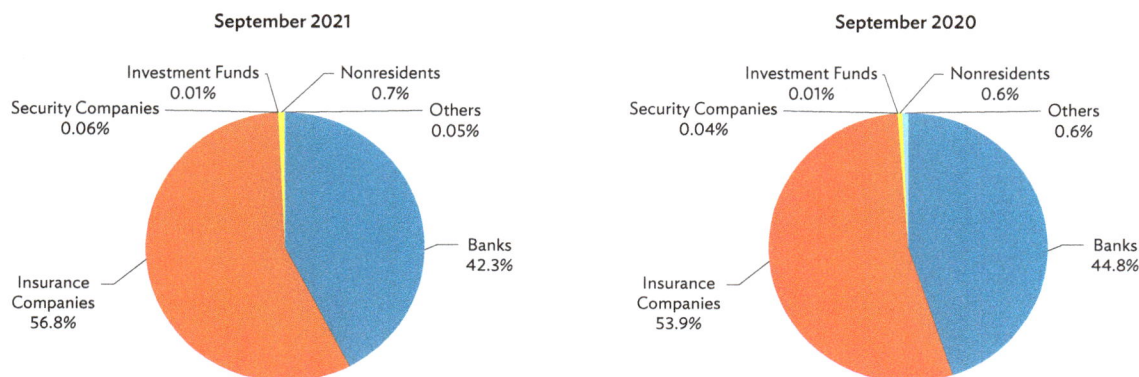

Figure 2: Local Currency Government Bonds Investor Profile

September 2021

Investment Funds 0.01%
Nonresidents 0.7%
Security Companies 0.06%
Others 0.05%
Banks 42.3%
Insurance Companies 56.8%

September 2020

Investment Funds 0.01%
Nonresidents 0.6%
Security Companies 0.04%
Others 0.6%
Banks 44.8%
Insurance Companies 53.9%

Source: Ministry of Finance, Government of Viet Nam.

Policy, Institutional, and Regulatory Developments

State Treasury Implements Multiple Price Auction for 5-Year Treasury Bonds

On 6 October, the State Treasury implemented a pilot auction using a multiple price method for 5-year Treasury bonds. In a multiple price auction, the successful bidders pay the price stated in their respective bids for the allotted quantity of securities. The expected offering volume for the 5-year Treasury bond auctions was VND1,000–VND2,000 billion per session. For the rest of the tenors, the auction followed the uniform price method.[14]

---

[14] *Vietnam Bond Market Association*. 2021. "The State Treasury to Implement Pilot Auctions of Government Bonds by Multi-Price Method." 21 September. https://vbma.org.vn/en/activities/kho-bac-nha-nuoc-thi-diem-trien-khai-phat-hanh-trai-phieu-chinh-phu-theo-phuong-thuc-dau-thau-da-gia.